英美文学佳作赏析

Highlights of British and American Literature

（第三版）

主　编　惠海峰
副主编　郭晶晶　王　群　陈先梅

华中科技大学出版社
中国·武汉

内 容 提 要

本书由华中科技大学外国语学院长期担任"英美文学佳作赏析"教学任务的教师根据多年的教学实践,在自编讲义的基础上修订增补,精心编写而成。为适应非英语专业学生的知识背景和实际需求,本书编者在选材时力求做到既适当涵盖经典,兼顾英美文学,又突出选文的时代性、趣味性和可读性。本书的适用读者,包括英语第二学位学生、高等学校英美文学公共选修课的学生,同时还可供具有一定英语水平的英美文学爱好者、自学者学习之用。

图书在版编目(CIP)数据

英美文学佳作赏析/惠海峰主编.-3 版.—武汉:华中科技大学出版社,2013.12
ISBN 978-7-5609-9494-9

Ⅰ.①英… Ⅱ.①惠… Ⅲ.①英语-阅读教学-高等学校-教材 ②文学-作品-介绍-英国 ③文学-作品-介绍-美国 Ⅳ.①H319.4:Ⅰ

中国版本图书馆 CIP 数据核字(2013)第 287038 号

英美文学佳作赏析(第三版)　　　　　　　　　　　　　　　惠海峰　主编

策划编辑:刘　平
责任编辑:刘　平
责任校对:张　琳
封面设计:范翠璇
责任监印:周治超

出版发行:华中科技大学出版社(中国・武汉)　　电话:(027)81321913
　　　　　武汉市东湖新技术开发区华工科技园　　邮编:430223
录　　排:华中科技大学惠友文印中心
印　　刷:北京虎彩文化传播有限公司
开　　本:710mm×1000mm　1/16
印　　张:19
字　　数:376 千字
版　　次:2019 年 6 月第 3 版第 3 次印刷
定　　价:58.00 元

本书若有印装质量问题,请向出版社营销中心调换
全国免费服务热线:400-6679-118　竭诚为您服务
版权所有　侵权必究

第三版前言

在中外交流日益频繁、全球一体化趋势不断加强的今天,学习英语、了解英美文化已成为中国大学生的共识。文学是文化的精华载体,通过赏析英美文学名篇,我们不仅能学习语言、了解文化,同时还能接受优秀英美作品精髓思想的熏陶,增强对社会生活的理解与感悟,加强自身的人文素质和修养。

华中科技大学外国语学院本着培养复合型素质人才的理念,面向本校及外校非英语专业学生开设英语第二学位,其中"英美文学佳作赏析"是一门重要的必修课。长期担任该课程教学的教师根据多年的教学实践,在自编讲义的基础上修订增补,精心编写成此书,这其中既包含对学术同仁最新成果的借鉴,又凝结着教师自己教学实践的总结创新。考虑到非英语专业学生的知识背景和实际需求,本书编者在选材时力求做到既适当涵盖经典、兼顾英美文学,又突出选文的时代性、趣味性和可读性。

该教材从最初的讲义到成书经历了七八年教学实践的检验,取得了很好的成效。随着国内外国文学研究和教学的发展,原有版本在选材和介绍方面已经不能完全满足新时期的需要,因此我们在前两版的基础上做了修订,主要是对散文、小说和诗歌的篇目进行了更新,力求在介绍名篇的基础上注重学生的学习难度和学习兴趣,引入一些学生更加喜闻乐见以及近些年课外阅读中流行的名篇,例如最新的007电影中引用的英国桂冠诗人丁尼生的诗句。

本书的适用读者,包括英语第二学位学生、高等学校英美文学公共选修课的学生,同时还可供具有一定英语水平的英美文学爱好者、自学者学习之用。

本书在编写的过程中得到了华中科技大学外国语学院各级领导的支持和鼓励,外国语学院英语系教授胡泓博士在本书的编写设计、选材及审稿各个环节都提供了有益的指导并提出了宝贵的意见,华中科技大学出版社的相关编辑在编辑加工、提高书稿质量方面做了许多细致的工作,在此,我们谨致衷心的谢意!

由于编者水平所限,书中难免有考虑不周之处,恳请批评指正。

惠海峰
2013 年 7 月于武汉

Contents

Introduction

- Enjoying Poetry 3
- Enjoying Drama 7
- Enjoying Fiction 11
- Enjoying Essay 14

Part One British Literature

Poetry 19

- Shall I Compare Thee to a Summer's Day 20
- The Flea 21
- The Definition of Love 23
- A Red, Red Rose 25
- My Heart's in the Highlands 26
- I Wandered Lonely as a Cloud 27
- Lines Composed a Few Miles Above Tintern Abbey, on Revisiting the Banks of the Wye During a Tour. July 13, 1798 29
- The Tyger 34
- The Lamb 35
- Frost at Midnight 36
- My Last Duchess 40
- How Do I Love Thee? 42
- When You Are Old 43
- The Second Coming 44

- Ulysses ... 45
- Hawk Roosting ... 48
- 40—Love ... 50

Drama ... 53
- Hamlet: Prince of Denmark ... 54
- The Importance of Being Earnest ... 65
- Pygmalion ... 74

Fiction ... 81
- The Picture of Dorian Gray ... 82
- The Horse Dealer's Daughter ... 91
- The Garden Party ... 110
- Dubliners ... 126

Essay ... 137
- Of Studies ... 138
- A Modest Proposal ... 141
- To the Right Honorable the Earl of Chesterfield ... 148
- The Idea of a University ... 152
- Tradition and the Individual Talent ... 157

Part Two　American Literature

Poetry ... 165
- To a Waterfowl ... 166
- Annabel Lee ... 167
- Beat! Beat! Drums! ... 169
- Because I Could Not Stop for Death ... 171
- Hope Is the Thing with Feathers ... 172
- I'm Nobody ... 173
- Stopping by Woods on a Snowy Evening ... 174
- The Road Not Taken ... 175
- Anecdote of the Jar ... 176
- The Red Wheelbarrow ... 177
- In a Station of the Metro ... 178
- Journey of the Magi ... 179
- l(a ... 181

    in Just— 181
    I, Too 183
    Dreams 184
Drama 185
    A Streetcar Named Desire 186
    Death of a Salesman 195
    True West 203
Fiction 213
    The Tell-Tale Heart 214
    The Egg 220
    Rip Van Winkle 231
    A Clean, Well-Lighted Place 245
    A Rose for Emily 251
Essay 263
    Sinners in the Hands of an Angry God 264
    Nature (excerpt) 271
    Walden 276
    Once More to the Lake 286
Bibliography 294

Introduction

Enjoying Poetry

Poetry is hard to define in exact words. However, it is instantly recognizable. Some of its qualities are special visual tips on the printed page: stanzas and forms, such as couplets, quatrains, sonnets, capitalized first lines and short lines. Some are special uses of language and rhythm: imagery, metaphor, symbol, repetition, onomatopoeia, rhyme, and meter. Others are compression of language, tension, tone, seriousness of ideas, or utter playfulness.

In some ways reading poetry is much like reading fiction, drama, and essay: we observe details of action and language, make connections and inferences, and draw conclusions. We also bring to poetry the same intellectual and emotional dispositions, the same general experience with life and literature that we draw on in reading drama, fiction, and essay. Yet there is something different about reading poems. We are supposed to be more attentive to the connotations of words, more receptive to the expressive qualities of sound and rhythm in line and stanza, more discerning about details of syntax and punctuation. This increased attention to linguistic detail is necessary because of the density and compression characteristic of poetry. More than fiction, drama, and essay, poetry is an art of condensation and implication; poems concentrate on meaning and distill feeling.

There are generally two kinds of poems: the narrative and the lyric. Narrative poems, which tell stories and describe actions, include epic, romance, and ballad. Lyric poems, combining speech and song to express feelings in varying degrees of verbal music, include elegy, epigraph, sonnet, sestina, villanelle, and many other ones that contain strong personal emotions.

Elements of Poetry

The close reading of a poem depends on observing the specific elements of the poem. Since all the elements of a poem work together harmoniously to convey feeling and embody meaning, we can learn to interpret and appreciate a poem by understanding these basic elements.

Voice: Speaker and Tone When we read or hear a poem, we hear a speaker's voice. It is this voice that conveys the poem's tone, its implied attitude toward its subject. When we listen to a poem's language and hear the voice of its speaker, we catch its tone and feeling and ultimately its meaning.

Image An image is a verbal picture of an object, action or abstract idea or sensation (feeling). Images appeal directly to one of the senses: touch, sight, hearing, smell, or taste. Poets make efforts to excite our responses through sensory experiences (what we see, hear, feel, smell, taste), rather than through abstract language, for it is through our senses that we perceive the world. Images trigger our memories, stimulate our feelings, and command our response. Imagery refers to a pattern of related details in a poem. When images cluster together to convey an idea or feeling beyond what the images literally describe, we call them metaphorical or symbolic.

Figurative Language Language can be classified as either literal or figurative. When we speak literally, we mean exactly what each word conveys; when we use figurative language, we mean something other than the actual meaning of the words. Poetry achieves many of its effects through this skill of language. Simile and metaphor, the two most commonly used rhetorical devices, are both making connections between normally unrelated things, seeing one thing in terms of another. However, simile establishes the comparison explicitly with the words "like" or "as", while metaphor employs no such explicit verbal clue, and is then more subtle and implied. Other kinds of figurative language include personification, giving inanimate objects or abstract concepts animate characteristics or qualities; metonymy, substituting an attribute of a thing for the thing itself; pun, a play on words; hyperbole, or exaggeration; paradox, to name only a few.

Symbol and Allegory A symbol is any object or action that means more than itself, any object or action that represents something beyond itself. A rose, for example, can represent beauty or love or transience. A tree may represent a family's roots and branches. A soaring bird might stand for freedom. Light might symbolize hope or knowledge or life. A symbol may be universal in its nature, as when we say that "sailing westward" usually symbolizes preparation for death. But a symbol can also be more private. Recognizing their use in poetry will help you see them in daily language, either spoken or written. Related to symbolism, allegory is a form of narrative in which people, places, and happenings have hidden or symbolic meaning. Allegory is thus a type of symbolism, but it differs from the former in establishing a strict system of correspondences between details of action and a pattern of meaning. Allegory is especially suitable as a vehicle for teaching.

Syntax Syntax refers to the grammatical structure of words in sentences and the deployment of sentences throughout the poem. It is an important element of a poem's tone and a guide to a speaker's state of mind. Speakers who repeat themselves or who break off abruptly in the midst of a thought, for example, reveal something about how they feel. When reading poetry, we should pay attention to such syntactical features as sentence length, sentence type, word order, complexity, and arrangement. Special attention should also go to some peculiarities like inversion, repetition, parallelism, omitting, adding, sentence fragments, rhetorical sentences (requiring no answer), exclamation sentences, coinage of new words and phrases, and even punctuation and capitalization. These are usually where special meaning lies.

Sound Effect Rhythm refers to the changing pattern of stressed and unstressed syllables in a line of a poem. It is the beat of music we feel in poetry that adds greatly to its aesthetic effect. The tempo of rhythm helps to express meaning and convey meaning. A certain combination of various syllables is called a foot or a meter. Rising meters like iambic and anapestic, and falling meters like trochaic and dactylic, are most frequently employed in English verse. Rhyme, the matching of final vowel and consonant sounds in two or more words at regular intervals, usually at the end of lines (end rhyme), and sometimes within lines (internal rhyme or middle rhyme). Two other forms of sound play prevail in poetry: alliteration or the repetition of consonant sounds, especially at the beginning of words, and assonance or the repetition of vowel sounds. These sound devices, having the music effect of onomatopoeia, make poetry pleasant to read and sweet to hear. Working together with other elements of poetry, they contribute to the meaning of the poetry.

Form When we analyze the form, or the structure of a poem, we focus on its patterns of organization. Form exists in poems on many levels from patterns of sound and image to structures of syntax and of thought; it is as much a matter of phrase and line as of stanza and whole poem. Some poems are strictly constrained in closed or fixed form and we can recognize them by their patterns of rhyme, meter, repetition, the shapes of their stanzas and the patterns of their line lengths. Shakespearean Sonnets are the most typical poems of fixed form. But not all poems are written in fixed forms. Many poets, resisting the limitations inherent in using a consistent and specific metrical pattern or in rhyming lines in a prescribed manner, developed and discovered looser, more open and free forms. Open or free form does not imply formlessness. It suggests that poets can either create their own forms or use the traditional fixed forms in more flexible ways. Walt Whitman is regarded as a pioneer experimenting with free verses.

Theme Theme is defined as an abstraction or generalization drawn from the details of a literary work. It is an idea or meaning inherent and implicit in a work. In determining a poem's theme we should be careful neither to oversimplify the poem nor to distort its meaning, and we also should recognize that sometimes poems can have multiple themes. Focusing on a poem's theme enables us to see a poem's significance—what it says, what it implies, and what it means.

Suggestions on Reading Poetry

1. Read the poem a few times slowly and deliberately. If possible read it aloud. Make sure you know the meaning of the words and the grammar so that you can follow what each sentence literally says.

2. Identify the speaker (who is speaking?), subject (about what?), situation and the tone (how does he feel?).

3. Pay attention to special language phenomena, figure of speech, syntax features, symbols, etc.

4. Consider the poem's form and how its structure shapes its thought and its emotion.

5. Test the poem against your own experience (do you have similar experiences and feelings?) or try to view things in the poet's feet. If you cannot understand very much, don't be too upset. Read it at some other time or with a friend.

6. Identify the social, cultural and moral values that emerge in the poem. Consider how your own values influence your interpretation and evaluation of its worth.

Enjoying Drama

Drama, unlike the other literary genres, is a staged art. Plays are written to be performed by actors before an audience. We can easily tell a play from other texts of literature for such peculiarities as dialogues, stage directions and the arrangement of acts and scenes. And of all the literary forms, drama is the one in which the dramatist almost never speaks directly to the audience/reader. For the most part, dramatists convey ideas through their characters and the plot, rather than in a direct embodiment of themselves in the way novelists do with narrators.

As a literary genre, drama share common qualities with fiction, poetry and the essay. Drama is most like fiction, possessing a narrative dimension: a play often narrates a story in the form of a plot. It shares features with poetry as well. Plays may be written in verse (Shakespeare wrote in blank verse), and are to be heard, as lyrical poems are, and on the other hand some poems contain dramatic elements. Also like essays, plays may be vehicles of persuasion. Drama is very often intended to discuss certain issues and convey ideas. With dramatic performance, however, we must read drama with special attention to its performance element. We can try to hear the voices of characters, and imagine tones and inflections. We can try to see mentally how characters look, where they stand in relation to one another, how they move and gesture. We can read, in short, as armchair directors and as aspiring actors and actresses considering the physical and practical realities of the performance.

Comedy Comic plays end happily, often with a celebration such as a marriage, success or good fortune. They celebrate (affirm) life, and are typically joyous and festival. Comic heroes are usually ordinary people, and are frequently one dimensional to the extent that many are stereotypes: the braggart, for example, or the hypocrite, the unfaithful wife, etc.

There are two major types of comedy: satiric and romantic. Satire exposes human folly, criticizes human conduct, and aims to correct it. Ridiculing the weakness of human nature, satiric comedy shows us the low level to which human behavior sink. Romantic comedy, on the other hand, portrays characters gently, even generously; its spirit is more tolerant and its tone more genial. The humor is more sympathetic than corrective, intending more to entertain than instruct, to delight than ridicule.

Tragedy In *Poetics*, Aristotle describes tragedy as "an imitation of an action that is serious, complete in itself, and has a certain magnitude". This definition suggests that tragedies are solemn plays concerned with grave human actions and their consequences. Tragic plays end sorrowfully, often with the death of the hero. They highlight life's sorrows and are typically brooding and solemn. Tragic heroes are usually grand, noble characters, men "of high estate". Their tragic ends are often resulted from flaws (weakness) in character, errors of judgment (tragedy of character). The heroes may also be doomed by fate, coincidence or circumstances beyond control (tragedy of circumstances). Despite the suffering and catastrophe, tragedies are not depressing. Aristotle suggested that the pity and fear aroused in the audience are purged or released and the audience experiences a cleansing of those emotions and a sense of relief that the action is over.

Tragicomedy Many modern plays mix elements of comedy and tragedy. Some plays may begin like a comedy but end more like a tragedy. Some other plays, which may end with a brutal murder, have some very funny moments. They are not so easy to classify and are often designated tragicomedies to identify their mode. Some twentieth century dramatists have found that tragicomedy is more suitable for representing a complex, uncertain, and often irrational world than either tragedy or comedy alone.

Elements of Drama

Plot Plot is the unified arrangement of the incidents of the play. Traditionally plot structure consists of an exposition, presentation of background information necessary for the development of the plot; rising action or the complication, a set of conflicts and crises; climax, the turning point and the play's most decisive crisis; falling action, a follow-up that moves toward the play's resolution or denouement. Whether playwrights use a traditional plot structure or vary the formula, they control our expectations about what is happening through plot. They decide when to present action and information, what to reveal and what to conceal. By arrangement of incidents, a dramatist may create suspense, evoke laughter, cause anxiety, or elicit surprise. Suspense is created by conflict. Drama is essentially the development and resolution of conflicts.

Introduction

Characters When reading plays, we are soon absorbed in the characters: how they look and what their appearance tells us about them; what they say and what their manner of saying expresses; what they do and how their actions reveal who they are and what they represent. Though the characters in plays are not real people, their human qualities are the most engaging feature that attracts the audience. Drama lives in the encounter of characters, and its essence is human relationships, the things men and women say and do to each other. Dramatic characters come together and affect each other, making things happen by coming into conflict.

Dialogue Plays are stories told in dialogue, and dramas are merely "persons moving about on a stage using words"(Ezra Pond), therefore the playwright's choices for dialogue are critical to the success of the drama. Dialogue in plays typically has three major functions: to advance plot, to establish setting (the time and place of the action), and to reveal character; and the last is the most important and consistent function. In some plays the dialogue is colloquial, resembling everyday speech, but in many poetic dramas, such as *Oedipus* and *Hamlet*, the dialogue avoids the conversational and aims at a more formal effect. Long passages of dialogue sometimes contain the philosophical parts of the play. Certain forms of dialogue are special to dramas. The soliloquy is a speech delivered while no one else is on stage. Soliloquies are important because we may assume that anything said in total private is truthful and revealing. Another special form of dialogue is the aside, a brief comment meant to be heard only by the audience that reveals the character's true feelings. Asides are not used very frequently because they break the spell of the drama, and they are usually included in the stage directions.

Staging By staging, we have in mind the spectacle a play presents in performance, its visual detail. This includes such things as the positions of actors onstage, their nonverbal gestures and movements, the scenic background, the props and costumes, lighting, and sound effects. Some playwrights, like Shakespeare, provide only scant suggestions for action. Others provide details of movement, such as "Picking up old newspapers and other trash from the floor", which may precede or coincide with a piece of dialogue. Some directions suggest emotions: "hostile", "strong", "increasing anger". Yet other directions are more complex and subtle, suggesting difficult actions for performance onstage. A playwright's stage directions will sometimes help us see and hear things. But with or without stage directions, we have to use our aural and visual imagination.

Theme From plot, character, dialogue and staging, we derive a sense of the play's meaning or significance. An abstraction of this meaning is its central idea or theme. When reading a play, we work back and forth between its details and our conception of its significance, letting the work modify and alter our notion of its theme, paying special attention to the dialogue of its characters, who frequently represent conflicting ideas and viewpoints. It is very likely that a play will include more than one theme.

Suggestions on Reading Drama

1. Read the opening stage directions carefully. Try to set the scene mentally. Read the opening scene slowly, referring back to the cast of characters if you become confused about who is who.

2. Note places in the action where conflicts develop most intensely. Consider what causes the conflict and how it might be resolved.

3. Decide what values the characters embody and believe in. Consider they may represent and examine their relationships with one another.

4. Listen carefully to the play's dialogue. Notice what the characters say and how they say things. Try to hear their tones of voice; consider what the characters' speeches reveal about them.

5. Try staging parts of the play in your mind. Try to visualize the play's setting from the dialogue and stage directions.

6. Try to sum up your sense of the play's central ideas. What point does it seem to make? What values emerge? What attitudes are taken toward these values by the playwright?

7. Consider the play's characters and action in relation to your own experience. Assess their values in the light of your own.

Enjoying Fiction

The literary genre of fiction, as we define today, roughly started in the 18th century. Judging by the length of writing, there are novels, novellas (short novels) and short stories. And with regard to the content of writing, we might figure out fairy tales and mystery stories, science fiction stories, and popular romance in this category. However, the earlier forms of fiction came into the world much earlier than we can accurately date. Those we might know include parables, fables and tales.

A parable is a brief story that teaches a lesson, often of a religious or spiritual nature. Likewise, fables are also brief stories that point to a certain moral. The difference between them lies in the fact that the moral of fables is stated explicitly, whereas the moral of parables is implied. For instance, at the end of each piece of the famous *Aesop's Fables* there must be a clear sentence to elucidate such morals like "goodness is the reward for good deeds"; but when Jesus speaks to his disciples in the *New Testament*, he will always choose to tell a story without stating out his true teaching verbally. Another earlier form, the tale, is a story that narrates strange or attention-grabbing happenings in a direct manner, without detailed descriptions of character. If we read a parable or a fable to get enlightened by its moral, we read a tale maybe just for fun, for the delight of reading.

It might be generally overviewed that novels, novellas and short stories can be distinguished from each other through their lengths. Yet this is not true. The short story developed and became popular in the 19th century. Parables, fables, and tales tend to summarize action, to tell what happens. Short stories, on the other hand, typically reveal character in dramatic scenes. The novella, the short novel, shares characteristics with both the novel and short story. Like the novel, the novella narrates incidents and portrays characters over a certain amount of time, which cannot be achieved by the short story due to the limitation of its scope. Yet like the short story, the novella also turns to moments of flashlights and quick turns of action to bring out a solidified theme.

Elements of Fiction

The basic elements of fiction are plot, character, setting, point of view, style and language, symbol, irony and theme. Each of them is worth plenty of discussion, but the reader should be aware that all the elements of a story work together to convey feeling and embody meaning.

Plot Plot, the action element in fiction, is the arrangement of events that make up a story. An enchanting plot is the magic that keeps us turning the pages of a story and even want to hold our breath to read on. A skillful writer knows how to manipulate his plot in such a pattern or order as to reveal his intentions and properly respond to the readers at the same time. Therefore, in examining plot, we are concerned with causality, with how one action leads into or has relation with another one.

Characters Characters are the imaginary people that writers create for a certain purpose, sometimes identifying with them and sometimes judging them. In fact, most of us read a story not only to find out what happens but also to follow the fortunes of the characters. We want to know not just "how did it happen" but "how did it happen to him or her". The well-forged characters often come alive when we read about them. We often make distinctions between major and minor, static and dynamic characters. Theoretically speaking, a major character centers the plot of the story yet minor characters support the development process. A static character is one whose depiction remains in congruity throughout the development of the plot, while a dynamic character is one who may have undergone a certain change, sometimes an abrupt psychological one, in the story.

Setting Setting refers to the place or location of a story's action along with the time in which it occurs. For writers like James Joyce or William Faulkner, setting is essential to meaning. Functioning as more than a simple backdrop for action, it provides a historical and cultural context that enhances our understanding of the theme or characters.

Point of View It is necessary to study the point of view in a story because we want to know who is telling the story and how that factor shapes our understanding. For example, in a story with an objective point of view, we seem to get an unbiased account of the happening. The narrator does not state clearly how we should form a judgment, so every single piece of knowledge has to be inferred from the fictional fact. Yet if the narrator also takes part in the story, we get a first-person point of view. It feels more personal and might affect the reader more directly, but certainly it has limitations of knowledge and vision.

Irony and Symbol Irony and symbol are two very important techniques used in many stories, but not in all. Writers have their own preferences. Irony is brought about by a contrast or discrepancy between one thing and another. For instance, the contrast may be between what is said and what is meant or between what happens and what is expected to happen. In some stories, the reader sees what is actually going on but some character may not see that. In that case, we see irony of circumstance. Symbols are simply objects, actions or events that convey meaning. The meaning will extend beyond their literal and superficial significance.

Theme A story's theme is its idea or point formulated as a generalization. Unlike earlier forms of fables or parables, modern fiction rarely reveals its theme openly so that it is abstracted from the details of characterization and action that compose the story. Different readers might see totally different themes in one story, because each of them inevitably relates the narration with their own life experience or vision.

Suggestions on Reading Fiction

1. Read the story a few times until you understand the plot and the characters. Some stories may not be designed for easy comprehension and immediate delight of the reader, for they demand thoughtfulness and wit.

2. Identify the setting and point of view of the story. Is there anything special about the setting? Why is the story told from this point of view?

3. Pay attention to special language phenomena, figure of speech, syntax features, symbols, irony, etc. Do they contribute to the weaving of the story? How?

4. Ponder over the theme of the story. What does the writer want to reveal through his artistic arrangement? What is the tone of him, serious or sarcastic?

5. Sometimes you may understand the theme or the story quickly because you have similar experience or you are utterly involved in it. Yet some other times you might feel lost in a maze. If this is the case, drop the story but pick it up a few days later or discuss it with your friends.

6. The social, cultural and ideological factors might play a fairly important role in the development of a story or the shaping of its characters. If possible, try to identify those factors so as to enhance your understanding of the story.

Enjoying Essay

The essay, a term originally taken from the French word "essai" (meaning "attempt"), is "a composition, usually in prose (Pope's *Moral Essays* in verse are an exception), which may be of only a few hundred words (like Bacon's *Essays*) or of book length (like Locke's *Essay Concerning Human Understanding*) and which discusses, formally or informally, a topic or a variety of topics". As one of the most flexible and adaptable of all literary forms, it "undertakes to discuss a matter, express a point of view, persuade us to accept a thesis on any subject, or simply entertain".

The Greeks Theophrastus and Plutarch and the Romans Cicero and Seneca practiced this literary form long before French philosopher Montaigne coined the word "essai" when, in 1580, he gave the title *Essais* to his first publication. The word means "attempts", and by its use Montaigne meant to indicate that his discussions were tentative compared with ordinary philosophical writings. When Francis Bacon published in 1597 his first collection of aphoristic essays, he used *Essays* as its title and became the first English "essayist". After Bacon, Alexander Pope adopted the term for his expository compositions in verse, *The Essay on Criticism* and *The Essay on Man*.

In the early eighteenth century Joseph Addison and Sir Richard Steel created in *Tatler* and *Spectator* the periodical essay, a new form that achieved great popularity and attracted some of the best writers of the time.

In the early nineteenth century the founding of new types of magazine, and their steady increase helped the development of essays and made them a major department of literature. Essayists as William Hazlitt, Thomas De Quincey, Charles Lamb, and, later in the century, Robert Louis Stevenson, brought the English essay, and especially the personal essay to a level that has not been surpassed. Major American essayists in this century include Washington Irving, Emerson, Thoreau, James Russell Lowell, and Mark Twain.

In the twentieth century, the essay in the tradition of Addison, Hazlitt and Lamb gradually gave place to constantly increasing journalism. But many writers, critics and philosophers continued to use the essay for their different purposes.

Concerning the matter of style, the essay falls into the category of nonfictional prose. It can be classified in different ways. One common classification is: the formal essay and the informal one. In terms of subjects and forms, it can be divided into moralizing, aphoristic, psychological, periodical, biographical, reflective, etc. According to Robert DiYanni, in his *Literature: Reading Fiction, Poetry, Drama and the Essay*, essays are classified in a rough way as speculative, argumentative, narrative, and expository. Narrative essays tell stories and chronicle event; expository essays explain ideas and attitudes; speculative essays explore ideas and feelings; argumentative essays make claims and present evidence to support them.

Elements of Essays

Due to the difference between the essay and the other literary forms, the genre has long had an uncertain status as literature. While we emphasize the primacy of ideas in the essay, we cannot deny that essays can be imaginative, dramatic, or poetic. Therefore, an essay, like a poem, play, or story, can also be studied from a number of perspectives: voice, style, structure, and thought—the basic elements of the essay as a literary form.

Voice When we read an essay we hear a writer's voice, someone speaking to us person to person. It is the essayist's voice that conveys his tone, his attitude toward his subject. The essayist's voice may be commanding or cajoling, intimate or reserved, urgent and insistent, witty and charming—to suggest a few possibilities.

Style When we talk about an essayist's works and the characteristic way he uses the resources of language to achieve certain effects, we are talking about style. A writer's style in an essay derives from choices he or she makes in diction (the individual words an author chooses), syntax (the arrangement of those words) and figurative language. Each essayist's style is unique. It distinguishes his work from that of others.

Structure The structural features of an essay are not as visible as the stanzas of poems or the acts and scenes of plays. In examining structure, we look for patterns, that is, the shape of the content that the essay as a whole possesses. Structure is important because it reflects thought and is closely connected with thought. The form of an essay, its structure of thought, is a clue to how we should read it; its form is an aspect of its meaning.

Thought When writers choose to write an essay rather than a poem, play, or story, it may be because they have something on their minds and want to express it. The very choice of factual rather than fictional discourse indicates the essayist's concern for expressing an idea. It is this primary of idea that makes an essay what it is. But thought does not exist independently of feeling. The ideas we discover in essays are felt, not merely thought out. They derive from the writer's emotions; they have their basis in feeling. Feeling, in fact, is mixed with thought expressed in language. Therefore, to some extent we can say that there is no thought without feeling.

Suggestions on Reading Essays

1. Read through the essay to get a feel for what it is about. Center on the subject and idea. During this reading, jot down your responses to the work and ask a few questions. Consider the essay in light of your own experience and how it affects you as you read it.

2. Read the essay a second time. During this reading, concentrate on the structure and the development of the argument. Pay special attention to shifts of direction, changes of language and tone, example and image, scene and point of view.

3. During your second reading—or possibly a third—concentrate on language and style. Notice diction, syntax, imagery and figurative language. Consider what the style reveals about the writer's purpose and the intended audience. Single out passages that highlight the central idea.

4. Consider the values the author expresses in the essay, as well as the essay's main assumption.

Part One British Literature

Poetry

Shall I Compare Thee to a Summer's Day

Shall I compare thee to a summer's day?
Thou art[①] more lovely and more temperate:
Rough winds do shake the darling buds of May,
And summer's lease hath all too short a date:
Sometime too hot the eye of heaven shines
And often is his gold complexion dimmed;
And every fair from fair sometime declines,
By chance or nature's changing course untrimmed;
But thy eternal summer shall not fade,
Nor lose possession of that fair thou ow'st;[②]
Nor shall death brag thou wander'st in his shade,
When in eternal lines to time thou grow'st:
So long as men can breathe or eyes can see,
So long lives this, and this gives life to thee.

Questions for Discussion

1. What makes the poet think "thou" are more lovely (fair), and can be immortal?
2. What is the theme of the poem?
3. What rhetorical devices are used in this sonnet?
4. Comment on the form of the poem, including the meter, rhyme, and the organization of the lines.

About the Author

William Shakespeare (1564—1616) is the greatest poet and dramatist in the English Renaissance period. Shakespeare produced 2 narrative poems, 154 sonnets and 38 plays. His writing has exerted tremendous influence on numerous later writers of England and the world. Sonnet is a poetic form in fourteen lines with one or more rhyming schemes. It was first introduced to England by

---

① You are.
② You own.

Thomas Wyatt from Italy. With some innovation of the borrowed Italian Peterachan Sonnet, Shakespeare made this poetic form very popular in England. There are various types of sonnets with different stylistic patterns. Shakespeare's sonnets, 154 in total number, are thought to be written between 1593—1599. Each sonnet contains three quadruplets and a final couplet as a conclusion. The lines are in iambic pentameter and the whole rhyming pattern is abab, cdcd, efef, gg. Shakespeare's sonnets, on the whole, focus on the theme of humanism: the praise of man, nature, life, beauty, love, friendship and virtues.

The Flea

Mark but this flea, and mark in this,
How little that which thou deny'st me is;
Me it sucked first, and now sucks thee,
And in this flea our two bloods mingled be;
Thou know'st that this cannot be said
A sin, or shame, or loss of maidenhead,
Yet this enjoys before it woo,
And pampered swells with one blood made of two,
And this, alas, is more than we would do. ①

Oh stay, three lives in one flea spare,
Where we almost, nay more than married are.
This flea is you and I, and this
Our marriage bed and marriage temple is;
Though parents grudge, and you, we are met,
And cloistered in these living walls of jet.
Though use② make you apt to kill me
Let not to that, self-murder added be,
And sacrilege, three sins in killing three.

Cruel and sudden, hast thou since

---

① We don't dare hope for this consummation of our love, which the flea freely accepts. The idea of swelling suggests pregnancy.
② Habit.

Purpled thy nail in blood of innocence?
Wherein could this flea guilty be,
Except in that drop which it sucked from thee?
Yet thou triumph'st, and say'st that thou
Find'st not thy self nor me the weaker now;
'Tis true; then learn how false fears be:
Just so much honor, when thou yield'st to me,
Will waste, as this flea's death took life from thee.

Questions for Discussion

1. Who is the speaker talking to? Guess what has happened before the poem begins?
2. What do you think of the speaker's assertion that the flea is their "marriage bed and marriage temple", and killing of it is "three sins in killing three"?
3. What do you think is the addressee's parents' attitude toward the wooing?
4. What happens in the third stanza? How does the speaker reason for his real purpose in the end?

About the Author

John Donne (1572—1631) is the most outstanding figure of the English Metaphysical Poetry. He was born in London to a prominent Roman Catholic family. He studied at Oxford, and began to study law at Lincoln's Inn, London, in 1592. Donne's poetry embraces a wide range of secular and religious subjects, and they reveal the typical characteristics of metaphysical poetry (a poetic style combining passion and intellect, displaying both feeling and learning): dazzling wordplay; paradox; subtle argumentation; surprising contrasts; intricate psychological analysis; and striking imagery selected from nontraditional areas such as law, physiology, philosophy, geography, astronomy and mathematics. Donne had the lively imagination to use unusual imagery in traditional situations, and the conceits are often startling. Besides, Donne frequently relies on conversational language and tone to give the lyrics a sense of immediacy. Donne's poetic collections include *Songs and Sonnets*, *Elegies* and *Holy Sonnets*. The selected poems, *Death, Be Not Proud* and *The Flea* are among the most famous.

The Definition of Love

My love is of a birth as rare
As 'tis for object strange and high①;
It was begotten by Despair
Upon Impossibility.

Magnanimous Despair alone
Could show me so divine a thing
Where feeble Hope could ne'er have flown,
But vainly flapp'd its tinsel② wing.

And yet I quickly might arrive
Where my extended soul is fixed③,
But Fate does iron wedges drive,
And always crowds itself betwixt.

For Fate with jealous eye does see
Two perfect loves, nor lets them close④;
Their union would her ruin be,
And her tyrannic pow'r depose⑤.

And therefore her decrees of steel
Us as the distant poles have plac'd,
(Though love's whole world on us doth wheel⑥)
Not by themselves to be embrac'd;

---

① I. e., my love's lineage is as rare as my love itself is strange and high.
② Glittering; also, flashy, with little or no intrinsic worth.
③ The speaker describes his soul as having gone out of his body ("extended") and attached ("fixed") itself to his mistress.
④ Unite.
⑤ A reference to the idea that an even mixture of pure elements formed an altogether stable compound, able to withstand any sudden change, and hence, in context, defying fate.
⑥ Though by decree of fate the lovers are as far apart as Earth's two poles, the relationship (literally, the line) between them forms the axis on which love's world turns.

Unless the giddy heaven fall,
And earth some new convulsion tear;
And, us to join, the world should all
Be cramp'd into a planisphere①.

As lines, so loves oblique may well
Themselves in every angle greet②;
But ours so truly parallel,
Though infinite, can never meet.

Therefore the love which us doth bind,
But Fate so enviously debars,
Is the conjunction of the mind,
And opposition of the stars③.

Questions for Discussion

1. What kind of metaphors have been used to describe love? What do they have in common?
2. What is the overall tone of the poem?

About the Author

Andrew Marvell (1621—1678), English poet, whose political reputation overshadowed that of his poetry until the 20th century. He is now considered to be one of the best Metaphysical poets. Marvell was educated at Hull grammar school and Trinity College, Cambridge, taking a B. A. in 1639. His father's death in 1641 may have ended Marvell's promising academic career. He was abroad for at least five years (1642—1646), presumably as a tutor. In 1651—

---

① A chart formed by the projection of a sphere on a plane; the two poles could come together only if the charted world were collapsed.

② I. e., the lines may converge at any angle. "Oblique" lovers, in one sense, might deviate from accepted behavior or thought.

③ In this astronomical image, the minds of the lovers are in accord (literally in "conjunction", or occupying the same celestial longitude), but the stars determining their destinies are entirely hostile (literally in "opposition", or 180 degrees apart).

1652 he was tutor to Mary, daughter of Lord Fairfax, the Parliamentary general, at Nun Appleton, Yorkshire, during which time he probably wrote his notable poems *Upon Appleton House* and *The Garden* as well as his series of Mower poems.

While Marvell's political reputation has faded and his reputation as a satirist is on a par with others of his time, his small body of lyric poems, first recommended in the 19th century by Charles Lamb, has since appealed to many readers, and in the 20th century he came to be considered one of the most notable poets of his century. Marvell was eclectic: his *To His Coy Mistress* is a classic of Metaphysical poetry; the Cromwell odes are the work of a classicist; his attitudes are sometimes those of the elegant Cavalier poets; and his nature poems resemble those of the Puritan Platonists. In *To His Coy Mistress*, which is one of the most famous poems in the English language, the impatient poet urges his mistress to abandon her false modesty and submit to his embraces before time and death rob them of the opportunity to love.

A Red, Red Rose

O my luve's① like a red, red rose,
That's newly sprung in June;
O my luve's like the melodie
That's sweetly play'd in tune.

As fair art thou, my bonnie lass,
So deep in luve am I;
And I will luve thee still, my dear,
Till a' the seas gang dry. ②

Till a' the seas gang dry, my dear,
And the rocks melt wi' the sun;
O I will luve thee still, my dear,
while the sands o'life shall run. ③

---

① Love.
② Till all the seas go dry.
③ The sands are allusive of the sands in the hourglass, hence, the moments of one's life.

And fare thee weel, my only luve,
And fare thee weel awhile!
And I will come again, my luve,
Though it were ten thousand mile.

Questions for Discussion

1. How does the speaker describe his love in the first stanza?
2. How does the speaker express his deep love for his girl?
3. What are the remarkable syntactical features of the poem?

My Heart's in the Highlands

My heart's in the Highlands,① my heart is not here;
My heart's in the Highlands, a-chasing the deer;
A-chasing the wild deer, and following the roe—
My heart's in the Highlands wherever I go.

Farewell to the Highlands, farewell to the North!
The birthplace of valor, the country of worth;
Wherever I wander, wherever I rove,
The hills of the Highlands for ever I love.

Farewell to the mountains high-cover'd with snow!
Farewell to the straths② and green valleys below!
Farewell to the forests and wild-hanging woods!
Farewell to the torrents and loud-pouring floods!

My heart's in the Highlands, my heart is not here;
My heart's in the Highlands a-chasing the deer;
A-chasing the wild deer, and following the roe—
My heart's in the Highlands wherever I go.

---

① The mountainous Northern area of Scotland.
② A flat, wide river valley.

Questions for Discussion

1. What is the poem mainly about? What emotion does the poet express in this poem?
2. Can you imagine the beautiful scenes of the Highlands? Describe them in your own words.
3. What are the functions of the repetition and parallel structures in this poem?

About the Author

Robert Burns (1759—1796) is the best-loved national poet of Scotland, and is celebrated throughout the world. Burns was born into a poor farming family in Ayrshire in 1759, and he began writing poems as a teenager while working on the farm. Burns tried publishing a collection of his early poems in 1786, and it turned out to be a great success. Then Burns settled down in Edinburgh, devoting himself mostly to collecting, revising and adapting traditional Scottish songs. Robert Burns is regarded as a forerunner of Romanticism poetry. He wrote his poems chiefly in the Scottish dialect, and his poetry is unsurpassed for its beautiful lyricism and sincerity of emotions. His themes vary: love and friendship; the natural beauty of Scotland; the life and labor of the common people; the patriotism and the struggle for liberty; satire on the corruption and hypocrisy of the high society. Burns played an important role in reviving and reserving the Scottish culture.

I Wandered Lonely as a Cloud

I wandered lonely as a cloud
That floats on high o'er vales and hills,
When all at once I saw a crowd,
A host, of golden daffodils;
Beside the lake, beneath the trees,
Fluttering and dancing in the breeze.

Continuous as the stars that shine
And twinkle on the milky way,

They stretched in never-ending line
Along the margin of a bay:
Ten thousand saw I at a glance,
Tossing their heads in sprightly dance.

The waves beside them danced; but they
Out-did the sparkling waves in glee;
A poet could not but be gay,
In such a jocund① company;
I gazed—and gazed—but little thought
What wealth the show to me had brought:

For oft, when on my couch I lie
In vacant or in pensive mood,
They flash upon that inward eye
Which is the bliss of solitude;
And then my heart with pleasure fills,
And dances with the daffodils.

Questions for Discussion

1. Compare the mood of the speaker in the beginning and in the end, and explain what leads to the change, in relating to the theme of the poem.
2. How does the poet describe the features of the daffodils in the poem? What rhetorical devices are used to make it so vivid and impressive?
3. Comment on the syntactical features and effects of the following two parts:

    Ten thousand saw I at a glance,
Tossing their heads in sprightly dance.

    ...

    I gazed—and gazed—but little thought
What wealth the show to me had brought.

---

① Cheerful.

Lines

Composed a Few Miles Above Tintern Abbey, on Revisiting the Banks of the Wye During a Tour. July 13, 1798

Five years have past; five summers, with the length
Of five long winters! and again I hear
These waters, rolling from their mountain-springs
With a soft inland murmur. —Once again
Do I behold these steep and lofty cliffs,
That on a wild secluded scene impress
Thoughts of more deep seclusion; and connect
The landscape with the quiet of the sky.
The day is come when I again repose
Here, under this dark sycamore, and view
These plots of cottage-ground, these orchard-tufts,
Which at this season, with their unripe fruits,
Are clad in one green hue, and lose themselves
'Mid groves and copses. Once again I see
These hedge-rows, hardly hedge-rows, little lines
Of sportive wood run wild: these pastoral farms,
Green to the very door; and wreaths of smoke
Sent up, in silence, from among the trees!

With some uncertain notice, as might seem
Of vagrant dwellers in the houseless woods,
Or of some Hermit's cave, where by his fire
The Hermit sits alone.

These beauteous forms,
Through a long absence, have not been to me
As is a landscape to a blind man's eye:
But oft, in lonely rooms, and 'mid the din
Of towns and cities, I have owed to them
In hours of weariness, sensations sweet,

Felt in the blood, and felt along the heart;
And passing even into my purer mind,
With tranquil restoration: — feelings too
Of unremembered pleasure: such, perhaps,
As have no slight or trivial influence
On that best portion of a good man's life,
His little, nameless, unremembered, acts
Of kindness and of love. Nor less, I trust,
To them I may have owed another gift,
Of aspect more sublime; that blessed mood
In which the burthen of the mystery,
In which the heavy and the weary weight
Of all this unintelligible world,
Is lightened: — that serene and blessed mood,
In which the affections gently lead us on, —
Until, the breath of this corporeal frame
And even the motion of our human blood
Almost suspended, we are laid asleep
In body, and become a living soul:
While with an eye made quiet by the power
Of harmony, and the deep power of joy,
We see into the life of things.

If this
Be but a vain belief, yet, oh! how oft —
In darkness and amid the many shapes
Of joyless daylight; when the fretful stir
Unprofitable, and the fever of the world,
Have hung upon the beatings of my heart —
How oft, in spirit, have I turned to thee,
O sylvan Wye! thou wanderer thro' the woods,
How often has my spirit turned to thee!

And now, with gleams of half-extinguished thought,
With many recognitions dim and faint,

And somewhat of a sad perplexity,
The picture of the mind revives again:
While here I stand, not only with the sense
Of present pleasure, but with pleasing thoughts
That in this moment there is life and food
For future years. And so I dare to hope,
Though changed, no doubt, from what I was when first
I came among these hills; when like a roe
I bounded o'er the mountains, by the sides
Of the deep rivers, and the lonely streams,
Wherever nature led: more like a man
Flying from something that he dreads than one
Who sought the thing he loved. For nature then
(The coarser pleasures of my boyish days,
And their glad animal movements all gone by)
To me was all in all. — I cannot paint
What then I was. The sounding cataract
Haunted me like a passion: the tall rock,
The mountain, and the deep and gloomy wood,
Their colours and their forms, were then to me
An appetite; a feeling and a love,
That had no need of a remoter charm,
By thought supplied, nor any interest
Unborrowed from the eye. — That time is past,
And all its aching joys are now no more,
And all its dizzy raptures. Not for this
Faint I, nor mourn nor murmur; other gifts
Have followed; for such loss, I would believe,
Abundant recompense. For I have learned
To look on nature, not as in the hour
Of thoughtless youth; but hearing oftentimes
The still, sad music of humanity,
Nor harsh nor grating, though of ample power
To chasten and subdue. And I have felt
A presence that disturbs me with the joy

Of elevated thoughts; a sense sublime
Of something far more deeply interfused,
Whose dwelling is the light of setting suns,
And the round ocean and the living air,
And the blue sky, and in the mind of man:
A motion and a spirit, that impels
All thinking things, all objects of all thought,
And rolls through all things. Therefore am I still
A lover of the meadows and the woods,
And mountains; and of all that we behold
From this green earth; of all the mighty world
Of eye, and ear, — both what they half create,
And what perceive; well pleased to recognise
In nature and the language of the sense
The anchor of my purest thoughts, the nurse,
The guide, the guardian of my heart, and soul
Of all my moral being.

Nor perchance,
If I were not thus taught, should I the more
Suffer my genial spirits to decay:
For thou art with me here upon the banks
Of this fair river; thou my dearest Friend,
My dear, dear Friend; and in thy voice I catch
The language of my former heart, and read
My former pleasures in the shooting lights
Of thy wild eyes. Oh! yet a little while
May I behold in thee what I was once,
My dear, dear Sister! and this prayer I make,
Knowing that Nature never did betray
The heart that loved her; 'tis her privilege,
Through all the years of this our life, to lead
From joy to joy; for she can so inform
The mind that is within us, so impress
With quietness and beauty, and so feed

With lofty thoughts, that neither evil tongues,
Rash judgments, nor the sneers of selfish men,
Nor greetings where no kindness is, nor all
The dreary intercourse of daily life,
Shall e'er prevail against us, or disturb
Our cheerful faith, that all which we behold
Is full of blessings. Therefore let the moon
Shine on thee in thy solitary walk;
And let the misty mountain-winds be free
To blow against thee: and, in after years,
When these wild ecstasies shall be matured
Into a sober pleasure; when thy mind
Shall be a mansion for all lovely forms,
Thy memory be as a dwelling-place
For all sweet sounds and harmonies; oh! then,
If solitude, or fear, or pain, or grief,
Should be thy portion, with what healing thoughts
Of tender joy wilt thou remember me,
And these my exhortations! Nor, perchance —
If I should be where I no more can hear
Thy voice, nor catch from thy wild eyes these gleams
Of past existence — wilt thou then forget
That on the banks of this delightful stream
We stood together; and that I, so long
A worshipper of Nature, hither came
Unwearied in that service: rather say
With warmer love — oh! with far deeper zeal
Of holier love. Nor wilt thou then forget,
That after many wanderings, many years
Of absence, these steep woods and lofty cliffs,
And this green pastoral landscape, were to me
More dear, both for themselves and for thy sake!

Questions for Discussion

1. Give a summary of the poem.

2. What's the general mood throughout the poem?
3. Wordsworth once said that "poetry is the overflow of powerful emotions recollected in tranquility." What kind of emotions are recollected here?

About the Author

William Wordsworth (1770—1850) attended Cambridge University, but remained rootless and virtually penniless until 1795, when a legacy made possible a reunion with his sister Dorothy Wordsworth. He became friends with S. T. Coleridge, with whom he wrote *Lyrical Ballads* (1798), the collection often considered to have launched the English Romantic movement. Wordsworth's contributions include *Tintern Abbey* and many lyrics controversial for their common, everyday language. Around 1798 he began writing the epic autobiographical poem that would absorb him intermittently for the next 40 years, *The Prelude* (1850). His second verse collection, *Poems, in Two Volumes* (1807), includes many of the rest of his finest works, including *Ode: Intimations of Immortality*. His poetry is perhaps most original in its vision of the almost divine power of the creative imagination reforging the links between man and man between humankind and the natural world. The most memorable poems of his middle and late years were often cast in elegaic mode; few match the best of his earlier works. By the time he became widely appreciated by the critics and the public, his poetry had lost much of its force and his radical politics had yielded to conservatism. In 1843 he became England's poet laureate. He is regarded as the central figure in the initiation of English Romanticism.

The Tyger

Tyger, tyger, burning bright
In the forests of the night,
What immortal hand or eye
Could frame thy fearful symmetry?

In what distant deeps or skies
Burnt the fire of thine eyes?
On what wings dare he aspire?
What the hand dare seize the fire?

And what shoulder and what art
Could twist the sinews of thy heart?
And when thy heart began to beat,
What dread hand? And what dread feet?

What the hammer? What the chain?
In what furnace was thy brain?
What the anvil? What dread grasp
Dare its deadly terrors clasp?

When the stars threw down their spears
And watered Heaven with their tears,
Did he smile his work to see?
Did he who made the Lamb make thee?
Tyger, tyger, burning bright
In the forests of the night,
What immortal hand or eye
Dare frame thy fearful symmetry?

The Lamb

Little lamb, who made thee?
Dost thou know who made thee,
Gave thee life and bid thee feed
By the stream and o'er the mead —
Gave thee clothing of delight,
Softest clothing, woolly bright,
Gave thee such a tender voice,
Making all the vales rejoice?
Little lamb, who made thee,
Dost thou know who made thee?

Little lamb, I'll tell thee,
Little lamb, I'll tell thee!

He is called by thy name,
For he calls himself a Lamb;
He is meek and he is mild,
He became a little child:
I a child, and thou a lamb,
We are called by his name.
Little lamb, God bless thee,
Little lamb, God bless thee!

Questions for Discussion

1. The two poems are from Blake's collection *Song of Innocence and Experience*. How can you make sense of these poems in consideration of the title of the collection?
2. What do the lamb and the tiger symbolize?

About the Author

William Blake (1757—1827), English poet, painter, engraver, and visionary. Though he did not attend school, he was trained as an engraver at the Royal Academy and opened a print shop in London in 1784. He developed an innovative technique for producing colored engravings and began producing his own illustrated books of poetry with his "illuminated printing," including *Songs of Innocence* (1789), *The Marriage of Heaven and Hell* (1793), and *Songs of Experience* (1794), *Jerusalem* (1804—1820), his third major epic treating of the fall and redemption of humanity, is his most richly decorated book. His other major works include *The Four Zoas* (1795—1804) and *Milton* (1804—1808). A late series of 22 watercolors inspired by *The Book of Job* includes some of his best-known pictures. He was called mad because he was single-minded and unworldly; he lived on the edge of poverty and died in neglect. His books form one of the most strikingly original and independent bodies of work in the Western cultural tradition. Ignored by the public of his day, he is now regarded as one of the earliest and greatest figures of Romanticism.

Frost at Midnight

The frost performs its secret ministry,

Unhelped by any wind. The owlet's cry
Came loud—and hark, again! loud as before.
The inmates of my cottage, all at rest,
Have left me to that solitude, which suits
Abstruser musings: save that at my side
My cradled infant① slumbers peacefully.
'Tis calm indeed! so calm, that it disturbs
And vexes meditation with its strange
And extreme silentness. Sea, hill, and wood,
This populous village! Sea, and hill, and wood,
With all the numberless goings on of life,
Inaudible as dreams! the thin blue flame
Lies on my low burnt fire, and quivers not;
Only that film②, which fluttered on the grate,
Still flutters there, the sole unquiet thing.
Methinks, its motion in this hush of nature
Gives it dim sympathies with me who live,
Making it a companionable form,
Whose puny flaps and freaks the idling Spirit
By its own moods interprets, every where
Echo or mirror seeking of itself,
And makes a toy of Thought.
But O! how oft,
How oft, at school, with most believing mind,
Presageful, have I gazed upon the bars,
To watch that fluttering stranger! and as oft
With unclosed lids, already had I dreamt
Of my sweet birth-place, and the old church-tower,
Whose bells, the poor man's only music, rang
From morn to evening, all the hot Fair-day③,
So sweetly, that they stirred and haunted me

---

① Coleridge's eldest son, Hartley.

② Bits of soot fluttering in a fireplace; in folklore, said to foretell the arrival of an unexpected guest, and hence called "strangers".

③ Market-day, often a time of festivities.

With a wild pleasure, falling on mine ear
Most like articulate sounds of things to come!
So gazed I, till the soothing things I dreamt
Lulled me to sleep, and sleep prolonged my dreams!
And so I brooded all the following morn,
Awed by the stern preceptor's face, mine eye
Fixed with mock study on my swimming book①:
Save if the door half opened, and I snatched
A hasty glance, and still my heart leaped up,
For still I hoped to see the stranger's face,
Townsman, or aunt, or sister more beloved,
My play-mate when we both were clothed alike!②

Dear Babe, that sleepest cradled by my side,
Whose gentle breathings, heard in this deep calm,
Fill up the interspersed vacancies
And momentary pauses of the thought!
My babe so beautiful! it thrills my heart
With tender gladness, thus to look at thee,
And think that thou shalt learn far other lore
And in far other scenes! For I was reared
In the great city, pent 'mid cloisters dim,
And saw nought lovely but the sky and stars.
But thou, my babe! shalt wander like a breeze
By lakes and sandy shores, beneath the crags
Of ancient mountain, and beneath the clouds,
Which image in their bulk both lakes and shores
And mountain crags: so shalt thou see and hear
The lovely shapes and sounds intelligible
Of that eternal language, which thy God
Utters, who from eternity doth teach
Himself in all, and all things in himself.

---

① I. e., seen unclearly because of emotion.
② In early childhood, when boys and girls wore the same kind of infants' clothing.

Great universal Teacher! he shall mould
Thy spirit, and by giving make it ask.

Therefore all seasons shall be sweet to thee,
Whether the summer clothe the general earth
With greenness, or the redbreast sit and sing
Betwixt the tufts of snow on the bare branch
Of mossy apple-tree, while the nigh thatch
Smokes in the sun-thaw; whether the eve-drops fall
Heard only in the trances of the blast,
Or if the secret ministry of frost
Shall hang them up in silent icicles,
Quietly shining to the quiet Moon.

Questions for Discussion

1. Please describe the scene in the poem.
2. How do you make sense of the title? What does the frost mean to the poet?

About the Author

Samuel Taylor Coleridge (1772—1834), English poet, critic, and philosopher. Born in Devonshire, he studied at Cambridge University, where he became closely associated with R. Southey. In his poetry he perfected a sensuous lyricism that was echoed by many later poets. *Lyrical Ballads* (1798, with W. Wordsworth), containing the famous *Rime of the Ancient Mariner* and *Frost at Midnight*, heralded the beginning of English Romanticism. Other poems in the "fantastical" style of the "Mariner" include the unfinished *Christabel* and the celebrated *Pleasure Dome of Kubla Khan*. While in a bad marriage and addicted to opium, he produced *Dejection: An Ode* (1802), in which he laments the loss of his power to produce poetry. Later, partly restored by his revived Anglican faith, he wrote *Biographia Literaria* (2 vols., 1817), the most significant work of general literary criticism of the Romantic period. Imaginative and complex, with a unique intellect, Coleridge led a restless life full of turmoil and unfulfilled possibilities.

My Last Duchess[①]

That's my last Duchess painted on the wall,
Looking as if she were alive. I call
That piece a wonder, now: Fra Pandolf's hands
Worked busily a day, and there she stands.
Will't please you sit and look at her? I said
"Fra Pandolf" by design, for never read
Strangers like you that pictured countenance,
The depth and passion of its earnest glance,
But to myself they turned (since none puts by
The curtain I have drawn for you, but I)
And seemed as they would ask me, if they durst,
How such a glance came there; so, not the first
Are you to turn and ask thus. Sir, 'twas not
Her husband's presence only, called that spot
Of joy into the Duchess' cheek: perhaps
Fra Pandolf chanced to say "Her mantle laps
"Over my Lady's wrist too much," or "Paint
"Must never hope to reproduce the faint
"Half-flush that dies along her throat": such stuff
Was courtesy, she thought, and cause enough
For calling up that spot of joy. She had
A heart—how shall I say? —too soon made glad,
Too easily impressed; she liked whate'er
She looked on, and her looks went everywhere.
Sir, 'twas all one! My favor at her breast,
The dropping of the daylight in the West,

---

① The events of Browning's poem parallel historical events, but its emphasis is rather on truth to Renaissance attitudes than on historic specificity. Alfonso II d'Este, Duke of Ferrara (born in 1533), in Northern Italy, had married his first wife, daughter of Cosimo I de'Medici, Duke of Florence, in 1558, when she was fourteen; she died on April 21, 1561, under suspicious circumstances, and soon afterwards he opened negotiations for the hand of the niece of the Count of Tyrol, the seat of whose court was at Innsbruck, in Austria. "Fra Pandolf" and "Claus of Innsbruck" are types rather than specific artists.

Part One   British Literature

The bough of cherries some officious fool
Broke in the orchard for her, the white mule
She rode with round the terrace—all and each
Would draw from her alike the approving speech,
Or blush, at least. She thanked men,—good! but thanked
Somehow—I know not how—as if she ranked
My gift of a nine-hundred-years-old name
With anybody's gift. Who'd stoop to blame
This sort of trifling? Even had you skill
In speech—which I have not—to make your will
Quite clear to such an one, and say, "Just this
"Or that in you disgusts me; here you miss,
"Or there exceed the mark"—and if she let
Herself be lessoned so, nor plainly set
Her wits to yours, forsooth, and made excuse,
—E'en then would be some stooping, and I choose
Never to stoop. Oh sir, she smiled, no doubt,
Whene'er I passed her; but who passed without
Much the same smile? This grew; I gave commands;
Then all smiles stopped together. There she stands
As if alive. Will't please you rise? We'll meet
The company below, then. I repeat,
The Count your master's known munificence
Is ample warrant that no just pretense
Of mine for dowry will be disallowed;
Though his fair daughter's self, as I avowed
At starting, is my object. Nay, we'll go
Together down, sir. Notice Neptune, though,
Taming a sea-horse, thought a rarity,
Which Claus of Innsbruck cast in bronze for me!

Questions for Discussion

1. Who is speaking in this poem? According to this passage, what happened to the duchess? Why?
2. What do you know about the character of the duke and his last duchess from

this passage? Illustrate how irony is effectively used in the poem.
3. This poem is in the form of dramatic dialogue. Who is the silent listener present? What is he here for? What is the purpose for the duke to show him the portrait of the last duchess?

About the Author

Robert Browning (1812—1889) is one of the most well-known Victorian poets. He was born in Camberwell, south London. His early poetical works attracted little attention, and the publication of his poems under the title *Bells and Pomegranates* between 1841 and 1846 brought him instant fame. The book contained several of his best-known poems, including *Pippa Passes* (1841), a dramatic poem depicting a silk winder and his wandering in Italy. In 1846 Browning married the poet Elizabeth Barrett, and settled with her in Florence. When Elizabeth died in 1861, he moved to London, and there he wrote his greatest work, *The Ring and the Book* (1869). Browning is best-known for his dramatic monologue technique (his contribution to English poetry). This is a type of poems in which an imaginary or historical character, at some critical moment, addresses an identifiable but silent audience, thereby unwittingly revealing his or her real personality.

How Do I Love Thee?

How do I love thee? Let me count the ways.
I loved thee to the depth and breadth and height
My soul can reach, when feeling out of sight
For the ends of Being and ideal Grace.
I love thee to the level of everyday's
Most quiet need, by sun and candle-light.
I love thee freely, as men strive for Right;
I love thee purely, as they turn from praise.
I love thee with the passion put to use
In my old griefs, and with my childhood's faith.
I love thee with a love I seemed to lose
With my lost saints—I love thee with the breath,
Smile, tears, of all my life! —and, if God choose,

I shall but love thee better after death.

Questions for Discussion

1. Who is the speaker addressing to? What is she talking about? Can you describe the tone of her speaking?
2. How many ways does she count in which she loves him?
3. What is the most remarkable syntactical feature of the poem? What effect does it achieve?

About the Author

Elizabeth Barrett Browning (1806—1861) is the most respected and successful woman poet of the Victorian period. An injury to her spine when she was fifteen confined young Elizabeth in her gloomy home, but she read and wrote. Her efforts in literature brought the publication of her famous volume of *Poems* in 1844, which changed her life dramatically. Robert Browning read the poems, loved them and loved her. He began corresponding with her by letter. This was the start of one of the world's most famous romances. They married and moved to Italy in 1846, and lived happily till the death of Mrs. Browning in 1861. Elizabeth's greatest work, *Sonnets from the Portuguese* (1850), is a sequence of love sonnets which exhibit not only her superb skill in writing poetry but her heart-felt love for the man she loved.

When You Are Old

When you are old and gray and full of sleep,
And nodding by the fire, take down this book,
And slowly read, and dream of the soft look
Your eyes had once, and of their shadows deep;

How many loved your moments of glad grace,
And loved your beauty with love false or true,
But one man loved the pilgrim soul in you,
And loved the sorrows of your changing face;

And bending down beside the glowing bars,
Murmur, a little sadly, how love fled
And paced upon the mountains overhead
And hid his face amid a crowd of stars.

Questions for Discussion

1. There is a very popular song adapted from this poem. Can you figure out what it is?
2. Compare the Chinese song with this poem. Do you see any differences?

The Second Coming

Turning and turning in the widening gyre
The falcon cannot hear the falconer;
Things fall apart; the centre cannot hold;
Mere anarchy is loosed upon the world,
The blood-dimmed tide is loosed, and everywhere
The ceremony of innocence is drowned;
The best lack all conviction, while the worst
Are full of passionate intensity.

Surely some revelation is at hand;
Surely the Second Coming is at hand.
The Second Coming! Hardly are those words out
When a vast image out of Spiritus Mundi
Troubles my sight: a waste of desert sand;
A shape with lion body and the head of a man,
A gaze blank and pitiless as the sun,
Is moving its slow thighs, while all about it
Wind shadows of the indignant desert birds.

The darkness drops again but now I know
That twenty centuries of stony sleep
Were vexed to nightmare by a rocking cradle,
And what rough beast, its hour come round at last,

Part One British Literature

Slouches towards Bethlehem to be born?

Questions for Discussion

1. The poem refers to the biblical event of the second coming of Jesus Christ. Please give a brief summary of the event.
2. How does the poet describe the second coming? What is the basic tone?

About the Author

William Butler Yeats (1865—1939) Irish poet, dramatist, and prose writer. The son of a well-known painter, Yeats early developed an interest in mysticism and visionary traditions as well as in Irish peasant folklore, and both interests would continue to be sources of poetic imagery for him. His early volumes include the poetry volume *The Wanderings of Oisin* (1889) and the essay collection *The Celtic Twilight* (1893). In 1889 he fell in love with Maud Gonne, a brilliant, beautiful Irish patriot who inspired his involvement in Irish nationalism but did not reciprocate his feelings. With Lady A. Gregory and others, he founded the theater that became the Abbey Theatre; throughout his life he would remain one of its directors. He contributed plays to its repertoire, including *The Countess Cathleen* (1899), *On Baile's Strand* (1905), and *Deirdre* (1907). His poetry changed decisively in the years 1909—1914: the otherworldly, ecstatic atmosphere of the early lyrics cleared and his work gained in concreteness and complexity, often dealing with political themes, though his interest in mysticism and his passion for Maud Gonne continued unabated. With *Responsibilities* (1914) and *The Wild Swans at Coole* (1917) he began the period of his highest achievement. Some of his greatest verse appears in *The Tower* (1928), *The Winding Stair* (1929), and *Last Poems* (1939), whose individual poems are largely held together by the system of symbolism he developed in *A Vision* (1925), which used astrological images to link individual psychology with the larger patterns of history. He was a member of the Irish Senate (1922—1928). He won the Nobel Prize in 1923, and he is regarded by some as the greatest English-language poet of the 20th century.

Ulysses

It little profits that an idle king,

By this still hearth, among these barren crags,
Match'd with an aged wife, I mete and dole
Unequal laws unto a savage race,
That hoard, and sleep, and feed, and know not me.

I cannot rest from travel: I will drink
Life to the lees: all times I have enjoy'd
Greatly, have suffer'd greatly, both with those
That loved me, and alone; on shore, and when
Thro' scudding drifts the rainy Hyades
Vext the dim sea: I am become a name;
For always roaming with a hungry heart
Much have I seen and known; cities of men
And manners, climates, councils, governments,
Myself not least, but honour'd of them all;
And drunk delight of battle with my peers,
Far on the ringing plains of windy Troy.

I am a part of all that I have met;
Yet all experience is an arch wherethro'
Gleams that untravell'd world, whose margin fades
For ever and for ever when I move.
How dull it is to pause, to make an end,
To rust unburnish'd, not to shine in use!
As tho' to breathe were life. Life piled on life
Were all too little, and of one to me
Little remains: but every hour is saved
From that eternal silence, something more,
A bringer of new things; and vile it were
For some three suns to store and hoard myself,
And this gray spirit yearning in desire
To follow knowledge like a sinking star,
Beyond the utmost bound of human thought.

This is my son, mine own Telemachus,

To whom I leave the sceptre and the isle—
Well-loved of me, discerning to fulfil
This labour, by slow prudence to make mild
A rugged people, and thro' soft degrees
Subdue them to the useful and the good.
Most blameless is he, centred in the sphere
Of common duties, decent not to fail
In offices of tenderness, and pay
Meet adoration to my household gods,
When I am gone. He works his work, I mine.

There lies the port; the vessel puffs her sail:
There gloom the dark broad seas. My mariners,
Souls that have toil'd, and wrought, and thought with me—
That ever with a frolic welcome took
The thunder and the sunshine, and opposed
Free hearts, free foreheads—you and I are old;
Old age hath yet his honour and his toil;
Death closes all: but something ere the end,
Some work of noble note, may yet be done,
Not unbecoming men that strove with Gods.
The lights begin to twinkle from the rocks:
The long day wanes: the slow moon climbs: the deep
Moans round with many voices. Come, my friends,
'Tis not too late to seek a newer world.
Push off, and sitting well in order smite
The sounding furrows; for my purpose holds
To sail beyond the sunset, and the baths
Of all the western stars, until I die.
It may be that the gulfs will wash us down:
It may be we shall touch the Happy Isles,
And see the great Achilles, whom we knew.
Tho' much is taken, much abides; and tho'
We are not now that strength which in old days
Moved earth and heaven; that which we are, we are—

One equal temper of heroic hearts,
Made weak by time and fate, but strong in will
To strive, to seek, to find, and not to yield.

Questions for Discussion

1. Please tell the relationship between this poem and the story of Ulysses.
2. The last few lines have been adopted in the latest James Bond film. In what kind of circumstance are they quoted in the film?

About the Author

Alfred, Lord Tennyson (1809—1892), English poet, the leading poet of the Victorian Age. While attending Cambridge University, Tennyson developed a deep friendship with Arthur Hallam and published *Poems, Chiefly Lyrical* (1830). Another volume, including *The Lotos-Eaters* and *The Lady of Shalott*, was published in 1832 (dated 1833). When Hallam died suddenly in 1833, the severe shock prompted Tennyson to write poems that eventually became part of the vast *In Memoriam* (1850) and lyrics that later appeared in the brooding *Maud* (1855), his favorite poem. *Poems* (1842), including *Ulysses*, *Morte d'Arthur*, and *Locksley Hall*, followed, then *The Princess* (1847), a long antifeminist fantasia that includes such lyrics as *Sweet and Low* and *Tears, Idle Tears*. In 1850 he married and was named poet laureate of England. Among his subsequent works are *The Charge of the Light Brigade* (1855); *Idylls of the King* (1859), treating the Arthurian legend; and *Enoch Arden* (1864). A consummate poetic artist who was inclined to melancholy, Tennyson was also regarded as a spokesman for the educated English middle class. His works often dealt with the difficulties of an age when traditional assumptions were increasingly called into question by science and modern progress.

Hawk Roosting

I sit in the top of the wood, my eyes closed.
Inaction, no falsifying dream
Between my hooked head and hooked feet:
Or in sleep rehearse perfect kills and eat.

The convenience of the high trees!
The air's buoyancy and the sun's ray
Are of advantage to me;
And the earth's face upward for my inspection.

My feet are locked upon the rough bark.
It took the whole of Creation
To produce my foot, my each feather:
Now I hold Creation in my foot

Or fly up, and revolve it all slowly—
I kill where I please because it is all mine.
There is no sophistry in my body:
My manners are tearing off heads—

The allotment of death.
For the one path of my flight is direct
Through the bones of the living.
No arguments assert my right:

The sun is behind me.
Nothing has changed since I began.
My eye has permitted no change.
I am going to keep things like this.

Questions for Discussion

1. What physical advantages does the hawk enjoy?
2. What does the monologue reveal about the nature of the hawk?
3. How do you understand the symbolic meaning of the hawk?

About the Author

Ted Hughes (1930—1998) is ranked as one of the best poets of his generation. He went to Cambridge in 1950. After graduation, he spent two years working a series of jobs in London, and then he returned to Cambridge to start a literary magazine with friends. Hughes wrote frequently of the mixture of beauty and violence in the natural world. Animals serve as a metaphor for his view on life: animals live out a struggle for the survival of the fittest in the same way that humans strive for ascendancy and success. A classic example is *Hawk Roosting*. His later work is heavily inflected with a modernist, existential and satirical viewpoint. Hughes' first collection, *Hawk in the Rain* (1957) attracted considerable critical acclaim. His most significant work is perhaps *Crow* (1970), which combines an apocalyptic, bitter, cynical and surreal view of the universe with what appears to be simple verse. He was British Poet Laureate from 1984 until his death.

40—Love

Middle   aged
couple   playing
ten   nis
when   the
game   ends
and   they
go   home
the   net
will   still
be   be
tween   them

Questions for Discussion

1. What does the poem say about?
2. The form of this poem speaks a lot. What does the poem look like?
3. What is special with the title?

About the Author

Roger McGough (1937—) is one of the most prominent British poets today. He belongs to the Liverpool Poets, who became renowned in the 1960s for their public performances of poetry (Their subject matter of popular culture and music, and the use of wit and colloquial language were inspired by the US Beat poets of the 1950s and the contemporary Liverpool music scene—chiefly The Beatles). McGough's unusual poetry challenges the imagination of his readers, and the speed of reading is often slowed in order to draw attention to the arrangement of the words on the page in contrast to the usual way of reading everyday texts. His writing is outgoing, and was often displayed in public places like the London Underground or local bus services.

Drama

Hamlet: Prince of Denmark

William Shakespeare

ACT Ⅲ (Excerpts)

SCENE Ⅰ. A room in the castle.

Enter KING CLAUDIUS, QUEEN GERTRUDE, POLONIUS, OPHELIA, ROSENCRANTZ, and GUILDENSTERN

KING CLAUDIUS

And can you, by no drift of conference,
Get from him why he puts on this confusion,
Grating so harshly all his days of quiet
With turbulent and dangerous lunacy?

ROSENCRANTZ

He does confess he feels himself distracted;
But from what cause he will by no means speak.

GUILDENSTERN

Nor do we find him forward to be sounded,
But, with a crafty madness, keeps aloof,
When we would bring him on to some confession
Of his true state.

QUEEN GERTRUDE

Did he receive you well?

ROSENCRANTZ

Most like a gentleman.

GUILDENSTERN

But with much forcing of his disposition.

ROSENCRANTZ

Niggard of question; but, of our demands,
Most free in his reply.

QUEEN GERTRUDE

Did you assay① him?
To any pastime?

ROSENCRANTZ

Madam, it so fell out, that certain players
We o'er-raught② on the way: of these we told him;
And there did seem in him a kind of joy
To hear of it: they are about the court,
And, as I think, they have already order
This night to play before him.

LORD POLONIUS

'Tis most true:
And he beseech'd me to entreat your majesties
To hear and see the matter.

KING CLAUDIUS

With all my heart; and it doth much content me
To hear him so inclined.
Good gentlemen, give him a further edge,
And drive his purpose on to these delights.

ROSENCRANTZ

We shall, my lord.
Exeunt ROSENCRANTZ and GUILDENSTERN

KING CLAUDIUS

Sweet Gertrude, leave us too;
For we have closely③ sent for Hamlet hither,
That he, as 'twere by accident, may here
Affront④ Ophelia:

---

① Try to win.
② Overtook and passed.
③ Privately.
④ Confront, meet.

Her father and myself, lawful espials,
Will so bestow ourselves that, seeing, unseen,
We may of their encounter frankly judge,
And gather by him, as he is behaved,
If 't be the affliction of his love or no
That thus he suffers for.

QUEEN GERTRUDE

I shall obey you.
And for your part, Ophelia, I do wish
That your good beauties be the happy cause
Of Hamlet's wildness: so shall I hope your virtues
Will bring him to his wonted way again,
To both your honours.

OPHELIA

Madam, I wish it may.
Exit QUEEN GERTRUDE

LORD POLONIUS

Ophelia, walk you here. Gracious, so please you,
We will bestow ourselves.
To OPHELIA
Read on this book;
That show of such an exercise may colour①
Your loneliness. We are oft to blame in this,—
'Tis too much proved—that with devotion's visage
And pious action we do sugar o'er
The devil himself.

KING CLAUDIUS

(Aside) O, 'tis too true!
How smart a lash that speech doth give my conscience!
The harlot's cheek, beautied with plastering art,

---

① In such a manner that shows your loneliness.

Is not more ugly to the thing that helps it
Than is my deed to my most painted word:
O heavy burthen!

LORD POLONIUS

I hear him coming: let's withdraw, my lord.
Exeunt KING CLAUDIUS and POLONIUS
Enter HAMLET

HAMLET

To be, or not to be: that is the question:
Whether 'tis nobler in the mind to suffer
The slings and arrows of outrageous fortune①,
Or to take arms against a sea of troubles,
And by opposing end them? To die: to sleep;
No more; and by a sleep to say we end
The heart-ache and the thousand natural shocks
That flesh is heir to? 'Tis a consummation②
Devoutly to be wish'd. To die, to sleep;
To sleep, perchance to dream: aye, there's the rub;
For in that sleep of death what dreams may come
When we have shuffled off this mortal coil③,
Must give us pause. There's the respect
That makes calamity of so long life;
For who would bear the whips and scorns of time,
The oppressor's wrong, the proud man's contumely,
The pangs of despised love, the law's delay,
The insolence of office and the spurns
That patient merit of the unworthy takes,
When he himself might his quietus make
With a bare bodkin④? Who would fardels bear,

---

① The fatal attacks of cruel destiny.
② End, a completion of one's life.
③ The trouble of mortal life.
④ Might make an end of his life with merely a dagger.

To grunt and sweat under a weary life,
But that the dread of something after death,
The undiscover'd country from whose bourn
No traveller returns, puzzles the will,
And makes us rather bear those ills we have
Than fly to others that we know not of?
Thus conscience does make cowards of us all;
And thus the native hue of resolution
Is sicklied o'er① with the pale cast of thought,
And enterprises of great pitch and moment
With this regard their currents turn awry,
And lose the name of action.—Soft you now!
The fair Ophelia! Nymph, in thy orisons
Be all my sins remember'd.

OPHELIA

Good my lord,
How does your honour for this many a day?

HAMLET

I humbly thank you; well, well, well.

OPHELIA

My lord, I have remembrances of yours,
That I have longed long to re-deliver;
I pray you, now receive them.

HAMLET

No, not I;
I never gave you aught②.

OPHELIA

My honour'd lord, you know right well you did;
And, with them, words of so sweet breath composed

---

① Cover with a sickly colour.
② Anything.

As made the things more rich: their perfume lost,
Take these again; for to the noble mind
Rich gifts wax poor when givers prove unkind.
There, my lord.

HAMLET

Ha, ha! Are you honest①?

OPHELIA

My lord?

HAMLET

Are you fair?

OPHELIA

What means your lordship?

HAMLET

That if you be honest and fair, your honesty should admit no discourse to your beauty.

OPHELIA

Could beauty, my lord, have better commerce② than with honesty?

HAMLET

Ay, truly; for the power of beauty will sooner transform honesty from what it is to a bawd than the force of honesty can translate beauty into his likeness: this was sometime a paradox, but now the time gives it proof. I did love you once.

OPHELIA

Indeed, my lord, you made me believe so.

---

① Truthful; chaste.
② Dealings.

HAMLET

You should not have believed me; for virtue cannot so inoculate our old stock① but we shall relish of it: I loved you not.

OPHELIA

I was the more deceived.

HAMLET

Get thee to a nunnery: why wouldst thou be a breeder of sinners? I am myself indifferent honest; but yet I could accuse me of such things that it were better my mother had not borne me: I am very proud, revengeful, ambitious, with more offences at my beck② than I have thoughts to put them in, imagination to give them shape, or time to act them in. What should such fellows as I do crawling between earth and heaven? We are arrant knaves, all; believe none of us. Go thy ways to a nunnery. Where's your father?

OPHELIA

At home, my lord.

HAMLET

Let the doors be shut upon him, that he may play the fool no where but in's own house. Farewell.

OPHELIA

O, help him, you sweet heavens!

HAMLET

If thou dost marry, I'll give thee this plague for thy dowry: be thou as chaste as ice, as pure as

---

① We do not still have the virtue of the old stock.
② At my command.

snow, thou shalt not escape calumny. Get thee to a
nunnery, go: farewell. Or, if thou wilt needs
marry, marry a fool; for wise men know well enough
what monsters you make of them①. To a nunnery, go,
and quickly too. Farewell.

OPHELIA

O heavenly powers, restore him!

HAMLET

I have heard of your paintings too, well enough; God
has given you one face, and you make yourselves
another: you jig, you amble, and you lisp, and
nick-name God's creatures, and make your wantonness
your ignorance②. Go to, I'll no more on't; it hath
made me mad. I say, we will have no more marriages:
those that are married already, all but one, shall
live; the rest shall keep as they are. To a nunnery, go.
Exit

OPHELIA

O, what a noble mind is here o'erthrown!
The courtier's, soldier's, scholar's, eye, tongue, sword;
The expectancy and rose of the fair state③,
The glass of fashion and the mould of form,
The observed of all observers, quite, quite down!
And I, of ladies most deject and wretched,
That suck'd the honey of his music vows,
Now see that noble and most sovereign reason,
Like sweet bells jangled, out of tune and harsh;
That unmatch'd form and feature of blown youth
Blasted with ecstasy④: O, woe is me,

---

① What cuckolds you women make them.
② Excuse your affection on the grounds of your ignorance.
③ The hope and ornament of the kingdom.
④ Madness.

To have seen what I have seen, see what I see!

Re-enter KING CLAUDIUS and POLONIUS

KING CLAUDIUS

Love! His affections do not that way tend;
Nor what he spake, though it lack'd form a little,
Was not like madness. There's something in his soul,
O'er which his melancholy sits on brood;
And I do doubt the hatch and the disclose
Will be some danger: which for to prevent,
I have in quick determination
Thus set it down: he shall with speed to England,
For the demand of our neglected tribute
Haply the seas and countries different
With variable objects shall expel
This something-settled matter in his heart,
Whereon his brains still beating puts him thus
From fashion of himself①. What think you on't?

LORD POLONIUS

It shall do well: but yet do I believe
The origin and commencement of his grief
Sprung from neglected love. How now, Ophelia!
You need not tell us what Lord Hamlet said;
We heard it all. My lord, do as you please;
But, if you hold it fit, after the play
Let his queen mother all alone entreat him
To show his grief: let her be round with him;
And I'll be placed, so please you, in the ear
Of all their conference. If she find him not,
To England send him, or confine him where
Your wisdom best shall think.

---

① Out of his natural manner.

Part One British Literature

KING CLAUDIUS

It shall be so:
Madness in great ones must not unwatch'd go.
Exeunt

Questions for Discussion

1. A great deal has been written on the meaning of the famous line "To be, or not to be." How do you understand this line in the context of the soliloquy and of the entire play?
2. Why does Hamlet urge Ophelia to go to a nunnery repeatedly in Act III, scene I ? How does this statement reflect Hamlet's views about the world around him?
3. Comment on Hamlet's paradoxical remarks that convince Ophelia his madness. Describe the character of Hamlet and Ophelia.
4. Describe the varied views of Claudius and Polonius on Hamlet's madness. What does this reveal about their character?
5. Illustrate how important this part is to the whole play.

About the Author

    William Shakespeare (1564—1616), one of the greatest giant of the Renaissance, holds the foremost place in the world's literature. He was born in Stratford-upon-Avon, Warwick, in central England. At the age of seven he attended the local grammar school and there learned Latin and a little Greek. At eighteen he married Anne Hathaway, who was eight years senior, and they had three children. About 1586 Shakespeare left his family for London. First he worked at odd jobs in a theater. Then he became an actor and later started to write for the stage. By the end of the 16th century he had already won the popularity of a successful writer. In 1611 he retired to his native town, and stayed there till his death in 1616.

    As a dramatist, Shakespeare's career is usually divided into three periods. In the first period (1590—1600), he wrote most of his historical plays and comedies, and a few early tragedies, and these plays are imbued with an optimistic atmosphere of humanism. The best-known plays of this period are *Romeo and Juliet* (1594) and *The Merchant of Venice* (1596). The second period (1601—1608), includes chiefly his great tragedies: *Hamlet* (1601), *Othello* (1604), *King Lear* (1605), *Macbeth* (1605) and *Timon of Athens* (1609), which reflect the social contradictions of the age. In the third period (1609—1612), Shakespeare chiefly wrote three tragic-comedies, of which *The Tempest* (1612) is the most significant. In these last plays we see Shakespeare's optimistic faith in the future of humanity, at the same time we also see the dramatist's Utopianism. Shakespeare's impact on English language, literature and thought is beyond calculation. According to his contemporary playwright, Ben Johnson, Shakespeare was "not of an age, but for all time."

Hamlet is undoubtedly the most famous of Shakespearean plays. Through a story of murder and revenge, Shakespeare depicts Hamlet as an image of typical idealist, who is ambitious to set right "the time that is out of joint". Hamlet embodies, with his action and speeches, a humanist desire for a comprehensive and thorough reformation of the social realities that are degenerated with various kinds of evils. The play also exhibits the playwright's masterly dramatic skills, like performance of a play within a play, the lunacy of major characters, the appearance of a ghost, heart-searching soliloquies, superb blank verse, which are components of his dramatic creation.

In Act Ⅲ, Scene Ⅰ, Claudius, suspicious of Hamlet's motive in the disguise of madness, decides to test him by arranging a meeting between Ophelia and Hamlet. This part includes the best known and most important of Hamlet's soliloquies, in which Shakespeare has Hamlet reveal his innermost thoughts and emotions, his hesitation in particular, before taking decisive action to revenge.

The Importance of Being Earnest

Oscar Wilde

ACT I. (Part 1)

...

(*Enter LANE.* [1])

LANE. Mr. Ernest Worthing.

(*Enter JACK*)

(*LANE goes out.*)

ALGERNON. How are you, my dear Ernest? What brings you up to town?

JACK. Oh, pleasure, pleasure! What else should bring one anywhere? Eating as usual, I see, Algy!

ALGERNON. (*Stiffly.*) I believe it is customary in good society to take some slight refreshment at five o'clock. Where have you been since last Thursday?

JACK. (*Sitting down on the sofa.*) In the country.

ALGERNON. What on earth do you do there?

JACK. (*Pulling off his gloves.*) When one is in town one amuses oneself. When one is in the country one amuses other people. It is excessively boring.

ALGERNON. And who are the people you amuse?

JACK. (*Airily.*) Oh, neighbours, neighbours.

ALGERNON. Got nice neighbours in your part of Shropshire?

JACK. Perfectly horrid! Never speak to one of them.

ALGERNON. How immensely you must amuse them! (*Goes over and takes sandwich.*) By the way, Shropshire is your county, is it not?

JACK. Eh? Shropshire? Yes, of course. Hallo! Why all these cups? Why cucumber sandwiches? Why such reckless extravagance in one so young? Who is coming to tea?

ALGERNON. Oh! merely Aunt Augusta and Gwendolen.

JACK. How perfectly delightful!

---

[1] Lane is the servant of Algernon.

ALGERNON. Yes, that is all very well; but I am afraid Aunt Augusta won't quite approve of your being here.

JACK. May I ask why?

ALGERNON. My dear fellow, the way you flirt with Gwendolen is perfectly disgraceful. It is almost as bad as the way Gwendolen flirts with you.

JACK. I am in love with Gwendolen. I have come up to town expressly to propose to her.

ALGERNON. I thought you had come up for pleasure?... I call that business.

JACK. How utterly unromantic you are!

ALGERNON. I really don't see anything romantic in proposing. It is very romantic to be in love. But there is nothing romantic about a definite proposal. Why, one may be accepted. One usually is, I believe. Then the excitement is all over. The very essence of romance is uncertainty. If ever I get married, I'll certainly try to forget the fact.

JACK. I have no doubt about that, dear Algy. The Divorce Court was specially invented for people whose memories are so curiously constituted.

ALGERNON. Oh! there is no use speculating on that subject. Divorces are made in Heaven—(*Jack puts out his hand to take a sandwich. Algernon at once interferes.*) Please don't touch the cucumber sandwiches. They are ordered specially for Aunt Augusta. (*Takes one and eats it.*)

JACK. Well, you have been eating them all the time.

ALGERNON. That is quite a different matter. She is my aunt. (*Takes plate from below.*) Have some bread and butter. The bread and butter is for Gwendolen. Gwendolen is devoted to bread and butter.

JACK. (*Advancing to table and helping himself.*) And very good bread and butter it is too.

ALGERNON. Well, my dear fellow, you need not eat as if you were going to eat it all. You behave as if you were married to her already. You are not married to her already, and I don't think you ever will be.

JACK. Why on earth do you say that?

ALGERNON. Well, in the first place girls never marry the men they flirt with. Girls don't think it right.

JACK. Oh, that is nonsense!

ALGERNON. It isn't. It is a great truth. It accounts for the extraordinary number of bachelors that one sees all over the place. In the second place, I don't give my consent.

JACK. Your consent!

ALGERNON. My dear fellow, Gwendolen is my first cousin. And before I allow you to marry her, you will have to clear up the whole question of Cecily. (*Rings bell.*)

JACK. Cecily! What on earth do you mean? What do you mean, Algy, by Cecily! I don't know any one of the name of Cecily.

(*Enter LANE.*)

ALGERNON. Bring me that cigarette case Mr. Worthing left in the smoking-room the last time he dined here.

LANE. Yes, sir. (*LANE goes out.*)

JACK. Do you mean to say you have had my cigarette case all this time? I wish to goodness you had let me know. I have been writing frantic letters to Scotland Yard about it. I was very nearly offering a large reward.

ALGERNON. Well, I wish you would offer one. I happen to be more than usually hard up.

JACK. There is no good offering a large reward now that the thing is found.

(*Enter LANE with the cigarette case on a salver. ALGERNON takes it at once. LANE goes out.*)

ALGERNON. I think that is rather mean of you, Ernest, I must say. (*Opens case and examines it.*) However, it makes no matter, for, now that I look at the inscription inside, I find that the thing isn't yours after all.

JACK. Of course it's mine. (*Moving to him.*) You have seen me with it a hundred times, and you have no right whatsoever to read what is written inside. It is a very ungentlemanly thing to read a private cigarette case.

ALGERNON. Oh! it is absurd to have a hard and fast rule about what one should read and what one shouldn't. More than half of modern culture depends on what one shouldn't read.

JACK. I am quite aware of the fact, and I don't propose to discuss modern culture. It isn't the sort of thing one should talk of in private. I simply want my cigarette case back.

ALGERNON. Yes, but this isn't your cigarette case. This cigarette case is a present from some one of the name of Cecily, and you said you didn't know any one of that name.

JACK. Well, if you want to know, Cecily happens to be my aunt.

ALGERNON. Your aunt!

JACK. Yes. Charming old lady she is, too. Lives at Tunbridge Wells. Just give it back to me, Algy.

ALGERNON. (*Retreating to back of sofa.*) But why does she call herself little Cecily if she is your aunt and lives at Tunbridge Wells? (*Reading.*) 'From little Cecily with her fondest love.'

JACK. (*Moving to sofa and kneeling upon it.*) My dear fellow, what on earth is there in that? Some aunts are tall, some aunts are not tall. That is a matter that surely an aunt may be allowed to decide for herself. You seem to think that every aunt should be exactly like your aunt! That is absurd! For Heaven's sake give me back my cigarette case. (*Follows Algernon round the room.*)

ALGERNON. Yes. But why does your aunt call you her uncle? 'From little Cecily, with her fondest love to her dear Uncle Jack.' There is no objection, I admit, to an aunt being a small aunt, but why an aunt, no matter what her size may be, should call her own nephew her uncle, I can't quite make out. Besides, your name isn't Jack at all; it is Ernest.

JACK. It isn't Ernest; it's Jack.

ALGERNON. You have always told me it was Ernest. I have introduced you to every one as Ernest. You answer to the name of Ernest. You look as if your name was Ernest. You are the most earnest-looking person I ever saw in my life. It is perfectly absurd your saying that your name isn't Ernest. It's on your cards. Here is one of them. (*Taking it from case.*) 'Mr. Ernest Worthing, B. 4, The Albany.' I'll keep this as a proof that your name is Ernest if ever you attempt to deny it to me, or to Gwendolen, or to any one else. (*Puts the card in his pocket.*)

JACK. Well, my name is Ernest in town and Jack in the country, and the cigarette case was given to me in the country.

ALGERNON. Yes, but that does not account for the fact that your small Aunt Cecily, who lives at Tunbridge Wells, calls you her dear uncle. Come, old boy, you had much better have the thing out at once.

JACK. My dear Algy, you talk exactly as if you were a dentist. It is very vulgar to talk like a dentist when one isn't a dentist. It produces a false impression.

ALGERNON. Well, that is exactly what dentists always do. Now, go on! Tell me the whole thing. I may mention that I have always suspected you of being a confirmed and secret Bunburyist; and I am quite sure of it now.

JACK. Bunburyist? What on earth do you mean by a Bunburyist?

ALGERNON. I'll reveal to you the meaning of that incomparable expression as soon as you are kind enough to inform me why you are Ernest in town and Jack in the country.

JACK. Well, produce my cigarette case first.

ALGERNON. Here it is. (*Hands cigarette case.*) Now produce your explanation, and pray make it improbable. (*Sits on sofa.*)

JACK. My dear fellow, there is nothing improbable about my explanation at all. In fact it's perfectly ordinary. Old Mr. Thomas Cardew, who adopted me when I was a little boy, made me in his will guardian to his grand-daughter, Miss Cecily Cardew. Cecily, who addresses me as her uncle from motives of respect that you could not possibly appreciate, lives at my place in the country under the charge of her admirable governess, Miss Prism.

ALGERNON. Where is that place in the country, by the way?

JACK. That is nothing to you, dear boy. You are not going to be invited... I may tell you candidly that the place is not in Shropshire.

ALGERNON. I suspected that, my dear fellow! I have Bunburyed all over Shropshire on two separate occasions. Now, go on. Why are you Ernest in town and Jack in the country?

JACK. My dear Algy, I don't know whether you will be able to understand my real motives. You are hardly serious enough. When one is placed in the position of guardian, one has to adopt a very high moral tone on all subjects. It's one's duty to do so. And as a high moral tone can hardly be said to conduce very much to either one's health or one's happiness, in order to get up to town I have always pretended to have a younger brother of the name of Ernest, who lives in the Albany, and gets into the most dreadful scrapes. That, my dear Algy, is the whole truth pure and simple.

ALGERNON. The truth is rarely pure and never simple. Modern life would be very tedious if it were either, and modern literature a complete impossibility!

JACK. That wouldn't be at all a bad thing.

ALGERNON. Literary criticism is not your forte, my dear fellow. Don't try it. You should leave that to people who haven't been at a university. They do it so well in the daily papers. What you really are is a Bunburyist. I was quite right in saying you were a Bunburyist. You are one of the most advanced Bunburyists I know.

JACK. What on earth do you mean?

ALGERNON. You have invented a very useful younger brother called Ernest, in order that you may be able to come up to town as often as you like. I have invented an invaluable permanent invalid called Bunbury, in order that I may be able to go down into the country whenever I choose. Bunbury is perfectly invaluable. If it wasn't for Bunbury's extraordinary bad health, for instance, I wouldn't be able to dine with you at Willis's to-night, for I have been really engaged to Aunt Augusta for more than a week.

JACK. I haven't asked you to dine with me anywhere to-night.

ALGERNON. I know. You are absurdly careless about sending out invitations. It is very foolish of you. Nothing annoys people so much as not receiving invitations.

JACK. You had much better dine with your Aunt Augusta.

ALGERNON. I haven't the smallest intention of doing anything of the kind. To begin with, I dined there on Monday, and once a week is quite enough to dine with one's own relations. In the second place, whenever I do dine there I am always treated as a member of the family, and sent down with either no woman at all, or two. In the third place, I know perfectly well whom she will place me next to, to-night. She will place me next Mary Farquhar, who always flirts with her own husband across the dinner-table. That is not very pleasant. Indeed, it is not even decent... and that sort of thing is enormously on the increase. The amount of women in London who flirt with their own husbands is perfectly scandalous. It looks so bad. It is simply washing one's clean linen in public. Besides, now that I know you to be a confirmed Bunburyist I naturally want to talk to you about Bunburying. I want to tell you the rules.

JACK. I'm not a Bunburyist at all. If Gwendolen accepts me, I am going to kill my brother, indeed I think I'll kill him in any case. Cecily is a little too much interested in him. It is rather a bore. So I am going to get rid of Ernest. And I strongly advise you to do the same with Mr... with your invalid friend who has the absurd name.

ALGERNON. Nothing will induce me to part with Bunbury, and if you ever get married, which seems to me extremely problematic, you will be very glad to know Bunbury. A man who marries without knowing Bunbury has a very tedious time of it.

JACK. That is nonsense. If I marry a charming girl like Gwendolen, and she is the only girl I ever saw in my life that I would marry, I certainly won't want to know Bunbury.

ALGERNON. Then your wife will. You don't seem to realize, that in married life three is company and two is none.

JACK. (*Sententiously.*) That, my dear young friend, is the theory that the corrupt French Drama has been propounding for the last fifty years.

ALGERNON. Yes; and that the happy English home has proved in half the time.

JACK. For heaven's sake, don't try to be cynical. It's perfectly easy to be cynical.

ALGERNON. My dear fellow, it isn't easy to be anything nowadays. There's such a lot of beastly competition about. (*The sound of an electric bell is heard.*) Ah! that must be Aunt Augusta. Only relatives, or creditors, ever ring in that Wagnerian manner. Now, if I get her out of the way for ten minutes, so that you can have an opportunity for proposing to Gwendolen, may I dine with you to-night at Willis's?

JACK. I suppose so, if you want to.

ALGERNON. Yes, but you must be serious about it. I hate people who are not serious about meals. It is so shallow of them.

Questions for Discussion

1. What is the main event of this selection? What do we learn about the play from the conversation between Algernon and Jack?
2. How is the cigarette case used for expository and comic purposes?
3. What does Algernon offer Jack in exchange for a free dinner?
4. What wordplay devices does Wilde use to make the dialogue humorous?
5. There are many paradoxical remarks in this selection. They seem to be absurd and illogical, but actually reveal much truth and satirize pointedly the manners of the society. Give instances.
6. What is the significance of the title of the play?

About the Author

Oscar Wilde (1854—1900) is a famous Irish poet, dramatist, novelist and essayist. He was born in Dublin, Ireland, in 1854. He went first to Trinity College, Dublin, majoring in classical studies, and then to Oxford, where he distinguished himself for his scholarship and wit, and also for his elegant eccentricity in dress, tastes, and manners. Influenced by the aesthetic teachings of his teachers John Ruskin and Walter Pater, Wilde later became the spokesman of the aestheticism (Art for art's sake) movement. Wilde was a dazzling conversationalist and a dandy in his life style. In 1895, he was sentenced to two year's imprisonment for alleged homosexual practice. After leaving jail, he emigrated to France. He died in Paris in poverty in 1900.

Wilde excelled in all genres of literature. The most remarkable of his works include: the novel *The Picture of Dorian Gray* (1891); the tragedy *Salome* (1892); a string of highly successful comedies: *Lady Windermere's Fan* (1893), *A Woman of No Importance* (1894), *An Ideal Husband* (1895) and *The Importance of Being Earnest* (1895); the long poem *The Ballad of Reading Gaol* (1898). Also noteworthy are his volume of fairy tales entitled *The Happy Prince* (1888) and his essays collected under the title *Intentions* (1891). Wilde's works contain elements of social protest and criticism despite his doctrine in writing: Art for art's sake. His brilliant comedies, for the witty paradoxes and epigrams in the dialogues and the cleverly constructed plots, have been acknowledged as his greatest contribution to English literature.

The Importance of Being Earnest (1895) is generally regarded as Wilde's greatest play. The primary characters of the play are John (Jack) Worthing and his friend Algernon Moncrieff, young gentlemen of marriageable age. Jack, who lives in the country, has invented a very useful young brother called "Ernest", living in London, in order that he may be able to go up to town to seek pleasure as often as he likes. Similarly, Algernon has invented an invalid country friend, "Bunbury" whose illness he uses as excuses to avoid social events he dislikes. In town, Jack announces to all his acquaintances that his name is "Ernest", including his friend Algernon and Algernon's cousin, Gwendolen, who falls in love with him because "her ideal has always been to love someone of the name of Ernest". Gwendolen's mother, Lady Bracknell rejects Jack because of his doubtful parenthood (he was found in a handbag in the cloak-room of Victorian

Station). Algernon introduces himself (during Jack's absence) as Jack's brother "Ernest" to his ward, an eighteen-year-old girl Cecily, who falls in love with him immediately. Gwendolen and Cecily discover they are both engaged to "Ernest". Finally, with the help of Cecily's governess, Miss Prism, who happens to be baby Jack's nurse 28 years ago, Lady Bracknell discovers that Jack is actually Algernon's long lost brother, whose Christian name is "Ernest John". The two pair of lovers can now wed happily.

    The play is subtitled "A Trivial Comedy for Serious People", which seems to indicate that the play is about little or nothing. It is true that the play is merely a farce with the stereotyped plot and the question of identity, disguise, and revelation. However, underneath we can get a glimpse of the manners of the Victorian society, the author's sharp satires and "earnest" commentary on a society that judges things only by appearance. The comedy consists of wonderful play, playing with roles, playing with words (bouts of clever remarks, repartee, puns, paradoxes, epigrams, etc.) and playing with ideas.

Pygmalion

George Bernard Shaw

ACT II （I）

THE FLOWER GIRL. ... He aint above giving lessons, not him: I heard him say so. Well, I aint come here to ask for any compliment; and if my money's not good enough I can go elsewhere.

HIGGINS. Good enough for what?

THE FLOWER GIRL. Good enough for ye-oo. Now you know, don't you? I'm come to have lessons, I am. And to pay for em too: make no mistake.

HIGGINS. (*stupent*) Well！！！ (*recovering his breath with a gasp*) What do you expect me to say to you?

THE FLOWER GIRL. Well, if you was a gentleman, you might ask me to sit down, I think. Dont I tell you I'm bringing you business?

HIGGINS. Pickering: Shall we ask this baggage① to sit down, or shall we throw her out of the window?

THE FLOWER GIRL. (*running away in terror to the piano, where she turns at bay②*) Ah-ah-oh-ow-ow-oo! (*wounded and whimpering*) I won't be called a baggage when I've offered to pay like any lady.

Motionless, the two men stare at her from the other side of the room, amazed.

PICKERING. (*gently*) What is it you want, my girl?

THE FLOWER GIRL. I want to be a lady in a flower shop stead of sellin at the corner of Tottenham Court Road. But they won't take me unless I can talk more genteel. He said he could teach me. Well, here I am ready to pay him—not asking any favor—and he treats me as if I was dirt.

MRS PEARCE. How can you be such a foolish ignorant girl as to think you could afford to pay Mr. Higgins?

THE FLOWER GIRL. Why shouldnt I? I know what lessons cost as well as you do; and I'm ready to pay.

HIGGINS. How much?

THE FLOWER GIRL. (*coming back to him, triumphant*) Now youre talking! I

---

① Slang word for "women".
② Said of a hunted animal under attack and having to fight for life.

thought youd come off it when you saw a chance of getting back a bit of what you chucked at me last night[①]. (*confidentially*) Youd had a drop in, hadnt you ?

HIGGINS. (*peremptorily*) Sit down.

THE FLOWER GIRL. Oh, if you're going to make a compliment of it—

HIGGINS. (*thundering at her*) Sit down.

MRS PEARCE. (*severely*) Sit down, girl. Do as youre told. (*She places the stray chair near the hearthrug between Higgins and Pickering, and stands behind it waiting for the girl to sit down.*)

THE FLOWER GIRL. Ah-ah-ah-ow-ow-oo! (*She stands, half rebellious, half bewildered.*)

PICKERING. (*very courteous*) Won't you sit down?

LIZA. (*coyly*) Don't mind if I do. (*She sits down. Pickering returns to the hearthrug.*)

HIGGINS. What's your name?

THE FLOWER GIRL. Liza Doolittle.

HIGGINS. (*declaiming gravely*)

    Eliza, Elizabeth, Betsy and Bess[②],

    They went to the woods to get a bird's nes':

PICKERING. They found a nest with four eggs in it:

HIGGINS. They took one apiece, and left three in it.

They laugh heartily at their own fun.

LIZA. Oh, don't be silly.

MRS PEARCE. You mustnt speak to the gentleman like that.

LIZA. Well, why won't he speak sensible to me ?

HIGGINS. Come back to business. How much do you propose to pay me for the lessons?

LIZA. Oh, I know whats right. A lady friend of mine gets French lessons for eighteen-pence an hour from a real French gentleman. Well, you wouldn't have the face to ask me the same for teaching me my own language as you would for French; so I won't give more than a shilling. Take it or leave it.

HIGGINS. (*walking up and down the room, rattling his keys and his cash in*

---

    ① Referring to the fact that Higgins threw a handful of money into the basket of the flower girl the previous night.

    ② All affectionate forms for Elizabeth.

    his pockets)

    You know, Pickering, if you consider a shilling, not as a simple shilling, but as a percentage of this girl's income, it works out as fully equivalent to sixty or seventy guineas from a millionaire.

PICKERING. How so?

HIGGINS. Figure it out. A millionaire has about £150 a day. She earns about half-a-crown.

LIZA. (*haughtily*) Who told you I only—

HIGGINS. (*continuing*) She offers me two fifths of her day's income for a lesson. Two fifths of a millionaire's income for a day would be somewhere about £60. It's handsome. By George, it's enormous! It's the biggest offer I ever had.

LIZA. (*rising, terrified*) Sixty pounds! What are you talking about? I never offered you sixty pounds. Where would I get—

HIGGINS. Hold your tongue.

LIZA. (*weeping*) But I ain't got sixty pound. Oh—

MRS PEARCE. Don't cry, you silly girl. Sit down. Nobody is going to touch your money.

HIGGINS. Somebody is going to touch you, with a broomstick, if you don't stop snivelling. Sit down.

LIZA. (*obeying slowly*) Ah-ah-ah-ow-oo-o ! One would think you was my father.

HIGGINS. If I decide to teach you, I'll be worse than two fathers to you. Here! (*He offers her his silk handkerchief.*)

LIZA. Whats this for?

HIGGINS. To wipe your eyes. To wipe any part of your face that feels moist. Remember; that's your sleeve. Dont mistake the one for the other if you wish to become a lady in a shop.

Liza, utterly bewildered, stares helplessly at him.

MRS PEARCE. It's no use talking to her like that, Mr. Higgins: she doesn't understand you. Besides, you're quite wrong: she doesn't do it that way at all. (*She takes the handkerchief.*)

LIZA. (*snatching it*) Here! You give me that handkerchief. He give it to me, not to you.

PICKERING. (*laughing*) He did. I think it must be regarded as her property,

Part One British Literature

Mrs. Pearce.

MRS PEARCE. (*resigning herself*) Serve you right, Mr. Higgins.

PICKERING. Higgins, I'm interested. What about the ambassador's garden party?① I'll say youre the greatest teacher alive if you make that good. I'll bet you all the expenses of the experiment you can't do it. And I'll pay for the lessons.

LIZA. Oh, you are real good. Thank you, Captain.

HIGGINS. (*tempted, looking to her*) It's almost irresistible. She's so deliciously low—so horribly dirty—

LIZA. (*protesting extremely*) Ah-ah-ah-ow-ow-oo-oo !!! I ain't dirty: I washed my face and hands afore I come, I did.

PICKERING. You're certainly not going to turn her head② with flattery, Higgins.

MRS PEARCE. (*uneasy*) Oh, don't say that, sir: there's more ways than one of turning a girl's head; and nobody can do it better than Mr Higgins, though he may not always mean it. I do hope, sir, you won't encourage him to do anything foolish.

HIGGINS. (*becoming excited as the idea grows on him*) What is life but a series of inspired follies? The difficulty is to find them to do. Never lose a chance; it doesn't come every day. I shall make a duchess of this draggletailed guttersnipe③.

LIZA. (*strongly deprecating this view of her*) Ah-ah-ah-ow-ow-oo!

HIGGINS. (*carried away*) Yes: in six months—in three if she has a good ear and a quick tongue—I'll take her anywhere and pass her off as anything. We'll start to-day: now ! this moment ! Take her away and clean her, Mrs Pearce. Monke Brand④ if it won't come off any other way. Is there a good fire in the kitchen?

MRS PEARCE. (*protesting*) Yes; but—

HIGGINS. (*storming on*) Take all her clothes off and burn them. Ring up

---

① Referring to what Higgins said the previous night (Act Ⅰ) that he could in three months pass the flower girl off as a duchess at an ambassador's garden party.
② Make her fall in love.
③ Dirty beggar.
④ Trade mark of a harsh detergent, commonly used for scouring cooking pans.

Whitcley① or somebody for new ones. Wrap her up in brown paper till they come.

LIZA. You're no gentleman, you're not, to talk of such things. I'm a good girl, I am; and I know what the like of you are, I do.

HIGGINS. We want none of your Lisson Grove② prudery here, young woman. Youve got to learn to behave like a duchess. Take her away, Mrs Pearce. If she gives you any trouble, wallop③ her.

Questions for Discussion

1. Describe the character of Eliza revealed from her words and actions.
2. Describe your impression of Higgins and some other people appearing in this part.
3. Give instances of vulgar speech (chiefly cockney—dialect of a part of London), as regards pronunciation, diction, and grammar.
4. Give instances of humorous and witty remarks.
5. Make a comment on how stage directions in this part help us visualize people and the whole story.

About the Author

George Bernard Shaw (1856—1950) is an outstanding realistic dramatist. Very much impressed by Ibsen's plays, Shaw handles social problems and takes drama as an effective weapon to attack the social evils. He was born in Dublin, Ireland. His father was a petty official and his mother was a talented musician. At twenty, Shaw went to London, devoting much time to self-education and doing odd jobs for small earnings. In 1879 he began to write novels, and in 1884 he joined the newly formed socialist Fabian Society, of which he became a leading member. Shaw's career as a dramatist began in 1892 and lasted substantially until 1939. During the First World War he denounced imperialism and in his *Heartbreak House* (1917) he tried to show the decline of the bourgeois civilization. In 1925 he received the Nobel Prize for literature. He visited China in 1932 and was warmly received by the revolutionary writers represented by Lu

---

① Name of a big department store.
② The flower girl is from Lisson Grove.
③ Beat soundly; the verb has a comic ring to it.

Xun and others. Shaw's best known works include: *Widowers' Houses*(1892), *Mrs. Warren's Profession* (1894), *Arms and the Man* (1894), *The Man of Destiny* (1895), *Caesar and Cleopatra* (1898), *Major Barbara* (1905), *Heartbreak Home* (1917), *The Apple Cart* (1922). In some of his plays, Shaw criticizes relentlessly the evils of the bourgeois society, and tears to pieces the masks of gentlemen and ladies.

Pygmalion (1912) tells the story of how Higgins, a linguist, turns Eliza, a flower girl in the street, into a cultured lady. The linguist succeeds in changing the outside of the girl. She learns the language and the manners of the cultured rich, but deeply rooted in her own cultural background, eventually she leaves Higgins and pursues her own way of life. The play is a poignant satire on middle-class morality, and also a criticism of any scientific attempt to change human beings into experimental objects. It is unique in that the different levels of English (educated and uneducated, colloquial, vulgar, slangy, cockney) are brought into sharp contrast on the stage, perhaps for the first time, in such a vivid and amusing manner. Note also the humorous and witty dialogues, the paradoxical statements. The play was adapted into an immensely popular musical *My Fair Lady* in 1956. Act II, Scene I tells how it has come that Higgins takes Eliza as a language experiment subject. It is a highlight part in which the characters fully exhibit their personalities and the ways of speaking.

Fiction

The Picture of Dorian Gray

Oscar Wilde

The Preface

The artist is the creator of beautiful things.

To reveal art and conceal the artist is art's aim.

The critic is he who can translate into another manner or a new material his impression of beautiful things.

The highest as the lowest form of criticism is a mode of autobiography. Those who find ugly meanings in beautiful things are corrupt without being charming.

This is a fault.

Those who find beautiful meanings in beautiful things are the cultivated. For these there is hope.

They are the elect to whom beautiful things mean only beauty.

There is no such thing as a moral or an immoral book. Books are well written, or badly written.

That is all.

The nineteenth century dislike of realism is the rage of Caliban seeing his own face in a glass.

The nineteenth century dislike of romanticism is the rage of Caliban not seeing his own face in a glass.

The moral life of man forms part of the subject-matter of the artist, but the morality of art consists in the perfect use of an imperfect medium. No artist desires to prove anything. Even things that are true can be proved.

No artist has ethical sympathies.

An ethical sympathy in an artist is an unpardonable mannerism of style. No artist is ever morbid. The artist can express everything.

Thought and language are to the artist instruments of an art.

Vice and virtue are to the artist materials for an art.

From the point of view of form, the type of all the arts is the art of the musician.

From the point of view of feeling, the actor's craft is the type.

All art is at once surface and symbol.

Those who go beneath the surface do so at their peril.

Those who read the symbol do so at their peril.

It is the spectator, and not life, that art really mirrors.

Diversity of opinion about a work of art shows that the work is new, complex, and vital.

When critics disagree, the artist is in accord with himself.

We can forgive a man for making a useful thing as long as he does not admire it. The only excuse for making a useless thing is that one admires it intensely.

All art is quite useless.

Chapter 1

The studio was filled with the rich odour of roses, and when the light summer wind stirred amidst the trees of the garden, there came through the open door the heavy scent of the lilac, or the more delicate perfume of the pink-flowering thorn.

From the corner of the divan of Persian saddle-bags on which he was lying, smoking, as was his custom, innumerable cigarettes, Lord Henry Wotton could just catch the gleam of the honey-sweet and honey-coloured blossoms of a laburnum, whose tremulous branches seemed hardly able to bear the burden of a beauty so flamelike as theirs; and now and then the fantastic shadows of birds in flight flitted across the long tussore-silk curtains that were stretched in front of the huge window, producing a kind of momentary Japanese effect, and making him think of those pallid, jade-faced painters of Tokyo who, through the medium of an art that is necessarily immobile, seek to convey the sense of swiftness and motion. The sullen murmur of the bees shouldering their way through the long unmown grass, or circling with monotonous insistence round the dusty gilt horns of the straggling woodbine, seemed to make the stillness more oppressive. The dim roar of London was like the bourdon note of a distant organ.

In the centre of the room, clamped to an upright easel, stood the full-length portrait of a young man of extraordinary personal beauty, and in front of it, some little distance away, was sitting the artist himself, Basil Hallward, whose sudden disappearance some years ago caused, at the time, such public excitement and gave rise to so many strange conjectures.

As the painter looked at the gracious and comely form he had so skillfully mirrored in his art, a smile of pleasure passed across his face, and seemed about to linger there. But he suddenly started up, and closing his eyes, placed his fingers upon the lids, as though he sought to imprison within his brain some curious dream from which he feared he might awake.

"It is your best work, Basil, the best thing you have ever done," said Lord Henry languidly. "You must certainly send it next year to the Grosvenor. The Academy is too large and too vulgar. Whenever I have gone there, there have been either so many people that I have not been able to see the pictures, which was dreadful, or so many pictures that I have not been able to see the people, which was worse. The Grosvenor is really the only place."

"I don't think I shall send it anywhere," he answered, tossing his head back in that odd way that used to make his friends laugh at him at Oxford. "No, I won't send it anywhere."

Lord Henry elevated his eyebrows and looked at him in amazement through the thin blue wreaths of smoke that curled up in such fanciful whorls from his heavy, opium-tainted cigarette. "Not send it anywhere? My dear fellow, why? Have you any reason? What odd chaps you painters are! You do anything in the world to gain a reputation. As soon as you have one, you seem to want to throw it away. It is silly of you, for there is only one thing in the world worse than being talked about, and that is not being talked about. A portrait like this would set you far above all the young men in England, and make the old men quite jealous, if old men are ever capable of any emotion."

"I know you will laugh at me," he replied, "but I really can't exhibit it. I have put too much of myself into it."

Lord Henry stretched himself out on the divan and laughed. "Yes, I knew you would; but it is quite true, all the same." "Too much of yourself in it! Upon my word, Basil, I didn't know you were so vain; and I really can't see any resemblance between you, with your rugged strong face and your coal-black hair, and this young Adonis, who looks as if he was made out of ivory and rose-leaves. Why, my dear Basil, he is a Narcissus, and you—well, of course you have an intellectual expression and all that. But beauty, real beauty, ends where an intellectual expression begins. Intellect is in itself a mode of exaggeration, and destroys the harmony of any face. The moment one sits down to think, one becomes all nose, or all forehead, or something horrid. Look at the successful men in any of the learned professions. How perfectly hideous they are! Except, of course, in the Church. But then in the Church they don't think. A bishop keeps on saying at the age of eighty what he was told to say when he was a boy of eighteen, and as a natural consequence he always looks absolutely delightful. Your mysterious young friend, whose name you have never told me, but whose picture really fascinates me, never thinks. I feel quite sure of that. He is some brainless beautiful creature who should be always here in winter when we have no flowers to look at, and always here in summer when we want something to chill our intelligence. Don't flatter yourself, Basil: you are not in the least like him."

"You don't understand me, Harry," answered the artist. "Of course I am not like him. I know that perfectly well. Indeed, I should be sorry to look like him. You shrug your shoulders? I am telling you the truth. There is a fatality about all physical and intellectual distinction, the sort of fatality that seems to dog through history the faltering steps of kings. It is better not to be different from one's fellows. The ugly and the stupid have the best of it in this world. They can sit at their ease and gape at the play. If they know nothing of victory, they are at least spared the knowledge of defeat. They live as we all should live—undisturbed, indifferent, and without disquiet. They neither bring ruin upon others, nor ever receive it from alien hands. Your rank and wealth, Harry; my brains, such as they are—my art, whatever it may be worth; Dorian Gray's good looks—we shall all suffer for what the gods have given us, suffer terribly."

"Dorian Gray? Is that his name?" asked Lord Henry, walking across the studio towards Basil Hallward.

"Yes, that is his name. I didn't intend to tell it to you."

"But why not?"

"Oh, I can't explain. When I like people immensely, I never tell their names to any one. It is like surrendering a part of them. I have grown to love secrecy. It seems to be the one thing that can make modern life mysterious or marvellous to us. The commonest thing is delightful if one only hides it. When I leave town now I never tell my people where I am going. If I did, I would lose all my pleasure. It is a silly habit, I dare say, but somehow it seems to bring a great deal of romance into one's life. I suppose you think me awfully foolish about it?"

"Not at all," answered Lord Henry, "not at all, my dear Basil. You seem to forget that I am married, and the one charm of marriage is that it makes a life of deception absolutely necessary for both parties. I never know where my wife is, and my wife never knows what I am doing. When we meet—we do meet occasionally, when we dine out together, or go down to the Duke's—we tell each other the most absurd stories with the most serious faces. My wife is very good at it—much better, in fact, than I am. She never gets confused over her dates, and I always do. But when she does find me out, she makes no row at all. I sometimes wish she would; but she merely laughs at me."

"I hate the way you talk about your married life, Harry," said Basil Hallward, strolling towards the door that led into the garden. "I believe that you are really a very good husband, but that you are thoroughly ashamed of your own virtues. You are an extraordinary fellow. You never say a moral thing, and you never do a wrong thing. Your cynicism is simply a pose."

"Being natural is simply a pose, and the most irritating pose I know," cried Lord Henry, laughing; and the two young men went out into the garden together and ensconced themselves on a long bamboo seat that stood in the shade of a tall laurel bush. The sunlight slipped over the polished leaves. In the grass, white daisies were tremulous.

After a pause, Lord Henry pulled out his watch. "I am afraid I must be going, Basil," he murmured, "and before I go, I insist on your answering a question I put to you some time ago."

"What is that?" said the painter, keeping his eyes fixed on the ground.

"You know quite well."

"I do not, Harry."

"Well, I will tell you what it is. I want you to explain to me why you won't exhibit Dorian Gray's picture. I want the real reason."

"I told you the real reason."

"No, you did not. You said it was because there was too much of yourself in it. Now, that is childish."

"Harry," said Basil Hallward, looking him straight in the face, "every portrait that is painted with feeling is a portrait of the artist, not of the sitter. The sitter is merely the accident, the occasion. It is not he who is revealed by the painter; it is rather the painter who, on the coloured canvas, reveals himself. The reason I will not exhibit this picture is that I am afraid that I have shown in it the secret of my own soul."

Lord Henry laughed. "And what is that?" he asked.

"I will tell you," said Hallward; but an expression of perplexity came over his face.

"I am all expectation, Basil," continued his companion, glancing at him.

"Oh, there is really very little to tell, Harry," answered the painter; "and I am afraid you will hardly understand it. Perhaps you will hardly believe it."

Lord Henry smiled, and leaning down, plucked a pink-petalled daisy from the grass and examined it. "I am quite sure I shall understand it," he replied, gazing intently at the little golden, white-feathered disk, "and as for believing things, I can believe anything, provided that it is quite incredible."

The wind shook some blossoms from the trees, and the heavy lilac-blooms, with their clustering stars, moved to and fro in the languid air. A grasshopper began to chirrup by the wall, and like a blue thread a long thin dragon-fly floated past on its brown gauze wings. Lord Henry felt as if he could hear Basil Hallward's heart beating, and wondered what was coming.

"The story is simply this," said the painter after some time. "Two months ago I went to a crush at Lady Brandon's. You know we poor artists have to show ourselves in society from time to time, just to remind the public that we are not savages. With an evening coat and a white tie, as you told me once, anybody, even a stock-broker, can gain a reputation for being civilized. Well, after I had been in the room about ten minutes, talking to huge overdressed dowagers and tedious academicians, I suddenly became conscious that some one was looking at me. I turned half-way round and saw Dorian Gray for the first time. When our eyes met, I felt that I was growing pale. A curious sensation of terror came over me. I knew that I had come face to face with some one whose mere personality was so fascinating that, if I allowed it to do so, it would absorb my whole nature, my whole soul, my very art itself. I did not want any external influence in my life. You know yourself, Harry, how independent I am by nature. I have always been my own master; had at least always been so, till I met Dorian Gray. Then— but I don't know how to explain it to you. Something seemed to tell me that I was on the verge of a terrible crisis in my life. I had a strange feeling that fate had in store for me exquisite joys and exquisite sorrows. I grew afraid and turned to quit the room. It was not conscience that made me do so: it was a sort of cowardice. I take no credit to myself for trying to escape."

"Conscience and cowardice are really the same things, Basil. Conscience is the trade-name of the firm. That is all."

"I don't believe that, Harry, and I don't believe you do either. However, whatever was my motive—and it may have been pride, for I used to be very proud—I certainly struggled to the door. There, of course, I stumbled against Lady Brandon. 'You are not going to run away so soon, Mr. Hallward?' she screamed out. You know her curiously shrill voice?"

"Yes; she is a peacock in everything but beauty," said Lord Henry, pulling the daisy to bits with his long nervous fingers.

"I could not get rid of her. She brought me up to royalties, and people with stars and garters, and elderly ladies with gigantic tiaras and parrot noses. She spoke of me as her dearest friend. I had only met her once before, but she took it into her head to lionize me. I believe some picture of mine had made a great success at the time, at least had been chattered about in the penny newspapers, which is the nineteenth-century standard of immortality. Suddenly I found myself face to face with the young man whose personality had so strangely stirred me. We were quite close, almost touching. Our eyes met again. It was reckless of me, but I asked Lady Brandon to introduce me to him. Perhaps it was not so reckless, after all. It was simply inevitable. We would have spoken to each other without any introduction. I am sure of that. Dorian told me so afterwards. He, too, felt that we were destined to know each other."

"And how did Lady Brandon describe this wonderful young man?" asked his companion. "I know she goes in for giving a rapid precis of all her guests. I remember her bringing me up to a truculent and red-faced old gentleman covered all over with orders and ribbons, and hissing into my ear, in a tragic whisper which must have been perfectly audible to everybody in the room, the most astounding details. I simply fled. I like to find out people for myself. But Lady Brandon treats her guests exactly as an auctioneer treats his goods. She either explains them entirely away, or tells one everything about them except what one wants to know."

"Poor Lady Brandon! You are hard on her, Harry!" said Hallward listlessly.

"My dear fellow, she tried to found a *salon*, and only succeeded in opening a restaurant. How could I admire her? But tell me, what did she say about Mr. Dorian Gray?"

"Oh, something like, 'Charming boy—poor dear mother and I absolutely inseparable. Quite forget what he does—afraid he—doesn't do anything—oh, yes, plays the piano—or is it the violin, dear Mr. Gray?' Neither of us could help laughing, and we became friends at once."

"Laughter is not at all a bad beginning for a friendship, and it is far the best ending for one," said the young lord, plucking another daisy.

Hallward shook his head. "You don't understand what friendship is, Harry," he murmured—"or what enmity is, for that matter. You like every one; that is to say, you are indifferent to every one."

"How horribly unjust of you!" cried Lord Henry, tilting his hat back and looking up at the little clouds that, like ravelled skeins of glossy white silk, were drifting across the hollowed turquoise of the summer sky. "Yes; horribly unjust of you. I make a great difference between people. I choose my friends for their good looks, my acquaintances for their good characters, and my enemies for their good intellects. A man cannot be too careful in the choice of his enemies. I have not got one who is a fool. They are all men of some intellectual power, and consequently they all appreciate me. Is that very vain of me? I think it is rather vain."

"I should think it was, Harry. But according to your category I must be merely an acquaintance."

"My dear old Basil, you are much more than an acquaintance."

"And much less than a friend. A sort of brother, I suppose?"

"Oh, brothers! I don't care for brothers. My elder brother won't die, and my younger brothers seem never to do anything else."

"Harry!" exclaimed Hallward, frowning.

"My dear fellow, I am not quite serious. But I can't help detesting my relations. I suppose it comes from the fact that none of us can stand other people having the same faults as ourselves. I quite sympathize with the rage of the English democracy against what they call the vices of the upper orders. The masses feel that drunkenness, stupidity, and immorality should be their own special property, and that if any one of us makes an ass of himself, he is poaching on their preserves. When poor Southwark got into the divorce court, their indignation was quite magnificent. And yet I don't suppose that ten per cent of the proletariat live correctly."

"I don't agree with a single word that you have said, and, what is more, Harry, I feel sure you don't either."

...

Questions for Discussion

1. Find the story and finish it. Then give a summary of the whole story.
2. Do you think there is anything different in theme in this novel from other novels that you have read?
3. What kind of person is Oscar Wilde?

About the Author

Oscar Wilde (1854—1900), was born and grew up in Dublin. After studying classics at Trinity College, Dublin, he won a scholarship to Oxford and there established a brilliant academic record. At Oxford he came under the influence of the aesthetic theories of John Ruskin. After graduating in 1878, Wilde moved to London, where his fellow Irishmen Bernard Shaw and William Butler Yeats were also to settle. Here Wilde quickly established himself both as a writer and as a spokesperson for the school of "art for art's sake." In Wilde's view this school included not only French poets and critics but also a line of English poets going back through Dante Gabriel Rossetti and the Pre-Raphaelites to John Keats. In 1882 he visited America for a long (and successful) lecture tour, during which he startled audiences by airing the gospel of the "aesthetic movement." In one of these lectures, he asserted that "to disagree with three fourths of all England on all points of view is one of the first elements of sanity."

Wilde's successes for seventeen years in England and America were, of course, not limited to his self-advertising stunts as a dandy. In the spring of 1895 this triumphant success suddenly crumbled when Wilde was arrested and sentenced to prison, with hard labor, for two years. Although Wilde was married and the father of two children, he did not hide his relationships with men, and in fact ended up shaping, to his personal cost, a long-standing public image of "the homosexual." When he began a romance (in 1891) with the handsome young poet Lord Alfred Douglas, he set in motion the events that brought about his ruin. In 1895 Lord Alfred's father, the marquis of Queensberry, accused Wilde of homosexuality; Wilde recklessly sued for libel, lost the case, and was thereupon arrested and convicted for what had only recently come onto the statute books as a serious offense. (A late addition to the Criminal Law Amendment Act of 1885, known as the Labouchere Amendment after the member of Parliament who had proposed it, effectively criminalized all forms of sexual relations between men.) The revulsion of feeling against him in Britain and America was violent, and the aesthetic movement suffered a severe setback not only with the public but among writers as well.

The Horse Dealer's Daughter

D. H. Lawrence

"Well, Mabel, and what are you going to do with yourself?" asked Joe, with foolish flippancy①. He felt quite safe himself. Without listening for an answer, he turned aside, worked a grain of tobacco to the tip of his tongue, and spat it out. He did not care about anything, since he felt safe himself.

The three brothers and the sister sat round the desolate breakfast-table, attempting some sort of desultory consultation. The morning's post had given the final tap to the family fortunes, and all was over. The dreary dining-room itself, with its heavy mahogany furniture, looked as if it were waiting to be done away with.

But the consultation amounted to nothing. There was a strange air of ineffectuality about the three men, as they sprawled② at table, smoking and reflecting vaguely on their own condition. The girl was alone, a rather short, sullen-looking young woman of twenty-seven. She did not share the same life as her brothers. She would have been good-looking, save for the impressive fixity of her face, "bull-dog", as her brothers called it.

There was a confused tramping of horses' feet outside. The three men all sprawled round in their chairs to watch. Beyond the dark holly bushes that separated the strip of lawn from the high-road, they could see a cavalcade③ of shire horses swinging out of their own yard, being taken for exercise. This was the last time. These were the last horses that would go through their hands. The young men watched with critical, callous④ look. They were all frightened at the collapse of their lives, and the sense of disaster in which they were involved left them no inner freedom.

Yet they were three fine, well-set⑤ fellows enough. Joe, the eldest, was a man of thirty-three, broad and handsome in a hot flushed way. His face was red,

---

① Inappropriate levity; insolence and rudeness.
② Sit or lie with one's limbs spread out.
③ A procession of people traveling on horseback.
④ Emotionally hardened.
⑤ Strongly and firmly constructed.

he twisted his black moustache over a thick finger, his eyes were shallow and restless. He had a sensual way of uncovering his teeth when he laughed, and his bearing was stupid. Now he watched the horses with a glazed look of helplessness in his eyes, a certain stupor of downfall.

The great drought-horses swung past. They were tied head to tail, four of them, and they heaved along to where a lane branched off from the high-road, planting their great roofs flouting in the fine black mud, swinging their great rounded haunches sumptuously, and trotting a few sudden steps as they were led into the lane, round the corner. Every movement showed a massive, slumberous strength, and a stupidity which held them in subjection. The groom at the head looked back, jerking the leading rope. And the cavalcade moved out of sight up the lane, the tail of the last horse, bobbed up tight and stiff, held out taut from the swinging great haunches as they rocked behind the hedges in a motion-like sleep.

Joe watched with glazed hopeless eyes. The horses were almost like his own body to him. He felt he was done for now. Luckily he was engaged to a woman as old as himself, and therefore her father, who was steward of a neighbouring estate, would provide him with a job. He would marry and go into harness. His life was over, and he would be a subject animal now.

He turned uneasily aside, the retreating steps of the horses echoing in his ears. Then, with foolish restlessness, he reached for the scraps of bacon-rind from the plates, and making a faint whistling sound, flung them to the terrier that lay against the fender. He watched the dog swallow them, and waited till the creature looked into his eyes. Then a faint grin came on his face, and in a high, foolish voice he said:

"You won't get much more bacon, shall you, you little b—?"

The dog faintly and dismally wagged its tail, then lowered its haunches, circled round, and lay down again.

There was another hopeless silence at the table. Joe sprawled uneasily in his seat, not willing to go till the family conclave① was dissolved. Fred Henry, the second brother, was erect, clean-limbed, alert. He had watched the passing of the horses with more sang-froid②. If he was an animal, like Joe, he was an

---

① A confidential or secret meeting.
② (French) Great coolness and composure under strain.

animal which controls, not one which is controlled. He was master of any horse, and he carried himself with a well-tempered air of mastery. But he was not master of the situation of life. He pushed his coarse brown moustache upwards, off his lip, and glanced irritably at his sister, who sat impassive and inscrutable.

"You'll go and stop with Lucy for a bit, shan't you?" he asked. The girl did not answer.

"I don't see what else you can do," persisted Fred Henry.

"Go as a skivvy①," Joe interpolated laconically.

The girl did not move a muscle.

"If I was her, I should go in for training for a nurse," said Malcolm, the youngest of them all. He was the baby of the family, a young man of twenty-two, with a fresh, jaunty *museau*②.

But Mabel did not take any notice of him. They had talked at her and round her for so many years, that she hardly heard them at all.

The marble clock on the mantelpiece softly chimed the half-hour, the dog rose uneasily from the hearth-rug and looked at the party at the breakfast-table. But still they sat on in ineffectual conclave.

"Oh, all right," said Joe suddenly, apropos of nothing. "Ill get a move on."

He pushed back his chair, straddled his knees with a downward jerk, to get them free, in horsey fashion, and went to the fire. Still, he did not go out of the room; he was curious to know what the others would do or say. He began to charge his pipe, looking down at the dog and saying in a high affected voice:

"Going wi' me ? Going wi' me are ter? Tha'rt goin' further than tha counts on just now, dost hear?"

The dog faintly wagged its tail, the man stuck out his jaw and covered his pipe with his hands, and puffed intently, losing himself in the tobacco, looking down all the while at the dog with an absent brown eye. The dog looked up at him in mournful distrust. Joe stood with his knees stuck out, in real horsey fashion.

"Have you had a letter from Lucy?" Fred Henry asked of his sister.

"Last week," came the neutral reply.

"And what does she say?"

---

① A female domestic servant who does all kinds of menial work.
② (French) Muzzle; here means face.

There was no answer.

"Does she *ask* you to go and stop there?" persisted Fred Henry.

"She says I can if I like."

"Well, then, you'd better. Tell her you'll come on Monday."

This was received in silence.

"That's what you'll do then, is it?" said Fred Henry, in some exasperation.

But she made no answer. There was a silence of futility and irritation in the room. Malcolm grinned fatuously①.

"You'll have to make up your mind between now and next Wednesday," said Joe loudly, "or else find your lodgings on the kerbstone.②"

The face of the young woman darkened, but she sat on immutable.

"Here's Jack Fergusson!" exclaimed Malcolm, who was looking aimlessly out of the window.

"Where?" exclaimed Joe loudly.

"Just gone past."

"Coming in?"

Malcolm craned his neck to see the gate.

"Yes," he said.

There was a silence. Mabel sat on like one condemned, at the head of the table. Then a whistle was heard from the kitchen. The dog got up and barked sharply. Joe opened the door and shouted:

"Come on."

After a moment a young man entered. He was muffled up in overcoat and a purple woollen scarf, and his tweed cap, which he did not remove, was pulled down on his head. He was of medium height, his face was rather long and pale, his eyes looked tired.

"Hello, Jack! Well, Jack!" exclaimed Malcolm and Joe. Fred Henry merely said: "Jack."

"What's doing?" asked the newcomer, evidently addressing Fred Henry.

"Same. We've got to be out by Wednesday. Got a cold?"

"I have—got it bad, too."

---

① Devoid of intelligence, in a stupid way.

② Or else you'll be homeless.

"Why don't you stop in?"

"*Me* stop in? When I can't stand on my legs, perhaps I shall have a chance." The young man spoke huskily. He had a slight Scotch accent.

"It's a knock-out, isn't it," said Joe, boisterously, "if a doctor goes round croaking with a cold. Looks bad for the patients, doesn't it?"

The young doctor looked at him slowly.

"Anything the matter with *you* then?" he asked sarcastically.

"Not as I know of. Damn your eyes, I hope not. Why?"

"I thought you were very concerned about the patients, wondered if you might be one yourself."

"Damn it, no, I've never been a patient to no flaming doctor, and hope I never shall be," returned Joe.

At this point Mabel rose from the table, and they all seemed to become aware of her existence. She began putting the dishes together. The young doctor looked at her, but did not address her. He had not greeted her. She went out the room with the tray, her face impassive and unchanged.

"When are you off then, all of you?" asked the doctor.

"I'm catching the eleven-forty," replied Malcolm. "Are you goin' down wi' th' trap, Joe?"

"Yes, I've told you I'm going down wi' th' trap, haven't I?"

"We'd better be getting in then. So long, Jack, if I don't see you before I go," said Malcolm, shaking hands.

He went out, followed by Joe, who seemed to have his tail between his legs.

"Well, this is the devil's own," exclaimed the doctor, when he was left alone with Fred Henry. "Going before Wednesday, are you?"

"That's the orders," replied the other.

"Where, to Northampton?"

"That's it."

"The devil!" exclaimed Fergusson, with quiet chagrin①.

And there was silence between the two.

"All settled up, are you?" asked Fergusson.

"About."

---

① Strong feelings of embarrassment.

There was another pause.

"Well, I shall miss yer, Freddy, boy," said the young doctor.

"And I shall miss thee, Jack," returned the other.

"Miss you like hell," mused the doctor.

Fred Henry turned aside. There was nothing to say. Mabel came in again, to finish clearing the table.

"What are *you* going to do, then, Miss Pervin?" asked Fergusson. "Going to your sister's, are you?"

Mabel looked at him with her steady, dangerous eyes, that always made him uncomfortable, unsettling his superficial ease.

"No," she said.

"Well, what in the name of fortune *are* you going to do? Say what you mean to do," cried Fred Henry, with futile intensity.

But she only averted her head, and continued her work. She folded the white table-cloth, and put on the chenille cloth.

"The sulkiest bitch that ever trod①!" muttered her brother.

But she finished her task with perfectly impassive face, the young doctor watching her interestedly all the while. Then she went out.

Fred Henry stared after her, clenching his lips, his blue eyes fixing in sharp antagonism, as he made a grimace of sour exasperation.

"You could bray② her into bits, and that's all you'd get out of her," he said, in a small, narrowed tone.

The doctor smiled faintly.

"What's she *going* to do, then?" he asked.

"Strike me if I know!" returned the other.

There was a pause. Then the doctor stirred.

"I'll be seeing you to-night, shall I?" he said to his friend.

"Ay—where's it to be? Are we going over to Jessdale?"

"I don't know. I've got such a cold on me. I'll come round to the 'Moon and Stars'③, anyway."

"Let Lizzie and May miss their night for once, eh?"

"That's it—if I feel as I do now."

---

① Angry curse words.
② Reduce to small pieces or particles by pounding or abrading.
③ Name of a pub.

Part One　British Literature

"All's one—"

The two young men went through the passage and down to the back door together. The house was large, but it was servantless now, and desolate. At the back was a small bricked house-yard and beyond that a big square, gravelled fine and red, and having stables on two sides. Sloping, dank, winter-dark fields stretched away on the open sides.

But the stables were empty. Joseph Pervin, the father of the family, had been a man of no education, who had become a fairly large horse-dealer. The stables had been full of horses, there was a great turmoil and come-and-go of horses and of dealers and grooms. Then the kitchen was full of servants. But of late things had declined. The old man had married a second time, to retrieve his fortunes. Now he was dead and everything was gone to the dogs①, and there was nothing but debt and threatening.

For months, Mabel had been servantless in the big house, keeping the home together in penury for her ineffectual brothers. She had kept house for ten years. But previously it was with unstinted means. Then, however brutal and coarse everything was, the sense of money had kept her proud, confident. The men might be foul-mouthed, the women in the kitchen might have bad reputations, her brothers might have illegitimate children. But so long as there was money, the girl felt herself established, and brutally proud, reserved.

No company came to the house, save dealers and coarse men. Mabel had no associates of her own sex, after her sister went away. But she did not mind. She went regularly to church, she attended to her father. And she lived in the memory of her mother, who had died when she was fourteen, and whom she had loved. She had loved her father, too, in a different way, depending upon him, and feeling secure in him, until at the age of fifty-four he married again. And then she had set hard against him. Now he had died and left them all hopelessly in debt.

She had suffered badly during the period of poverty. Nothing, however, could shake the curious, sullen, animal pride that dominated each member of the family. Now, for Mabel, the end had come. Still she would not cast about her. She would follow her own way just the same. She would always hold the keys of her own situation. Mindless and persistent, she endured from day to day. Why

---

① (slang) Gone wrong.

should she think? Why should she answer anybody? It was enough that this was the end, and there was no way out. She need not pass any more darkly along the main street of the small town, avoiding every eye. She need not demean herself any more, going into the shops and buying the cheapest food. This was at an end. She thought of nobody, not even herself. Mindless and persistent, she seemed in a sort of ecstasy to be coming nearer to her fulfilment, her own glorification, approaching her dead mother, who was glorified.

In the afternoon she took a little bag, with shears and sponge and a small scrubbing-brush, and went out. It was a grey, wintry day, with saddened, dark green fields and an atmosphere blackened by the smoke of foundries① not far off. She went quickly, darkly along the causeway②, heeding nobody, through the town to the churchyard.

There she always felt secure, as if no one could see her, although as a matter of fact she was exposed to the stare of everyone who passed along the churchyard wall. Nevertheless, once under the shadow of the great looming church, among the graves, she felt immune from the world, reserved within the thick churchyard wall as in another country.

Carefully she clipped the grass from the grave, and arranged the pinky white, small chrysanthemums in the tin cross. When this was done, she took an empty jar from a neighbouring grave, brought water, and carefully, most scrupulously sponged the marble headstone and the coping-stone.

It gave her sincere satisfaction to do this. She felt in immediate contact with the world of her mother. She took minute pains, went through the park in a state bordering on pure happiness, as if in performing this task she came into a subtle, intimate connection with her mother. For the life she followed here in the world was far less real than the world of death she inherited from her mother.

The doctor's house was just by the church. Fergusson, being a mere hired assistant, was slave to the country-side. As he hurried now to attend to the out-patients in the surgery, glancing across the graveyard with his quick eye, he saw the girl at her task at the grave. She seemed so intent and remote, and it was looking into another world. Some mystical element was touched in him. He slowed down as he walked, watching her as if spellbound.

---

① Factory where metal castings are produced.
② A road that is raised above water or marshland or sand.

She lifted her eyes, feeling him looking. Their eyes met. And each looked again at once, each feeling, in some way, found out by the other. He lifted his cap and passed on down the road. There remained distinct in consciousness, like a vision, the memory of her face, lifted from the tombstone in the churchyard, and looking at him with slow, large, portentous eyes. It *was* portentous, her face. It seemed to mesmerise① him. There was a heavy power in her eyes which laid hold of his whole being, as if he had drunk some powerful drug. He had been feeling weak and done before. Now the life came back into him, he felt delivered from his own fretted, daily self.

He finished his duties at the surgery as quickly as might be, hastily filling up the bottles of the waiting people with cheap drugs. Then, in perpetual haste, he set off again to visit several cases in another part of his round, before tea-time. At all times he preferred to walk if he could, but particularly when he was not well. He fancied the motion restored him.

The afternoon was falling. It was grey, deadened, and wintry, with a slow, moist, heavy coldness sinking in and deadening all the faculties. But why should he think or notice? He hastily climbed the hill and turned across the dark green fields, following the black cinder-track. In the distance, across a shallow dip in the country, the small town was clustered like smouldering ash, a tower, a spire, a heap of low, raw, extinct houses. And on the nearest fringe of the town, sloping into the dip, was Oldmeadow, the Pervins' house. He could see the stables and the out buildings distinctly, as they lay towards him on the slope. Well, he would not go there many more times! Another resource would be lost to him, another place gone: the only company he cared for in the alien, ugly little town he was losing. Nothing but work, drudgery, constant hastening from dwelling to dwelling among the colliers and the iron-workers. It wore him out, but at the same time he had a craving for it. It was a stimulant to him to be in the homes of the working people, moving, as it were, through the innermost body of their life. His nerves were excited and gratified. He could come so near, into the very lives of the rough, inarticulate, powerfully emotional men and women. He grumbled, he said he hated the hellish hole. But as a matter of fact it excited him, the contact with the rough, strongly-feeling people was a stimulant applied direct to his nerves.

---

① Attract strongly, as if with a magnet.

Below Oldmeadow, in the green, shallow, saddened hollow of fields, lay a square, deep pond. Roving across the landscape, the doctor's quick eye detected a figure in black passing through the gate of the field, down towards the pond. He looked again. It would be Mabel Pervin. His mind suddenly became alive and attentive.

Why was she going down there? He pulled up on the path on the slope above, and stood staring. He could just make sure of the small black figure moving in the hollow of the failing day. He seemed to see her in the midst of such obscurity, that he was like a clairvoyant①, seeing rather with the mind's eye than with ordinary sight. Yet he could see her positively enough, whilst he kept his eye attentive. He felt, if he looked away from her, in the thick, ugly falling dusk, he would lose her altogether.

He followed her minutely as she moved, direct and intent, like something transmitted rather than stirring in voluntary activity, straight down the field towards the pond. There she stood on the bank for a moment. She never raised her head. Then she waded slowly into the water.

He stood motionless as the small black figure walked slowly and deliberately towards the centre of the pond, very slowly, gradually moving deeper into the motionless water, and still moving forward as the water got up to her breast. Then he could see her no more in the dusk of the dead afternoon.

"There!" he exclaimed. "Would you believe it?"

And he hastened straight down, running over the wet, soddened fields, pushing through the hedges, down into the depression of callous wintry obscurity. It took him several minutes to come to the pond. He stood on the bank, breathing heavily. He could see nothing. His eyes seemed to penetrate the dead water. Yes, perhaps that was the dark shadow of her black clothing beneath the surface of water.

He slowly ventured into the pond. The bottom was deep, soft clay, he sank in, and the water clasped dead cold round his legs. As he stirred he could smell the cold, rotten clay that fouled up into the water. It was objectionable in his lungs. Still, repelled and yet not heeding, he moved deeper into the pond. The cold water rose over his thighs, over his loins, upon his abdomen. The lower part of his body was all sunk in the hideous cold element. And the bottom was so

---

① Someone who perceives things beyond the natural range of the senses.

deeply soft and uncertain, he was afraid of pitching with his mouth underneath. He could not swim, and was afraid.

He crouched a little, spreading his hands under the water and moving them round, trying to feel for her. The dead cold pond swayed upon his chest. He moved again, a little deeper, and again, with his hands underneath, he felt all around under the water. And he touched her clothing. But it evaded his fingers. He made a desperate effort to grasp it.

And so doing he lost his balance and went under, horribly, suffocating in the foul earthy water, struggling madly for a few moments. At last, after what seemed an eternity, he got his footing, rose again into the air and looked around. He gasped, and knew he was in the world. Then he looked at the water. She had risen near him. He grasped her clothing, and drawing her nearer, turned to take his way to land again.

He went very slowly, carefully, absorbed in the slow progress. He rose higher, climbing out of the pond. The water was now only about his legs; he was thankful, full of relief to be out of the clutches of the pond. He lifted her and staggered on to the bank, out of the horror of wet, grey clay.

He laid her down on the bank. She was quite unconscious and running with water. He made the water come from her mouth, he worked to restore her. He did not have to work very long before he could feel the breathing begin again in her; she was breathing naturally. He worked a little longer. He could feel her live beneath his hands; she was coming back. He wiped her face, wrapped her in his overcoat, looked round into the dim, dark grey world, then lifted her and staggered down the bank and across the fields.

It seemed an unthinkably long way, and his burden so heavy he felt he would never get to the house. But at last he was in the stable-yard, and then in the house-yard. He opened the door and went into the house. In the kitchen he laid her down on the hearth-rug and called. The house was empty. But the fire was burning in the grate.

Then again he kneeled to attend to her. She was breathing regularly, her eyes were wide open and as if conscious, but there seemed something missing in her look. She was conscious in herself, but unconscious of her surroundings.

He ran upstairs, took blankets from a bed, and put them before the fire to warm. Then he removed her saturated, earthy-smelling clothing, rubbed her dry with a towel, and wrapped her naked in the blankets. Then he went into the dining-room, to look for spirits. There was a little whisky. He drank a gulp himself, and put some into her mouth.

The effect was instantaneous. She looked full into his face, as if she had been seeing him for some time, and yet had only just become conscious of him.

"Dr. Fergusson?" she said.

"What?" he answered.

He was divesting himself of his coat, intending to find some dry clothing upstairs. He could not bear the smell of the dead, clayey water, and he was mortally afraid for his own health.

"What did I do?" she asked.

"Walked into the pond," he replied. He had begun to shudder like one sick, and could hardly attend to her. Her eyes remained full on him, he seemed to be going dark in his mind, looking back at her helplessly. The shuddering became quieter in him, his life came back to him, dark and unknowing, but strong again.

"Was I out of my mind?" she asked, while her eyes were fixed on him all the time.

"Maybe, for the moment," he replied. He felt quiet, because his strength had come back. The strange fretful strain had left him.

"Am I out of my mind now?" she asked.

"Are you?" he reflected a moment. "No," he answered truthfully, "I don't see that you are." He turned his face aside. He was afraid now, because he felt dazed, and felt dimly that her power was stronger than his, in this issue. And she continued to look at him fixedly all the time. "Can you tell me where I shall find some dry things to put on?" he asked.

"Did you dive into the pond for me?" she asked.

"No," he answered. "I walked in. But I went in overhead as well."

There was silence for a moment. He hesitated. He very much wanted to go upstairs to get into dry clothing. But there was another desire in him. And she seemed to hold him. His will seemed to have gone to sleep, and left him, standing there slack before her. But he felt warm inside himself. He did not shudder at all, though his clothes were sodden on him.

"Why did you?" she asked.

"Because I didn't want you to do such a foolish thing," he said.

"It wasn't foolish," she said, still gazing at him as she lay on the floor, with a sofa cushion under her head. "It was the right thing to do. I knew best, then."

"I'll go and shift these wet things," he said. But still he had not the power to move out of her presence, until she sent him. It was as if she had the life of his body in her hands, and he could not extricate himself. Or perhaps he did not want to.

Suddenly she sat up. Then she became aware of her own immediate condition. She felt the blankets about her, she knew her own limbs. For a moment it seemed as if her reason were going. She looked round, with wild eye, as if seeking something. He stood still with fear. She saw her clothing lying scattered.

"Who undressed me?" she asked, her eyes resting full and inevitable on his face.

"I did," he replied, "to bring you round."

For some moments she sat and gazed at him awfully, her lips parted.

"Do you love me, then?" she asked.

He only stood and stared at her, fascinated. His soul seemed to melt.

She shuffled forward on her knees, and put her arms round him, round his legs, as he stood there, pressing her breasts against his knees and thighs, clutching him with strange, convulsive certainty, pressing his thighs against her, drawing him to her face, her throat, as she looked up at him with flaring, humble eyes and transfiguration, triumphant in first possession.

"You love me," she murmured, in strange transport①, yearning and triumphant and confident. "You love me. I know you love me, I know."

And she was passionately kissing his knees, through the wet clothing, passionately and indiscriminately kissing his knees, his legs, as if unaware of everything.

He looked down at the tangled wet hair, the wild, bare, animal shoulders. He was amazed, bewildered and afraid. He had never thought of loving her. He had never wanted to love her. When he rescued her and restored her, he was a doctor, and she was a patient. He had had no single personal thought of her. Nay, this introduction of the personal element was very distasteful to him, a violation of his professional honour. It was horrible to have her there embracing

---

① A state of being carried away by overwhelming emotion.

his knees. It was horrible. He revolted from it, violently. And yet—and yet—he had not the power to break away.

She looked at him again, with the same supplication of powerful love, and that same transcendent, frightening light of triumph. In view of the delicate flame which seemed to come from her face like a light, he was powerless. And yet he had never intended to love her. He had never intended. And something stubborn in him could not give way.

"You love me," she repeated, in a murmur of deep, rhapsodic① assurance. "You love me."

Her hands were drawing him, drawing him down to her. He was afraid, even a little horrified. For he had, really, no intention of loving her. Yet her hands were drawing him towards her. He put out his hand quickly to steady himself, and grasped her bare shoulder. A flame seemed to burn the hand that grasped her soft shoulder. He had no intention of loving her: his whole will was against his yielding. It was horrible. And yet wonderful was the touch of her shoulders, beautiful the shining of her face. Was she perhaps mad? He had a horror of yielding to her. Yet something in him ached also.

He had been staring away at the door, away from her. But his hand remained on her shoulder. She had gone suddenly very still. He looked down at her. Her eyes were now wide with fear, with doubt, the light was dying from her face, a shadow of terrible greyness was returning. He could not bear the touch of her eyes' question upon him, and the look of death behind the question.

With an inward groan he gave way, and let his heart yield towards her. A sudden gentle smile came on his face. And her eyes, which never left his face, slowly, slowly filled with tears. He watched the strange water rise in her eyes, like some slow fountain coming up. And his heart seemed to burn and melt away in his breast.

He could not bear to look at her any more. He dropped on his knees and caught her head with his arms and pressed her face against his throat. She was very still. His heart, which seemed to have broken, was burning with a kind of agony in his breast. And he felt her slow, hot tears wetting his throat. But he could not move.

He felt the hot tears wet his neck and the hollows of his neck, and he

---

① Feeling great rapture or delight.

remained motionless, suspended through one of man's eternities. Only now it had become indispensable to him to have her face pressed close to him; he could never let her go again. He could never let her head go away from the close crutch of his arm. He wanted to remain like that for ever, with his heart hurting him in a pain that was also life to him. Without knowing, he was looking down on her damp, soft brown hair.

Then, as it were suddenly, he smelt the horrid stagnant smell of that water. And at the same moment she drew away from him and looked at him. Her eyes were wistful and unfathomable. He was afraid of them, and he fell to kissing her, not knowing what he was doing. He wanted her eyes not to have that terrible, wistful, unfathomable look.

When she turned her face to him again, a faint delicate flush was glowing, and there was again dawning that terrible shining of joy in her eyes, which really terrified him, and yet which he now wanted to see, because he feared the look of doubt still more.

"You love me?" she said, rather faltering.

"Yes." The word cost him a painful effort. Not because it wasn't true. But because it was too newly true, the *saying* seemed to tear open again his newly-torn heart. And he hardly wanted it to be true, even now.

She lifted her face to him, and he bent forward and kissed her on the mouth, gently, with the one kiss that is an eternal pledge①. And as he kissed her his heart strained again in his breast. He never intended to love her. But now it was over. He had crossed over the gulf to her, and all that he had left behind had shrivelled and become void.

After the kiss, her eyes again slowly filled with tears. She sat still, away from him, with her face drooped aside, and her hands folded in her lap. The tears fell very slowly. There was complete silence. He too sat there motionless and silent on the hearth-rug. The strange pain of his heart that was broken seemed to consume him. That he should love her? That this was love! That he should be ripped open in this way! Him, a doctor! How they would all jeer if they knew! It was agony to him to think they might know.

In the curious naked pain of the thought he looked again to her. She was sitting there drooped into a muse. He saw a tear fall, and his heart flared hot.

---

① A deposit of personal property as security for a debt.

He saw for the first time that one of her shoulders was quite uncovered, one arm bare, he could see one of her small breasts; dimly, because it had become almost dark in the room.

"Why are you crying?" he asked, in an altered voice.

She looked up at him, and behind her tears the consciousness of her situation for the first time brought a dark look of shame to her eyes.

"I'm not crying, really," she said, watching him, half-frightened.

He reached his hand, and softly closed it on her bare arm.

"I love you! I love you!" he said in a soft, low vibrating voice, unlike himself.

She shrank, and dropped her head. The soft, penetrating grip of his hand on her arm distressed her. She looked up at him.

"I want to go," she said. "I want to go and get you some dry things."

"Why?" he said. "I'm all right."

"But I want to go," she said. "And I want you to change your things."

He released her arm, and she wrapped herself in the blanket, looking at him rather frightened. And still she did not rise.

"Kiss me," she said wistfully.

He kissed her, but briefly, half in anger.

Then, after a second, she rose nervously, all mixed up in the blanket. He watched her in her confusion as she tried to extricate herself and wrap herself up so that she could walk. He watched her relentlessly, as she knew. And as she went, the blanket trailing, and he saw a glimpse of her feet and her white leg, he tried to remember her as she was when he had wrapped her up in the blanket. But then he didn't want to remember, because she had been nothing to him then, and his nature revolted from remembering her as she was when she was nothing to him.

A tumbling, muffled noise from within the dark house startled him. Then he heard her voice: "There are clothes." He rose and went to the foot of the stairs, and gathered up the garments she had thrown down. Then he came back to the fire, to rub himself down and dress. He grinned at his own appearance when he had finished.

The fire was sinking, so he put on coal. The house was now quite dark, save for the light of a street-lamp that shone in faintly from beyond the holly trees. He lit the gas with matches he found on the mantelpiece. Then he emptied the pockets of his own clothes, and threw all his wet things in a heap into the scullery. After which he gathered up her sodden clothes, gently, and put them in a separate heap on the copper-top in the scullery.

It was six o'clock on the clock. His own watch had stopped. He ought to go back to the surgery. He waited, and still she did not come down. So he went to the foot of the stairs and called:

"I shall have to go."

Almost immediately he heard her coming down. She had on her best dress of black voile, and her hair was tidy, but still damp. She looked at him—and in spite of herself, smiled.

"I don't like you in those clothes," she said.

"Do I look a sight?" he answered.

They were shy of one another.

"I'll make you some tea," she said.

"No, I must go."

"Must you?" And she looked at him again with the wide, strained, doubtful eyes. And again, from the pain of his breast, he knew how he loved her. He went and bent to kiss her, gently, passionately, with his heart's painful kiss.

"And my hair smells so horrible," she murmured in distraction. "And I'm so awful, I'm so awful! Oh no, I'm too awful." And she broke into bitter, heart-broken sobbing. "You can't want to love me, I'm horrible."

"Don't be silly, don't be silly," he said, trying to comfort her, kissing her, holding her in his arms. "I want you, I want to marry you, we're going to be married, quickly, quickly—to-morrow if I can."

But she only sobbed terribly, and cried:

"I feel awful. I feel awful. I feel I'm horrible to you."

"No, I want you, I want you," was all he answered, blindly, with that terrible intonation which frightened her almost more than her horror lest he should *not* want her.

Questions for Discussion

1. What can we learn about Mabel through the title? What kind of character is she like? How is the story organized? Is it centered around Mabel's action and movement? How is the relationship between her and people around her, especially the male characters?

2. Before the family's bankruptcy, what gave Mabel Pervin her sense of independence and integrity? How authentic was that sense—in other words, was it something that needed to be stripped away so that Mabel could arrive at a more accurate understanding of herself and her situation, or not?
3. What first draws Dr. Ferguson towards Mabel? And how does Lawrence represent the nature and value of love, based on the way he describes the encounter between Mabel and Dr. Ferguson?
4. Do you think Lawrence's way of representing love is authentic and accurate, or do you find it contrived? Explain your response.
5. What is the point of view of the story? Can the narrator be trusted in telling all the information needed to be known?

About the Author

David Herbert Lawrence (1885—1930), English novelist, storywriter, critic, poet and painter, one of the greatest figures in 20th-century English literature. Lawrence saw sex and intuition as ways to undistorted perception of reality and means to respond to the inhumanity of the industrial culture. From Lawrence's doctrines of sexual freedom arose obscenity trials, which had a deep effect on the relationship between literature and society. In 1912 he wrote: "What the blood feels, and believes, and says, is always true."

Lawrence was born in the mining town of Eastwood, Nottinghamshire, in central England. He was the fourth child of a struggling coal miner who was a heavy drinker. His mother was a former school teacher, whose family had fallen in hard times. However, she was greatly superior in education to her husband. Lawrence's childhood was dominated by poverty and friction between his parents. In a letter from 1910 to the poet Rachel Annand Taylor he later wrote: "Their marriage life has been one carnal, bloody fight. I was born hating my father: as early as ever I can remember, I shivered with horror when he touched me. He was very bad before I was born." This can probably explain why the male characters in his works either turn out to be almost beastly or never exist at all.

Encouraged by his mother, with whom he had a deep emotional bond and who figures as Mrs Morel in his first masterpiece, Lawrence became interested in arts. The appearance of his first novel, *The White Peacock* (1911), launched Lawrence as a writer at the age of 25. And his major fiction includes: *Sons and*

Lovers (1913), *The Rainbow* (1915), *The Lost Girl* (1920) and *Lady Chatterley's Lover* (1928). In addition, he also published a number of poems. However, at his time the public were still too sensitive to allow frank discussions of sex, psychology and religion, and that led to the banning of some of his works in both UK and the US.

The Horse Dealer's Daughter is about Mabel, who tries to commit suicide by drowning herself in a pond when she discovers that there is literally no way to go in her reality. A young doctor, Jack Ferguson, saves her. She then believes that he loves her. This idea is not a first thought to Jack, but he begins to find that he does love her. However, Mabel thinks she is "too awful" to be loved. Lawrence's marvelous story shows through passive natures, obedient attitudes, and shattered egos a woman struggling to live her life in a morbid and desolate environment.

The Garden Party

Katherine Mansfield

And after all the weather was ideal. They could not have had a more perfect day for a garden-party if they had ordered it. Windless, warm, the sky without a cloud. Only the blue was veiled with a haze of light gold, as it is sometimes in early summer. The gardener had been up since dawn, mowing the lawns and sweeping them, until the grass and the dark flat rosettes where the daisy plants had been seemed to shine. As for the roses, you could not help feeling they understood that roses are the only flowers that impress people at garden-parties; the only flowers that everybody is certain of knowing. Hundreds, yes, literally hundreds, had come out in a single night; the green bushes bowed down as though they had been visited by archangels.

Breakfast was not yet over before the men came to put up the marquee①.

"Where do you want the marquee put, mother?"

"My dear child, it's no use asking me. I'm determined to leave everything to you children this year. Forget I am your mother. Treat me as an honoured guest."

But Meg could not possibly go and supervise the men. She had washed her hair before breakfast, and she sat drinking her coffee in a green turban, with a dark wet curl stamped on each cheek. Jose, the butterfly, always came down in a silk petticoat and a kimono jacket.

"You'll have to go, Laura; you're the artistic one."

Away Laura flew, still holding her piece of bread-and-butter. It's so delicious to have an excuse for eating out of doors, and besides, she loved having to arrange things; she always felt she could do it so much better than anybody else.

Four men in their shirt-sleeves② stood grouped together on the garden path. They carried staves covered with rolls of canvas, and they had big tool-bags slung on their backs. They looked impressive. Laura wished now that she had

---

① Large and often sumptuous tent. 雨盖,大华盖

② Not wearing a jacket. 本来指的是衬衣袖子,而这里说的是这些工人们干的是体力活,所以不像上流社会的绅士们那样穿着西服外套,不是很体面。

not got the bread-and-butter, but there was nowhere to put it, and she couldn't possibly throw it away. She blushed and tried to look severe and even a little bit short-sighted as she came up to them.

"Good morning," she said, copying her mother's voice. But that sounded so fearfully affected that she was ashamed, and stammered like a little girl, "Oh—er—have you come—is it about the marquee?"

"That's right, miss," said the tallest of the men, a lanky, freckled fellow, and he shifted his tool-bag, knocked back his straw hat and smiled down at her. "That's about it."

His smile was so easy, so friendly that Laura recovered. What nice eyes he had, small, but such a dark blue! And now she looked at the others, they were smiling too. "Cheer up, we won't bite," their smile seemed to say. How very nice workmen were! And what a beautiful morning! She mustn't mention the morning; she must be business-like. The marquee.

"Well, what about the lily-lawn? Would that do?"

And she pointed to the lily-lawn with the hand that didn't hold the bread-and-butter. They turned, they stared in the direction. A little fat chap thrust out his under-lip, and the tall fellow frowned.

"I don't fancy it," said he. "Not conspicuous enough. You see, with a thing like a marquee," and he turned to Laura in his easy way, "you want to put it somewhere where it'll give you a bang slap in the eye, if you follow me①."

Laura's upbringing made her wonder for a moment whether it was quite respectful of a workman to talk to her of bangs slap in the eye. But she did quite follow him.

"A corner of the tennis-court," she suggested. "But the band's going to be in one corner."

"H'm, going to have a band, are you?" said another of the workmen. He was pale. He had a haggard look as his dark eyes scanned the tennis-court. What was he thinking?

"Only a very small band," said Laura gently. Perhaps he wouldn't mind so much if the band was quite small. But the tall fellow interrupted.

"Look here, miss, that's the place. Against those trees. Over there. That'll do fine."

---

① If you understand what I mean.

Against the karakas. Then the karaka-trees would be hidden. And they were so lovely, with their broad, gleaming leaves, and their clusters of yellow fruit. They were like trees you imagined growing on a desert island, proud, solitary, lifting their leaves and fruits to the sun in a kind of silent splendour. Must they be hidden by a marquee?

They must. Already the men had shouldered their staves and were making for the place. Only the tall fellow was left. He bent down, pinched a sprig of lavender, put his thumb and forefinger to his nose and snuffed up the smell. When Laura saw that gesture she forgot all about the karakas in her wonder at him caring for things like that—caring for the smell of lavender. How many men that she knew would have done such a thing? Oh, how extraordinarily nice workmen were, she thought. Why couldn't she have workmen for her friends rather than the silly boys she danced with and who came to Sunday night supper? She would get on much better with men like these.

It's all the fault, she decided, as the tall fellow drew something on the back of an envelope, something that was to be looped up or left to hang, of these absurd class distinctions. Well, for her part, she didn't feel them. Not a bit, not an atom... And now there came the chock-chock of wooden hammers. Some one whistled, some one sang out, "Are you right there, matey?" "Matey!" The friendliness of it, the—the—Just to prove how happy she was, just to show the tall fellow how at home she felt, and how she despised stupid conventions, Laura took a big bite of her bread-and-butter as she stared at the little drawing. She felt just like a work-girl.

"Laura, Laura, where are you? Telephone, Laura!" a voice cried from the house.

"Coming!" Away she skimmed, over the lawn, up the path, up the steps, across the veranda, and into the porch. In the hall her father and Laurie were brushing their hats ready to go to the office.

"I say, Laura," said Laurie very fast, "you might just give a squiz at my coat before this afternoon. See if it wants pressing."

"I will," said she. Suddenly she couldn't stop herself. She ran at Laurie and gave him a small, quick squeeze. "Oh, I do love parties, don't you?" gasped Laura.

"Ra-ther," said Laurie's warm, boyish voice, and he squeezed his sister too, and gave her a gentle push. "Dash off to the telephone, old girl."

The telephone. "Yes, yes; oh yes. Kitty? Good morning, dear. Come to lunch? Do, dear. Delighted of course. It will only be a very scratch meal—just the sandwich crusts and broken meringue-shells and what's left over. Yes, isn't it a perfect morning? Your white? Oh, I certainly should. One moment—hold the line. Mother's calling." And Laura sat back. "What, mother? Can't hear."

Mrs. Sheridan's voice floated down the stairs. "Tell her to wear that sweet hat she had on last Sunday."

"Mother says you're to wear that sweet hat you had on last Sunday. Good. One o'clock. Bye-bye."

Laura put back the receiver, flung her arms over her head, took a deep breath, stretched and let them fall. "Huh," she sighed, and the moment after the sigh she sat up quickly. She was still, listening. All the doors in the house seemed to be open. The house was alive with soft, quick steps and running voices. The green baize door that led to the kitchen regions swung open and shut with a muffled thud. And now there came a long, chuckling absurd sound. It was the heavy piano being moved on its stiff castors. But the air! If you stopped to notice, was the air always like this? Little faint winds were playing chase, in at the tops of the windows, out at the doors. And there were two tiny spots of sun, one on the inkpot, one on a silver photograph frame, playing too. Darling little spots. Especially the one on the inkpot lid. It was quite warm. A warm little silver star. She could have kissed it.

The front door bell pealed, and there sounded the rustle of Sadie's print skirt on the stairs. A man's voice murmured; Sadie answered, careless, "I'm sure I don't know. Wait. I'll ask Mrs Sheridan."

"What is it, Sadie?" Laura came into the hall.

"It's the florist, Miss Laura."

It was, indeed. There, just inside the door, stood a wide, shallow tray full of pots of pink lilies. No other kind. Nothing but lilies—canna lilies, big pink flowers, wide open, radiant, almost frighteningly alive on bright crimson stems.

"O-oh, Sadie!" said Laura, and the sound was like a little moan. She crouched down as if to warm herself at that blaze of lilies; she felt they were in her fingers, on her lips, growing in her breast.

"It's some mistake," she said faintly. "Nobody ever ordered so many. Sadie, go and find mother."

But at that moment Mrs. Sheridan joined them.

"It's quite right," she said calmly. "Yes, I ordered them. Aren't they lovely?" She pressed Laura's arm. "I was passing the shop yesterday, and I saw them in the window. And I suddenly thought for once in my life I shall have enough canna lilies. The garden-party will be a good excuse."

"But I thought you said you didn't mean to interfere," said Laura. Sadie had gone. The florist's man was still outside at his van. She put her arm round her mother's neck and gently, very gently, she bit her mother's ear.

"My darling child, you wouldn't like a logical mother, would you? Don't do that. Here's the man."

He carried more lilies still, another whole tray.

"Bank them up, just inside the door, on both sides of the porch, please," said Mrs. Sheridan. "Don't you agree, Laura?"

"Oh, I do, mother."

In the drawing-room Meg, Jose and good little Hans had at last succeeded in moving the piano.

"Now, if we put this chesterfield against the wall and move everything out of the room except the chairs, don't you think?"

"Quite."

"Hans, move these tables into the smoking-room, and bring a sweeper to take these marks off the carpet and—one moment, Hans—" Jose loved giving orders to the servants, and they loved obeying her. She always made them feel they were taking part in some drama. "Tell mother and Miss Laura to come here at once.

"Very good, Miss Jose."

She turned to Meg. "I want to hear what the piano sounds like, just in case I'm asked to sing this afternoon. Let's try over 'This life is Weary.'"

Pom! Ta-ta-ta Tee-ta! The piano burst out so passionately that Jose's face changed. She clasped her hands. She looked mournfully and enigmatically[①] at her mother and Laura as they came in.

"This Life is Wee-ary,

A Tear—a Sigh.

A Love that Chan-ges,

This Life is Wee-ary,

---

① Like a riddle.

A Tear—a Sigh.

A Love that Chan-ges,

And then... Good-bye!"

But at the word "Good-bye," and although the piano sounded more desperate than ever, her face broke into a brilliant, dreadfully unsympathetic smile.

"Aren't I in good voice, mummy?" she beamed.

"This Life is Wee-ary,

Hope comes to Die.

A Dream—a Wa-kening."

But now Sadie interrupted them. "What is it, Sadie?"

"If you please, m'm, cook says have you got the flags for the sandwiches?"

"The flags for the sandwiches, Sadie?" echoed Mrs. Sheridan dreamily. And the children knew by her face that she hadn't got them. "Let me see." And she said to Sadie firmly, "Tell cook I'll let her have them in ten minutes."

Sadie went.

"Now, Laura," said her mother quickly, "come with me into the smoking-room. I've got the names somewhere on the back of an envelope. You'll have to write them out for me. Meg, go upstairs this minute and take that wet thing off your head. Jose, run and finish dressing this instant. Do you hear me, children, or shall I have to tell your father when he comes home to-night? And—and, Jose, pacify cook if you do go into the kitchen, will you? I'm terrified of her this morning."

The envelope was found at last behind the dining-room clock, though how it had got there Mrs. Sheridan could not imagine.

"One of you children must have stolen it out of my bag, because I remember vividly—cream cheese and lemon-curd. Have you done that?"

"Yes."

"Egg and—" Mrs. Sheridan held the envelope away from her. "It looks like mice. It can't be mice, can it?"

"Olive, pet," said Laura, looking over her shoulder.

"Yes, of course, olive. What a horrible combination it sounds. Egg and olive."

They were finished at last, and Laura took them off to the kitchen. She found Jose there pacifying the cook, who did not look at all terrifying.

"I have never seen such exquisite sandwiches," said Jose's rapturous voice. "How many kinds did you say there were, cook? Fifteen?"

"Fifteen, Miss Jose."

"Well, cook, I congratulate you."

Cook swept up crusts with the long sandwich knife, and smiled broadly.

"Godber's has come," announced Sadie, issuing out of the pantry①. She had seen the man pass the window.

That meant the cream puffs had come. Godber's were famous for their cream puffs. Nobody ever thought of making them at home.

"Bring them in and put them on the table, my girl," ordered cook.

Sadie brought them in and went back to the door. Of course Laura and Jose were far too grown-up to really care about such things. All the same, they couldn't help agreeing that the puffs looked very attractive. Very. Cook began arranging them, shaking off the extra icing sugar.

"Don't they carry one back② to all one's parties?" said Laura.

"I suppose they do," said practical Jose, who never liked to be carried back. "They look beautifully light and feathery, I must say."

"Have one each, my dears," said cook in her comfortable voice. "Yer ma won't know."

Oh, impossible. Fancy cream puffs so soon after breakfast. The very idea made one shudder. All the same, two minutes later Jose and Laura were licking their fingers with that absorbed inward look that only comes from whipped cream.

"Let's go into the garden, out by the back way," suggested Laura. "I want to see how the men are getting on with the marquee. They're such awfully nice men."

But the back door was blocked by cook, Sadie, Godber's man and Hans.

Something had happened.

"Tuk-tuk-tuk," clucked cook like an agitated hen. Sadie had her hand clapped to her cheek as though she had toothache. Hans's face was screwed up in the effort to understand. Only Godber's man seemed to be enjoying himself; it was his story.

---

① A room where the food and dishes are kept.
② Make one remember, think of.

Part One　British Literature

"What's the matter? What's happened?"

"There's been a horrible accident," said Cook. "A man killed."

"A man killed! Where? How? When?"

But Godber's man wasn't going to have his story snatched from under his very nose.

"Know those little cottages just below here, miss?" Know them? Of course, she knew them. "Well, there's a young chap living there, name of Scott, a carter. His horse shied at a traction-engine, corner of Hawke Street this morning, and he was thrown out on the back of his head. Killed."

"Dead!" Laura stared at Godber's man.

"Dead when they picked him up," said Godber's man with relish. "They were taking the body home as I come up here." And he said to the cook, "He's left a wife and five little ones."

"Jose, come here." Laura caught hold of her sister's sleeve and dragged her through the kitchen to the other side of the green baize door. There she paused and leaned against it. "Jose!" she said, horrified, "however are we going to stop everything?"

"Stop everything, Laura!" cried Jose in astonishment. "What do you mean?"

"Stop the garden-party, of course." Why did Jose pretend?

But Jose was still more amazed. "Stop the garden-party? My dear Laura, don't be so absurd. Of course we can't do anything of the kind. Nobody expects us to. Don't be so extravagant."

"But we can't possibly have a garden-party with a man dead just outside the front gate."

That really was extravagant, for the little cottages were in a lane to themselves at the very bottom of a steep rise that led up to the house. A broad road ran between. True, they were far too near. They were the greatest possible eyesore, and they had no right to be in that neighbourhood at all. They were little mean dwellings painted a chocolate brown. In the garden patches there was nothing but cabbage stalks, sick hens and tomato cans. The very smoke coming out of their chimneys was poverty-stricken. Little rags and shreds of smoke, so unlike the great silvery plumes that uncurled from the Sheridans' chimneys. Washerwomen lived in the lane and sweeps and a cobbler, and a man whose house-front was studded all over with minute bird-cages. Children swarmed.

When the Sheridans were little they were forbidden to set foot there because of the revolting language and of what they might catch. But since they were grown up, Laura and Laurie on their prowls sometimes walked through. It was disgusting and sordid. They came out with a shudder. But still one must go everywhere; one must see everything. So through they went.

"And just think of what the band would sound like to that poor woman," said Laura.

"Oh, Laura!" Jose began to be seriously annoyed. "If you're going to stop a band playing every time some one has an accident, you'll lead a very strenuous life. I'm every bit as sorry about it as you. I feel just as sympathetic." Her eyes hardened. She looked at her sister just as she used to when they were little and fighting together. "You won't bring a drunken workman back to life by being sentimental," she said softly.

"Drunk! Who said he was drunk?" Laura turned furiously on Jose. She said, just as they had used to say on those occasions, "I'm going straight up to tell mother."

"Do, dear," cooed Jose.

"Mother, can I come into your room?" Laura turned the big glass door-knob.

"Of course, child. Why, what's the matter? What's given you such a colour?" And Mrs. Sheridan turned round from her dressing-table. She was trying on a new hat.

"Mother, a man's been killed," began Laura.

"Not in the garden?" interrupted her mother.

"No, no!"

"Oh, what a fright you gave me!" Mrs. Sheridan sighed with relief, and took off the big hat and held it on her knees.

"But listen, mother," said Laura. Breathless, half-choking, she told the dreadful story.

"Of course, we can't have our party, can we?" she pleaded. "The band and everybody arriving. They'd hear us, mother; they're nearly neighbours!"

To Laura's astonishment her mother behaved just like Jose; it was harder to bear because she seemed amused. She refused to take Laura seriously.

"But, my dear child, use your common sense. It's only by accident we've heard of it. If some one had died there normally—and I can't understand how they keep alive in those poky little holes—we should still be having our party, shouldn't we?"

Laura had to say "yes" to that, but she felt it was all wrong. She sat down on her mother's sofa and pinched the cushion frill.

"Mother, isn't it terribly heartless of us?" she asked.

"Darling!" Mrs. Sheridan got up and came over to her, carrying the hat. Before Laura could stop her she had popped it on. "My child!" said her mother, "the hat is yours. It's made for you. It's much too young for me. I have never seen you look such a picture. Look at yourself!" And she held up her hand-mirror.

"But, mother," Laura began again. She couldn't look at herself; she turned aside.

This time Mrs. Sheridan lost patience just as Jose had done.

"You are being very absurd, Laura," she said coldly. "People like that don't expect sacrifices from us. And it's not very sympathetic to spoil everybody's enjoyment as you're doing now."

"I don't understand," said Laura, and she walked quickly out of the room into her own bedroom. There, quite by chance, the first thing she saw was this charming girl in the mirror, in her black hat trimmed with gold daisies, and a long black velvet ribbon. Never had she imagined she could look like that. Is mother right? she thought. And now she hoped her mother was right. Am I being extravagant? Perhaps it was extravagant. Just for a moment she had another glimpse of that poor woman and those little children, and the body being carried into the house. But it all seemed blurred, unreal, like a picture in the newspaper. I'll remember it again after the party's over, she decided. And somehow that seemed quite the best plan...

Lunch was over by half past one. By half past two they were all ready for the fray. The green-coated band had arrived and was established in a corner of the tennis-court.

"My dear!" trilled Kitty Maitland, "aren't they too like frogs for words? You ought to have arranged them round the pond with the conductor in the middle on a leaf."

Laurie arrived and hailed them on his way to dress. At the sight of him Laura remembered the accident again. She wanted to tell him. If Laurie agreed with the others, then it was bound to be all right. And she followed him into the hall.

"Laurie!"

"Hallo!" He was half-way upstairs, but when he turned round and saw Laura he suddenly puffed out his cheeks and goggled his eyes at her. "My word, Laura! You do look stunning," said Laurie. "What an absolutely topping hat!"

Laura said faintly "Is it?" and smiled up at Laurie, and didn't tell him after all.

Soon after that people began coming in streams. The band struck up; the hired waiters ran from the house to the marquee. Wherever you looked there were couples strolling, bending to the flowers, greeting, moving on over the lawn. They were like bright birds that had alighted in the Sheridans' garden for this one afternoon, on their way to—where? Ah, what happiness it is to be with people who all are happy, to press hands, press cheeks, smile into eyes.

"Darling Laura, how well you look!"

"What a becoming① hat, child!"

"Laura, you look quite Spanish. I've never seen you look so striking."

And Laura, glowing, answered softly, "Have you had tea? Won't you have an ice? The passion-fruit ices really are rather special." She ran to her father and begged him. "Daddy darling, can't the band have something to drink?"

And the perfect afternoon slowly ripened, slowly faded, slowly its petals closed.

"Never a more delightful garden-party..." "The greatest success..." "Quite the most..."

Laura helped her mother with the good-byes. They stood side by side in the porch till it was all over.

"All over, all over, thank heaven," said Mrs. Sheridan. "Round up the others, Laura. Let's go and have some fresh coffee. I'm exhausted. Yes, it's been very successful. But oh, these parties, these parties! Why will you children insist on giving parties!" And they all of them sat down in the deserted marquee.

"Have a sandwich, daddy dear. I wrote the flag."

"Thanks." Mr. Sheridan took a bite and the sandwich was gone. He took another. "I suppose you didn't hear of a beastly accident that happened to-day?" he said.

---

① Fit, suitable.

"My dear," said Mrs. Sheridan, holding up her hand, "we did. It nearly ruined the party. Laura insisted we should put it off."

"Oh, mother!" Laura didn't want to be teased about it.

"It was a horrible affair all the same," said Mr. Sheridan. "The chap was married too. Lived just below in the lane, and leaves a wife and half a dozen kiddies, so they say."

An awkward little silence fell. Mrs. Sheridan fidgeted with her cup. Really, it was very tactless of father...

Suddenly she looked up. There on the table were all those sandwiches, cakes, puffs, all uneaten, all going to be wasted. She had one of her brilliant ideas.

"I know," she said. "Let's make up a basket. Let's send that poor creature some of this perfectly good food. At any rate, it will be the greatest treat for the children. Don't you agree? And she's sure to have neighbours calling in and so on. What a point to have it all ready prepared. Laura!" She jumped up. "Get me the big basket out of the stairs cupboard."

"But, mother, do you really think it's a good idea?" said Laura.

Again, how curious, she seemed to be different from them all. To take scraps from their party. Would the poor woman really like that?

"Of course! What's the matter with you today? An hour or two ago you were insisting on us being sympathetic, and now—"

Oh well! Laura ran for the basket. It was filled, it was heaped by her mother.

"Take it yourself, darling," said she. "Run down just as you are. No, wait, take the arum lilies too. People of that class are so impressed by arum lilies."

"The stems will ruin her lace frock," said practical Jose.

So they would. Just in time. "Only the basket, then. And, Laura!"—her mother followed her out of the marquee—"don't on any account—"

"What mother?"

No, better not put such ideas into the child's head! "Nothing! Run along."

It was just growing dusky as Laura shut their garden gates. A big dog ran by like a shadow. The road gleamed white, and down below in the hollow the little cottages were in deep shade. How quiet it seemed after the afternoon. Here she was going down the hill to somewhere where a man lay dead, and she

121

couldn't realize it. Why couldn't she? She stopped a minute. And it seemed to her that kisses, voices, tinkling spoons, laughter, the smell of crushed grass were somehow inside her. She had no room for anything else. How strange! She looked up at the pale sky, and all she thought was, "Yes, it was the most successful party."

Now the broad road was crossed. The lane began, smoky and dark. Women in shawls and men's tweed caps hurried by. Men hung over the palings; the children played in the doorways. A low hum came from the mean little cottages. In some of them there was a flicker of light, and a shadow, crab-like, moved across the window. Laura bent her head and hurried on. She wished now she had put on a coat. How her frock shone! And the big hat with the velvet streamer—if only it was another hat! Were the people looking at her? They must be. It was a mistake to have come; she knew all along it was a mistake. Should she go back even now?

No, too late. This was the house. It must be. A dark knot of people stood outside. Beside the gate an old, old woman with a crutch sat in a chair, watching. She had her feet on a newspaper. The voices stopped as Laura drew near. The group parted. It was as though she was expected, as though they had known she was coming here.

Laura was terribly nervous. Tossing the velvet ribbon over her shoulder, she said to a woman standing by, "Is this Mrs. Scott's house?" and the woman, smiling queerly, said, "It is, my lass."

Oh, to be away from this! She actually said, "Help me, God," as she walked up the tiny path and knocked. To be away from those staring eyes, or to be covered up in anything, one of those women's shawls even. I'll just leave the basket and go, she decided. I shan't even wait for it to be emptied.

Then the door opened. A little woman in black showed in the gloom.

Laura said, "Are you Mrs. Scott?" But to her horror the woman answered, "Walk in please, miss," and she was shut in the passage.

"No," said Laura, "I don't want to come in. I only want to leave this basket. Mother sent—"

The little woman in the gloomy passage seemed not to have heard her. "Step this way, please, miss," she said in an oily① voice, and Laura followed her.

---

① Tactful.

Part One British Literature

She found herself in a wretched little low kitchen, lighted by a smoky lamp. There was a woman sitting before the fire.

"Em," said the little creature who had let her in. "Em! It's a young lady." She turned to Laura. She said meaningly, "I'm 'er sister, miss. You'll excuse 'er, won't you?"

"Oh, but of course!" said Laura. "Please, please don't disturb her. I—I only want to leave—"

But at that moment the woman at the fire turned round. Her face, puffed up, red, with swollen eyes and swollen lips, looked terrible. She seemed as though she couldn't understand why Laura was there. What did it mean? Why was this stranger standing in the kitchen with a basket? What was it all about? And the poor face puckered up again.

"All right, my dear," said the other. "I'll thank the young lady."

And again she began, "You'll excuse her, miss, I'm sure," and her face, swollen too, tried an oily smile.

Laura only wanted to get out, to get away. She was back in the passage. The door opened. She walked straight through into the bedroom, where the dead man was lying.

"You'd like a look at 'im, wouldn't you?" said Em's sister, and she brushed past Laura over to the bed. "Don't be afraid, my lass,"—and now her voice sounded fond and sly, and fondly she drew down the sheet—"'e looks a picture. There's nothing to show. Come along, my dear."

Laura came.

There lay a young man, fast asleep—sleeping so soundly, so deeply, that he was far, far away from them both. Oh, so remote, so peaceful. He was dreaming. Never wake him up again. His head was sunk in the pillow, his eyes were closed; they were blind under the closed eyelids. He was given up to his dream. What did garden-parties and baskets and lace frocks matter to him? He was far from all those things. He was wonderful, beautiful. While they were laughing and while the band was playing, this marvel had come to the lane. Happy... happy... All is well, said that sleeping face. This is just as it should be. I am content.

But all the same you had to cry, and she couldn't go out of the room without saying something to him. Laura gave a loud childish sob.

"Forgive my hat," she said.

And this time she didn't wait for Em's sister. She found her way out of the door, down the path, past all those dark people. At the corner of the lane she met Laurie.

He stepped out of the shadow. "Is that you, Laura?"

"Yes."

"Mother was getting anxious. Was it all right?"

"Yes, quite. Oh, Laurie!" She took his arm, she pressed up against him.

"I say, you're not crying, are you?" asked her brother.

Laura shook her head. She was.

Laurie put his arm round her shoulder. "Don't cry," he said in his warm, loving voice. "Was it awful?"

"No," sobbed Laura. "It was simply marvellous. But Laurie—" She stopped, she looked at her brother. "Isn't life," she stammered, "isn't life—" But what life was she couldn't explain. No matter. He quite understood.

"Isn't it, darling?" said Laurie.

Questions for Discussion

1. Summarize the plot of the story.
2. Why is there a garden party? What kind of lifestyle does that show? Does the author give a clear picture of the party in process? Why is there such a big proportion of the preparations for the garden party? Do you think the detailed descriptions are necessary for the development of the story?
3. What kind of person is Laura? Do you feel that she is different from other members of her family? How do you characterize her family, such as her mother, father, Jose, and Laurie?
4. What are the themes for this story?
5. What has Laura learned about life and people through the garden party? What is she trying to say in the end about "isn't life—"?

About the Author

Katherine Mansfield (1888—1923) is New Zealand's most famous writer, closely associated with D. H. Lawrence and something of a rival of Virginia Woolf. Mansfield's creative years were burdened with loneliness, illness, jealousy, and alienation—all this reflected in her work with the bitter depiction of marital and family relationships of her middle-class characters. Her short stories are also notable for their use of stream of consciousness. Like the Russian writer Anton Chekhov, Mansfield depicted trivial events and subtle changes in human behavior.

Born in Wellington, New Zealand, into a middle-class colonial family, her father was a banker and her mother of genteel origins. She lived for six years in the rural village of Karori. Later on Mansfield said, "I imagine I was always writing. Twaddle it was, too. But better far write twaddle or anything, anything, than nothing at all." At the age of nine she had her first text published. As a first step to her rebellion against her background, she withdrew to London in 1903 and studied at Queen's College, where she joined the staff of the *College Magazine*. Back in New Zealand in 1906, she then took up music, and had affairs with both men and women. Her father denied her the opportunity to become a professional cello player—she was an accomplished violoncellist. In 1908 she studied typing and bookkeeping at Wellington Technical College. Later her father was persuaded to allow Katherine to move back to England, with an allowance of £100 a year. There she devoted herself to writing. Mansfield never visited New Zealand again.

In March 1907 Katherine's mother gave a garden party in their Wellington house; a fatal street accident to a neighbour living in a poor quarter nearby nearly spoiled the festival atmosphere of the day. This was to form the basis of her story *The Garden Party*, but Laura's sensibility as portrayed in that story is subtler and finer than anything that the author appears to have herself felt at that time. This story, like so much of Mansfiled's reworking of her New Zealand experiences in her last years, represents a kind of atonement for her younger self.

Dubliners

James Joyce

Two Gallants

The grey warm evening of August had descended upon the city, and a mild warm air, a memory of summer, circulated in the streets. The streets, shuttered for the repose of Sunday, swarmed with a gaily coloured crowd. Like illumined pearls the lamps shone from the summits of their tall poles upon the living texture below, which, changing shape and hue unceasingly, sent up into the warm grey evening air an unchanging, unceasing murmur.

Two young men came down the hill of Rutland Square. One of them was just bringing a long monologue to a close. The other, who walked on the verge of the path and was at times obliged to step on to the road, owing to his companion's rudeness, wore an amused, listening face. He was squat and ruddy. A yachting cap was shoved far back from his forehead, and the narrative to which he listened made constant waves of expression break forth over his face from the corners of his nose and eyes and mouth. Little jets of wheezing laughter followed one another out of his convulsed body. His eyes, twinkling with cunning enjoyment, glanced at every moment towards his companion's face. Once or twice he rearranged the light waterproof which he had slung over one shoulder in toreador fashion. His breeches, his white rubber shoes, and his jauntily slung waterproof expressed youth. But his figure fell into rotundity at the waist, his hair was scant and grey, and his face, when the waves of expression had passed over it, had a ravaged look.

When he was quite sure that the narrative had ended he laughed noiselessly for fully half a minute. Then he said:

"Well!... That takes the biscuit!"

His voice seemed winnowed of vigour; and to enforce his words he added with humour:

"That takes the solitary, unique, and, if I may so call it, *recherché* biscuit!"

He became serious and silent when he had said this. His tongue was tired, for he had been talking all the afternoon in a public-house in Dorset Street. Most people considered Lenehan a leech, but in spite of this reputation, his adroitness and eloquence had always prevented his friends from forming any general policy against him. He had a brave manner of coming up to a party of them in a bar and of holding himself nimbly at the borders of the company until he was included in a round. He was a sporting vagrant armed with a vast stock of stories, limericks, and riddles. He was insensitive to all kinds of discourtesy. No one knew how he achieved the stern task of living, but his name was vaguely associated with racing tissues.

"And where did you pick her up, Corley?" he asked.

Corley ran his tongue swiftly along his upper lip.

"One night, man," he said, "I was going along Dame Street and I spotted a fine tart under Waterhouse's clock, and said good night, you know. So we went for a walk round by the canal, and she told me she was a slavey in a house in Baggot Street. I put my arm round her and squeezed her a bit that night. Then next Sunday, man, I met her by appointment. We went out to Donnybrook and I brought her into a field there. She told me she used to go with a dairyman... It was fine, man. Cigarettes every night she'd bring me, and paying the tram out and back. And one night she brought me two bloody fine cigars—O, the real cheese, you known that the old fellow used to smoke... I was afraid, man, she'd get in the family way. But she's up to the dodge."

"Maybe she thinks you'll marry her," said Lenehan.

"I told her I was out of a job," said Corley. "I told her I was in Pim's. She doesn't know my name. I was too hairy to tell her that. But she thinks I'm a bit of class, you know."

Lenehan laughed again, noiselessly.

"Of all the good ones ever I heard," he said, "that emphatically takes the biscuit."

Corley's stride acknowledged the compliment. The swing of his burly body made his friend execute a few light skips from the path to the roadway and back again. Corley was the son of an inspector of police, and he had inherited his father's frame and gait. He walked with his hands by his sides, holding himself erect and swaying his head from side to side. His head was large, globular, and oily; it sweated in all weathers; and his large round hat, set upon it sideways, looked like a bulb which had grown out of another. He always stared straight before him as if he were on parade, and when he wished to gaze after someone in the street, it was necessary for him to move his body from the hips. At present he was about town. Whenever any job was vacant a friend was always ready to give him the hard word. He was often to be seen walking with policemen in plain clothes, talking earnestly. He knew the inner side of all affairs and was fond of delivering final judgments. He spoke without listening to the speech of his companions. His conversation was mainly about himself: what he had said to such a person and what such a person had said to him, and what he had said to settle the matter. When he reported these dialogues he aspirated the first letter of his name after the manner of Florentines.

Lenehan offered his friend a cigarette. As the two young men walked on through the crowd Corley occasionally turned to smile at some of the passing girls, but Lenehan's gaze was fixed on the large faint moon circled with a double halo. He watched earnestly the passing of the grey web of twilight across its face. At length he said:

"Well... tell me, Corley, I suppose you'll be able to pull it off all right, eh?"

Corley closed one eye expressively as an answer.

"Is she game for that?" asked Lenehan dubiously. "You can never know women."

"She's all right," said Corley. "I know the way to get around her, man. She's a bit gone on me."

"You're what I call a gay Lothario," said Lenehan. "And the proper kind of a Lothario, too!"

A shade of mockery relieved the servility of his manner. To save himself he had the habit of leaving his flattery open to the interpretation of raillery. But Corley had not a subtle mind.

"There's nothing to touch a good slavery," he affirmed. "Take my tip for it."

"By one who has tried them all," said Lenehan.

"First I used to go with girls, you know," said Corley, unbosoming; "girls off the South Circular. I used to take them out, man, on the tram somewhere and pay the tram, or take them to a band or a play at the theatre, or buy them chocolate and sweets or something that way. I used to spend money on them right enough," he added, in a convincing tone, as if he was conscious of being disbelieved.

But Lenehan could well believe it; he nodded gravely.

"I know that game," he said, "and it's a mug's game."

"And damn the thing I ever got out of it," said Corley.

"Ditto here," said Lenehan.

"Only off of one of them," said Corley.

He moistened his upper lip by running his tongue along it. The recollection brightened his eyes. He, too, gazed at the pale disc of the moon, now nearly veiled, and seemed to meditate.

"She was... a bit of all right," he said regretfully.

He was silent again. Then he added:

"She's on the turf now. I saw her driving down Earl Street one night with two fellows with her on a car."

"I suppose that's your doing," said Lenehan.

"There was others at her before me," said Corley philosophically.

This time Lenehan was inclined to disbelieve. He shook his head to and fro and smiled.

"You know you can't kid me, Corley," he said.

"Honest to God!" said Corley. "Didn't she tell me herself?"

Lenehan made a tragic gesture.

"Base betrayer!" he said.

As they passed along the railings of Trinity College, Lenehan skipped out into the road and peered up at the clock.

"Twenty after," he said.

"Time enough," said Corley. "She'll be there all right. I always let her wait a bit."

Lenehan laughed quietly.

"Ecod! Corley, you know how to take them," he said.

"I'm up to all their little tricks," Corley confessed.

"But tell me," said Lenehan again, "are you sure you can bring it off all right? You know it's a ticklish job. They're damn close on that point. Eh?... What?"

His bright small eyes searched his companion's face for reassurance. Corley swung his head to and fro as if to toss aside an insistent insect, and his brows gathered.

"I'll pull it off," he said. "Leave it to me, can't you?"

Lenehan said no more. He did not wish to ruffle his friend's temper, to be sent to the devil and told that his advice was not wanted. A little tact was necessary. But Corley's brow was soon smooth again. His thoughts were running another way.

"She's a fine decent tart," he said, with appreciation; "that's what she is."

They walked along Nassau Street and then turned into Kildare Street. Not far from the porch of the club a harpist stood in the roadway, playing to a little ring of listeners. He plucked at the wires heedlessly, glancing quickly from time to time at the face of each new-comer and from time to time, wearily also, at the sky. His harp, too, heedless that her coverings had fallen about her knees, seemed weary alike of the eyes of strangers and of her master's hands. One hand played in the bass the melody of *Silent, O Moyle*, while the other hand careered in the treble after each group of notes. The notes of the air sounded deep and full.

The two young men walked up the street without speaking, the mournful music following them. When they reached Stephen's Green they crossed the road. Here the noise of trams, the lights, and the crowd, released them from their silence.

"There she is!" said Corley.

At the corner of Hume Street a young woman was standing. She wore a blue dress and a white sailor hat. She stood on the kerbstone, swinging a sunshade in one hand. Lenehan grew lively.

"Let's have a look at her, Corley," he said.

Corley glanced sideways at his friend, and an unpleasant grin appeared on his face.

"Are you trying to get inside me?" he asked.

"Damn it!" said Lenehan boldly, "I don't want an introduction. All I want is to have a look at her. I'm not going to eat her."

"O... A look at her?" said Corley, more amiably. "Well. I'll tell you what. I'll go over and talk to her and you can pass by."

"Right!" said Lenehan.

Corley had already thrown one leg over the chains when Lenehan called out:

"And after? Where will we meet?"

"Half ten," answered Corley, bringing over his other leg.

"Where?"

"Corner of Merrion Street. We'll be coming back."

"Work it all right now," said Lenehan in farewell.

Corley did not answer. He sauntered across the road swaying his head from side to side. His bulk, his easy pace, and the solid sound of his boots had something of the conqueror in them. He approached the young woman and, without saluting, began at once to converse with her. She swung her umbrella more quickly and executed half turns on her heels. Once or twice when he spoke to her at close quarters she laughed and bent her head.

Lenehan observed them for a few minutes. Then he walked rapidly along beside the chains at some distance and crossed the road obliquely. As he approached Hume Street corner he found the air heavily scented, and his eyes made a swift anxious scrutiny of the young woman's appearance. She had her Sunday finery on. Her blue serge skirt was held at the waist by a belt of black leather. The great silver buckle of her belt seemed to depress the centre of her body, catching the light stuff of her white blouse like a clip. She wore a short black jacket with mother-of-pearl buttons, and a ragged black boa. The ends of her tulle collarette had been carefully disordered and a big bunch of red flowers was pinned in her bosom stems upwards. Lenehan's eyes noted approvingly her stout short muscular body. Frank rude health glowed in her face, on her fat red cheeks and in her unabashed blue eyes. Her features were blunt. She had broad nostrils, a straggling mouth which lay open in a contented leer, and two projecting front teeth. As he passed Lenehan took off his cap, and, after about ten seconds, Corley returned a salute to the air. This he did by raising his hand vaguely and pensively changing the angle of position of his hat.

Lenehan walked as far as the Shelbourne Hotel, where he halted and waited. After waiting for a little time he saw them coming towards him and, when they turned to the right, he followed them, stepping lightly in his white shoes, down one side of Merrion Square. As he walked on slowly, timing his pace to theirs, he watched Corley's head which turned at every moment towards the young woman's face like a big ball revolving on a pivot. He kept the pair in view until he had seen them climbing the stairs of the Donnybrook tram; then he turned about and went back the way he had come.

Now that he was alone his face looked older. His gaiety seemed to forsake him, and as he came by the railings of the Duke's Lawn he allowed his hand to run along them. The air which the harpist had played began to control his movements. His softly padded feet played the melody while his fingers swept a scale of variations idly along the railings after each group of notes.

He walked listlessly round Stephen's Green and then down Grafton Street. Though his eyes took note of many elements of the crowd through which he passed, they did so morosely. He found trivial all that was meant to charm him, and did not answer the glances which invited him to be bold. He knew that he would have to speak a great deal, to invent and to amuse, and his brain and throat were too dry for such a task. The problem of how he could pass the hours till he met Corley again troubled him a little. He could think of no way of passing them but to keep on walking. He turned to the left when he came to the corner of Rutland Square, and felt more at ease in the dark quiet street, the sombre look of which suited his mood. He paused at last before the window of a poor-looking shop over which the words *Refreshment Bar* were printed in white letters. On the glass of the window were two flying inscriptions: *Ginger Beer* and *Ginger Ale*. A Cut ham was exposed on a great blue dish, while near it on a plate lay a segment of very light plum-pudding. He eyed this food earnestly for some time, and then, after glancing warily up and down the street, went into the shop quickly.

He was hungry, for, except some biscuits which he had asked two grudging curates to bring him, he had eaten nothing since breakfast-time. He sat down at an uncovered wooden table opposite two work-girls and a mechanic. A slatternly girl waited on him.

"How much is a plate of peas?" he asked.

"Three halfpence, sir," said the girl.

"Bring me a plate of peas," he said, "and a bottle of ginger beer."

He spoke roughly in order to belie his air of gentility, for his entry had been followed by a pause of talk. His face was heated. To appear natural he pushed his cap back on his head and planted his elbows on the table. The mechanic and the two work-girls examined him point by point before resuming their conversation in a subdued voice. The girl brought him a plate of grocer's hot peas, seasoned with pepper and vinegar, a fork, and his ginger beer. He ate his food greedily and found it so good that he made a note of the shop mentally. When he had eaten all the peas he sipped his ginger beer and sat for some time thinking of Corley's adventure. In his imagination he beheld the pair of lovers walking along some dark road; he heard Corley's voice in deep energetic gallantries, and saw again the leer of the young woman's mouth. This vision made him feel keenly his own poverty of purse and spirit. He was tired of knocking about, of pulling the devil by the tail, of shifts and intrigues. He would be thirty-one in November. Would he never get a good job? Would he never have a home of his own? He thought how pleasant it would be to have a warm fire to sit by and a good dinner to sit down to. He had walked the streets long enough with friends and with girls. He knew what those friends were worth: he knew the girls too. Experience had embittered his heart against the world. But all hope had not left him. He felt better after having eaten than he had felt before, less weary of his life, less vanquished in spirit. He might yet be able to settle down in some snug corner and live happily if he could only come across some good simple-minded girl with a little of the ready.

He paid twopence halfpenny to the slatternly girl, and went out of the shop to begin his wandering again. He went into Capel Street and walked along towards the City Hall. Then he turned into Dame Street. At the corner of George's Street he met two friends of his, and stopped to converse with them. He was glad that he could rest from all his walking. His friends asked him had he seen Corley, and what was the latest. He replied that he had spent the day with Corley. His friends talked very little. They looked vacantly after some figures in the crowd, and sometimes made a critical remark. One said that he had seen Mac an hour before in Westmoreland Street. At this Lenehan said that he had been with Mac the night before in Egan's. The young man who had seen Mac in Westmoreland Street asked was it true that Mac had won a bit over a billiards match. Lenehan did not know: he said that Holohan had stood them drinks in Egan's.

He left his friends at a quarter to ten and went up George's Street. He turned to the left at the City Markets and walked on into Grafton Street. The crowd of girls and young men had thinned, and on his way up the street he heard many groups and couples bidding one another good night. He went as far as the clock of the College of Surgeons: it was on the stroke of ten. He set off briskly along the northern side of the Green, hurrying for fear Corley should return too soon. When he reached the corner of Merrion Street he took his stand in the shadow of a lamp, and brought out one of the cigarettes which he had reserved and lit it. He leaned against the lamp-post and kept his gaze fixed on the part from which he expected to see Corley and the young woman return.

His mind became active again. He wondered had Corley managed it successfully. He wondered if he had asked her yet or if he would leave it to the last. He suffered all the pangs and thrills of his friend's situation as well as those of his own. But the memory of Corley's slowly revolving head calmed him somewhat: he was sure Corley would pull it off all right. All at once the idea struck him that perhaps Corley had seen her home by another way, and given him the slip. His eyes searched the street: there was no sign of them. Yet it was surely half an hour since he had seen the clock of the College of Surgeons. Would Corley do a thing like that? He lit his Fast cigarette and began to smoke it nervously. He strained his eyes as each tram stopped at the far corner of the square. They must have gone home by another way. The paper of his cigarette broke and he flung it into the road with a curse.

Suddenly he saw them coming towards him. He started with delight, and keeping close to his lamp-post tried to read the result in their walk. They were walking quickly, the young woman taking quick short steps, while Corley kept beside her with his long stride. They did not seem to be speaking. An intimation of the result pricked him like the point of a sharp instrument. He knew Corley would fail; he knew it was no go.

They turned down Baggot Street, and he followed them at once, taking the other footpath. When they stopped he stopped too. They talked for a few moments, and then the young woman went down the steps into the area of a house. Corley remained standing at the edge of the path, a little distance from the front steps. Some minutes passed. Then the hall-door was opened slowly and cautiously. A woman came running down the front steps and coughed. Corley turned and went towards her. His broad figure hid hers from view for a few seconds and then she reappeared, running up the steps. The door closed on her, and Corley began to walk swiftly towards Stephen's Green.

Lenehan hurried on in the same direction. Some drops of light rain fell. He took them as a warning, and glancing back towards the house which the young woman had entered to see that he was not observed, he ran eagerly across the road. Anxiety and his swift run made him pant. He called out:

"Hallo, Corley!"

Corley turned his head to see who had called him, and then continued walking as before. Lenehan ran after him, settling the waterproof on his shoulders with one hand.

"Hallo, Corley!" he cried again.

Part One British Literature

He came level with his friend and looked keenly in his face. He could see nothing there.

"Well?" he said. "Did it come off?"

They had reached the corner of Ely Place. Still without answering, Corley swerved to the left and went up the side street. His features were composed in stern calm. Lenehan kept up with his friend, breathing uneasily. He was baffled, and a note of menace pierced through his voice.

"Can't you tell us?" he said. "Did you try her?"

Corley halted at the first lamp and stared grimly before him. Then with a grave gesture he extended a hand towards the light and, smiling, opened it slowly to the gaze of his disciple. A small gold coin shone in the palm.

Questions for Discussion

1. What do you think is the theme of the story?
2. What kind of people is the protagonist Lenehan? What is the narrator's attitude towards him?

About the Author

James Joyce (1882—1941), Irish novelist, noted for his experimental use of language in such works as *Ulysses* (1922) and *Finneganns Wake* (1939). Joyce's technical innovations in the art of the novel include an extensive use of interior monologue; he used a complex network of symbolic parallels drawn from the mythology, history, and literature, and created a unique language of invented words, puns, and allusions.

Joyce was born in Dublin, which kept haunting his dream throughout his life. In 1914 he published his most noted short story collection *The Dubliners*, which is a cycle of stories all set up in the city Dublin. It seems that Joyce was drawing a series of sketches of his fellow countrymen. In each, the detail is so chosen and organized that carefully interacting symbolic meanings are set up, and as a result, *The Dubliners* is also a book about human fate. A literary experiment, the stories are as refreshingly original and astonishing today, as when they were first published when Joyce was just twenty-five years old. Moreover, the stories are presented in a particular order so that new meanings arise from the relation between them.

Essay

Of Studies

Francis Bacon

Studies serve for delight, for ornament, and for ability. Their chief use for delight, is in privateness and retiring①; for ornament, is in discourse; and for ability, is in the judgment, and disposition of business. For expert men② can execute, and perhaps judge of particulars, one by one; but the general counsels, and the plots③ and marshalling of affairs, come best, from those that are learned. To spend too much time in studies is sloth; to use them too much for ornament, is affectation; to make judgment wholly by their rules, is the humor④ of a scholar. They perfect nature, and are perfected by experience: for natural abilities are like natural plants, that need proyning⑤, by study; and studies themselves, do give forth directions too much at large, except they be bounded in by experience. Crafty men contemn studies, simple men admire them, and wise men use them; for they teach not their own use; but that is a wisdom without them, and above them, won by observation. Read not to contradict and confute; nor to believe and take for granted; nor to find talk and discourse; but to weigh and consider. Some books are to be tasted, others to be swallowed, and some few to be chewed and digested; that is, some books are to be read only in parts; others to be read, but not curiously⑥; and some few to be read wholly, and with diligence and attention. Some books also may be read by deputy, and extracts made of them by others; but that would be only in the less important arguments, and the meaner sort of books, else distilled books are like common distilled waters, flashy things. Reading maketh a full man; conference a ready man; and writing an exact man. And therefore, if a man write little, he had need have a great memory; if he confer little, he had need have a present wit: and if he read little, he had need have much cunning, to seem to know that he doth not. Histories make men wise; poets

---

① When alone and away from work.
② Experienced (rather than learned) men.
③ Plan.
④ Mannerism.
⑤ Old spelling for "pruning".
⑥ With care.

witty; the mathematics subtitle; natural philosophy deep; moral grave; logic and rhetoric able to contend. Abeunt studia in mores①. Nay, there is no stond② or impediment in the wit, but may be wrought out by fit studies; like as③ diseases of the body, may have appropriate exercises. Bowling is good for the stone and reins④; shooting for the lungs and breast; gentle walking for the stomach; riding for the head; and the like. So if a man's wit be wandering, let him study the mathematics; for in demonstrations, if his wit be called away never so little, he must begin again. If his wit be not apt to distinguish or find differences, let him study the Schoolmen⑤; for they are cymini sectores⑥. If he be not apt to beat over matters, and to call up one thing to prove and illustrate another, let him study the lawyers' cases. So every defect of the mind, may have a special receipt⑦.

Questions for Discussion

1. Why does the author say that "To spend too much time in studies is sloth"?
2. Make a comment on the statement "crafty men contemn studies; simple men admire them and wise men use them".
3. According to your own experience, what kind of books are "to be tasted", what kind of books are "to be swallowed", and what kind of books are "to be chewed and digested"?
4. Do you agree that different human characters can be perfected by studying various subjects?
5. What are some characteristics of this essay? And what skills are used by the author to achieve them?

About the Author

　　Francis Bacon (1561—1626), a representative of the Renaissance in

---

① Abeunt studia in mores (Latin): The phrase, quoted from the *Heroides* (XV. 83) by Ovid, means that studies pass into character.
② Drawback.
③ (archaic use) As.
④ The bladder and kidneys.
⑤ Medieval theologians and academics.
⑥ (Latin) Hair-splitters.
⑦ Recipe.

England, is an English philosopher, statesman, essayist and one of the pioneers of modern scientific thought. He lays the foundation for modern science with his insistence on scientific way of thinking and fresh observation rather than authority as a basis for obtaining knowledge. He is believed to be the first to write essays in English, and his *Essays* has been recognized as an important landmark in the development of English prose.

Born on January 22, 1561, at York House, in the Strand, London, Bacon was educated at Trinity College, University of Cambridge. In 1584, he entered the House of Commons and gradually established his reputation. At the height of his career, under King James, he became Lord Keeper and then Lord Chancellor of England. But later he was accused of taking bribes in office. After a token imprisonment, Bacon retired in disgrace to his estate of Gornhambry to spend the last five years of his life. In the early spring of 1626 he died of a cold caught while he was making an experiment in a snowstorm, to see if snow might be used as a new preservative instead of salt in preserving meat.

Bacon's works mainly fall into two categories, the philosophical and the literary. The best of his philosophical works are *The Advancement of Learning* (1605), a review in English of the state of knowledge in his own time, and *Novum Organum; or, Indications Respecting the Interpretation of Nature* (1620). Bacon's literary power and success find expression chiefly in his essays. They were published at various times between 1597 and 1625, and characterized by their conciseness and brevity, simplicity and forcefulness, practicality and versatility. Short as they are, these essays show Bacon's profundity in understanding man and society. Some phrases in his essays have entered the English literary tradition and become very popular. *Of Studies* is the 50th of Bacon's *Essays*.

A Modest Proposal

FOR PREVENTING THE CHILDREN OF POOR PEOPLE IN IRELAND
FROM BEING A BURDEN TO THEIR PARENTS OR COUNTRY,
AND FOR MAKING THEM BENEFICIAL TO THE PUBLIC

Jonathan Swift

It is a melancholy object to those who walk through this great town① or travel in the country, when they see the streets, the roads, and cabin doors, crowded with beggars of the female sex, followed by three, four, or six children, all in rags, and importuning every passenger for an alms②. These mothers, instead of being able to work for their honest livelihood, are forced to employ all their time in strolling to beg sustenance for their helpless infants, who, as they grow up, either turn thieves for want of work, or leave their dear native country to fight for the Pretender in Spain③, or sell themselves to the Barbadoes.

I think it is agreed by all parties that this prodigious number of children in the arms, or on the backs, or at the heels of their mothers, and frequently of their fathers, is in the present deplorable state of the kingdom a very great additional grievance; and, therefore, whoever could find out a fair, cheap, and easy method of making these children sound, useful members of the commonwealth, would deserve so well of the public as to have his statue set up for a preserver of the nation④.

But my intention is very far from being confined to provide only for the children of professed beggars; it is of a much greater extent, and shall take in the whole number of infants at a certain age who are born of parents in effect as little able to support them as those who demand our charity in the streets.

As to my own part, having turned my thoughts for many years upon this

---

① The town refers to Dublin, the capital of Ireland.
② Money or goods contributed to the poor.
③ Refers to James Edward Stuart, the son of James Ⅱ. 英国光荣革命时期,英国国王 James Ⅱ 被迫流亡国外,但其子 James Edward Stuart 仍力图夺取英国王位,自称 James Ⅲ,世人称为 Pretender(僭位者)。当时爱尔兰的天主教徒和贫民因反英情绪强烈而充作雇佣军。
④ A savior of the nation Ireland. 这里是嘲讽的口吻,说的是谁能解决这些孩子的问题一定值得人民为他竖起纪念碑当做英雄来膜拜。

important subject, and maturely weighed the several schemes of other projectors①, I have always found them grossly mistaken in the computation. It is true, a child just dropped from its dam② may be supported by her milk for a solar year, with little other nourishment; at most not above the value of 2 shillings, which the mother may certainly get, or the value in scraps③, by her lawful occupation of begging; and it is exactly at one year old that I propose to provide for them in such a manner as instead of being a charge upon their parents or the parish, or wanting food and raiment④ for the rest of their lives, they shall on the contrary contribute to the feeding, and partly to the clothing, of many thousands.

There is likewise another great advantage in my scheme, that it will prevent those voluntary abortions, and that horrid practice of women murdering their bastard children, alas! too frequent among us! sacrificing the poor innocent babes I doubt more to avoid the expense than the shame, which would move tears and pity in the most savage and inhuman breast.

The number of souls in this kingdom being usually reckoned one million and a half, of these I calculate there may be about two hundred thousand couple whose wives are breeders; from which number I subtract thirty thousand couples who are able to maintain their own children, although I apprehend there cannot be so many, under the present distresses of the kingdom; but this being granted⑤, there will remain a hundred and seventy thousand breeders. I again subtract fifty thousand for those women who miscarry, or whose children die by accident or disease within the year. There only remain one hundred and twenty thousand children of poor parents annually born. The question therefore is, how this number shall be reared and provided for, which, as I have already said, under the present situation of affairs, is utterly impossible by all the methods hitherto⑥ proposed. For we can neither employ them in handicraft or agriculture; we neither build houses (I mean in the country) nor cultivate land: they can very seldom pick up a livelihood by stealing, till they arrive at six years

---

① Adviser.
② A female parent. Used of a four-legged animal.
③ Leftover bits of food.
④ Clothing; garments.
⑤ If this can be granted.
⑥ Up to this or that time.

old, except where they are of towardly parts①, although I confess they learn the rudiments much earlier, during which time, they can however be properly looked upon only as probationers②, as I have been informed by a principal gentleman in the county of Cavan, who protested to me that he never knew above one or two instances under the age of six, even in a part of the kingdom so renowned for the quickest proficiency in that art③.

I am assured by our merchants, that a boy or a girl before twelve years old is no salable commodity; and even when they come to this age they will not yield above three pounds, or three pounds and half-a-crown at most on the exchange; which cannot turn to account either to the parents or kingdom, the charge of nutriment and rags having been at least four times that value.

I shall now therefore humbly propose my own thoughts, which I hope will not be liable to the least objection.

I have been assured by a very knowing American of my acquaintance in London, that a young healthy child well nursed is at a year old a most delicious, nourishing, and wholesome food, whether stewed, roasted, baked, or boiled; and I make no doubt that it will equally serve in a fricassee or a ragout④.

I do therefore humbly offer it to public consideration that of the hundred and twenty thousand children already computed, twenty thousand may be reserved for breed, whereof only one-fourth part to be males; which is more than we allow to sheep, black cattle or swine; and myreason is, that these children are seldom the fruits of marriage, a circumstance not much regarded by our savages, therefore one male will be sufficient to serve four females. That the remaining hundred thousand may, at a year old, be offered in the sale to the persons of quality and fortune through the kingdom; always advising the mother to let them suck plentifully in the last month, so as to render them plump and fat for a good table. A child will make two dishes at an entertainment for friends; and when the family dines alone, the fore or hind quarter will make a reasonable dish, and seasoned with a little pepper or salt will be very good boiled on the fourth day, especially in winter.

---

① Towardly, promising; parts, aility, endowment. 这部分的意思是除非他们具有这方面(偷窃)的天赋,否则满 6 岁之前,他们很少能够靠做贼为生。
② Intern.
③ Here it refers to stealing.
④ Names of two French dishes. 这是两道法式菜名:原汁炖肉块和浓味蔬菜炖肉片。

I have reckoned upon a medium that a child just born will weigh 12 pounds, and in a solar year, if tolerably nursed, will increase to 28 pounds.

I grant this food will be somewhat dear, and therefore very proper for landlords, who, as they have already devoured most of the parents, seem to have the best title to the children.

Infant's flesh will be in season throughout the year, but more plentiful in March, and a little before and after; for we are told by a grave author, an eminent French physician①, that fish being a prolific diet②, there are more children born in Roman Catholic countries about nine months after Lent③ than at any other season; therefore, reckoning a year after Lent, the markets will be more glutted than usual, because the number of popish infants is at least three to one in this kingdom, and therefore it will have one other collateral advantage, by lessening the number of papists among us.

I have already computed the charge of nursing a beggar's child (in which list I reckon all cottagers, laborers, and four-fifths of the farmers) to be about two shillings per annum, rags included; and I believe no gentleman would repine to give ten shillings for the carcass of a good fat child, which, as I have said, will make four dishes of excellent nutritive meat, when he hath only some particular friend or his own family to dine with him. Thus the squire will learn to be a good landlord, and grow popular among his tenants; the mother will have eight shillings net profit, and be fit for work till she produces another child.

Those who are more thrifty (as I must confess the times require) may flay the carcass; the skin of which artificially dressed will make admirable gloves for ladies, and summer boots for fine gentlemen.

As to our city of Dublin, shambles④ may be appointed for this purpose in the most convenient parts of it, and butchers we may be assured will not be wanting; although I rather recommend buying the children alive, and dressing them hot from the knife, as we do roasting pigs.

A very worthy person, a true lover of his country, and whose virtues I

---

① It refers to Francois Rabelais (1494—1553), a major French Renaissance writer, doctor and humanist. He was regarded as a writer of fantasy, satire, the grotesque, dirty jokes and bawdy songs.

② 这句话可能出自拉伯雷。因为鱼多卵，所以古代欧洲人认为吃鱼可以促进生殖力。

③ The 40 weekdays from Ash Wednesday to Easter observed by the Roman Catholic, Eastern, and some Protestant churches as a period of penitence and fasting.【基督教】大斋节（亦称"齐斋节"，自圣灰星期三开始至复活节前的40天，在此期间进行斋戒和忏悔）

④ Slautherhouses.

highly esteem, was lately pleased in discoursing on this matter to offer a refinement upon my scheme. He said that many gentlemen of this kingdom, having of late destroyed their deer, he conceived that the want of venison might be well supplied by the bodies of young lads and maidens, not exceeding fourteen years of age nor under twelve; so great a number of both sexes in every country being now ready to starve for want of work and service; and these to be disposed of by their parents, if alive, or otherwise by their nearest relations. But with due deference to so excellent a friend and so deserving a patriot, I cannot be altogether in his sentiments; for as to the males, my American acquaintance assured me, from frequent experience, that their flesh was generally tough and lean, like that of our schoolboys by continual exercise, and their taste disagreeable; and to fatten them would not answer the charge. Then as to the females, it would, I think, with humble submission be a loss to the public, because they soon would become breeders themselves; and besides, it is not improbable that some scrupulous people might be apt to censure such a practice (although indeed very unjustly), as a little bordering upon cruelty; which, I confess, hath always been with me the strongest objection against any project, however so well intended.

...

Questions for Discussion

1. "For this kind of commodity will not bear exportation, the flesh being of too tender a consistence, to admit a long continuance in salt, although perhaps I could name <u>a country,</u> which would be glad to eat up our whole nation without it." Which country does the author imply? What does this sentence mean?
2. What is meant by the title "A Modest Proposal"? Why does the writer say "modest"?
3. Satire and irony are what Swift is noted for. During the reading can you figure out some examples of his satire? What is his aiming target?
4. Swift laid out his proposal in a controlled, logical and serious manner. Scheme out the line of his reason. What is the ultimate message that he is trying to convey to his fellow Irish people? What is his attitude towards the poor people in his country?

About the Author

Jonathan Swift (1667—1745) is an Anglo-Irish satirist, essayist, political pamphleteer (first for the Whigs then for the Tories), poet and cleric who became Dean of St. Patrick's, Dublin. He is remembered for works such as *Gulliver's Travels*, *A Modest Proposal*, *A Journal to Stella*, *Drapier's Letters*, *The Battle of the Books*, *An Argument Against Abolishing Christianity*, and *A Tale of a Tub*. Swift is probably the foremost prose satirist in the English language, known for being a master of two styles of satire: the Horatian and Juvenalian styles.

Swift was born in Dublin, Ireland; he was the son of Protestant Anglo-Irish parents. Young Jonathan was a sickly child, and it is said he later developed Meniere's Disease, which affects the inner ear and causes dizziness, vertigo, nausea, and hearing loss. After his father died, Jonathan's mother was left without an income but she did her best to provide care for him. He later had to live with his paternal uncle Godwin Swift Esquire, who would support him and provide him with the best education possible, although it is said Jonathan was an unhappy young man and did not excel in his studies.

The political unrest surrounding the Glorious Revolution of 1688, and the loss of financial support from his Uncle caused him to travel to England to stay with his mother. There Swift obtained a position as Secretary to retired diplomat Sir William Temple (1628—1699). It was a dramatic turn of events for Swift, who soon became acquainted with many politically influential figures of the day and was bestowed a great deal of responsibility by Temple. Temple was a powerful and influential figure and assisted Swift in gaining entrance to Oxford University, where he earned his M. A. in 1692.

In 1700 Swift became Chaplain to Lord Berkeley and was instituted as Vicar to Laracor, Agher, and Rathbeggan just outside Dublin. In 1701 he was awarded Doctor of Divinity from Trinity College, Dublin. In 1704 his satirical look at religion *A Tale of a Tub* was published. Busy with clerical duties, Swift was also immersed in Dublin society and politics. Becoming an outspoken critic, and with the intent of improving things in Ireland, he often travelled to London. In 1707, among many other matters, he sought the removal of taxation on the income of the Irish clergy, which was duly rejected by the Whigs. He thus severed his association with them. In 1710 he joined the Tories and his first of many political pamphlets appeared including *The Conduct of the Allies* (1711) and *The Public Spirit of the Whigs* (1714). Often tinged with bitter irony, Swift began to hone his abilities at innuendo and metaphor, and he sharpened his wit in his prodigious output of various articles, essays, and pamphlets including *Meditation on a Broomstick* (1703) and *A Modest Proposal* (1729) wherein he suggested that the children of the Irish poor be put to good use providing sustenance to the rich English.

To the Right Honorable the Earl of Chesterfield

Samuel Johnson

MY LORD,

I have been lately informed, by the proprietor of *The World*, that two papers, in which my dictionary is recommended to the public, were written by your Lordship. To be so distinguished, is an honor, which, being very little accustomed to favors from the great, I know not well how to receive, or in what terms to acknowledge. When, upon some slight encouragement, I first visited your Lordship, I was overpowered, like the rest of mankind, by the enchantment of your address; and could not forbear to wish that I might boast myself *Le vainqueur du vainqueur de la terre*①—that I might obtain that regard for which I saw the world contending; but I found my attendance so little encouraged that neither pride nor modesty would suffer me to continue it.

When I had once addressed your Lordship in public, I had exhausted all the art of pleasing which a retired and uncourtly scholar can possess. I had done all that I could; and no man is well pleased to have his all neglected, be it ever so little.

Seven years, my Lord, have now passed since I waited in your outward rooms, or was repulsed from your door; during which time 1 have been pushing on my work through difficulties of which it is useless to complain, and have brought it, at last, to the verge of publication, without one act of assistance, one word of encouragement, or one smile of favor. Such treatment I did not expect, for I never had a patron before.

The shepherd in Virgil grew at last acquainted with Love, and found him a native of the rocks.

Is not a patron, my Lord, one who looks with unconcern on a man struggling for life in the water, and, when he has reached ground, encumbers him with help? The notice which you have been pleased to take of my labors, had it been early, had been kind; but it has been delayed till I am indifferent, and

---

① The conqueror of the conqueror of the earth (French). From the first line of Scuderv's epic *Alaric* (1654).

cannot enjoy it; till I am solitary, and cannot impart it; till I am known, and do not want it. I hope it is no very cynical asperity not to confess obligations where no benefit has been received, or to be unwilling that the public should consider me as owing that to a patron which Providence has enabled me to do for myself.

Having carried on my work thus far with so little obligation to any favorer of learning, I shall not be disappointed though I should conclude it, if less be possible, with less; for I have been long wakened from that dream of hope in which I once boasted myself with so much exultation, my Lord, your Lordship's most humble, most obedient servant,

SAM. JOHNSON

Questions for Discussion

1. Please summarize the main idea of each paragraph.
2. Which paragraph do you think is the grandest?

About the Author

Samuel Johnson was famous as a talker in his own time, and his conversation (preserved by James Boswell and others) has been famous ever since. But his wisdom survives above all in his writings: a few superb poems; the grave *Rambler* essays, which established his reputation as a stylist and a moralist; the lessons about life in *Rasselas* and the *Lives of the Poets*; and literary criticism that ranks among the best in English. The virtues of the talk and the writings are the same. They come hot from a mind well stored with knowledge, searingly honest, humane, and quick to seize the unexpected but appropriate image of truth. Johnson's wit is timeless, for it deals with the great facts of human experience, with hope and happiness and loss and duty and the fear of death. Whatever topic he addresses, whatever the form in which he writes, he holds to one commanding purpose: to see life as it is.

In 1747 Johnson published the plan of his dictionary, and he spent the next seven years compiling it—although he had expected to finish it in three. When in 1748 Dr. Adams, a friend from Oxford days, questioned his ability to carry out such a work alone so fast and reminded him that the dictionary of the French Academy had needed forty academicians working for forty years, Johnson replied with humorous jingoism: "Sir, thus it is. This is the proportion. Let me see;

forty times forty is sixteen hundred. As three to sixteen hundred, so is the proportion of an Englishman to a Frenchman."

Johnson's achievement in compiling the dictionary seems even greater when we realize that he was writing some of his best essays and poems during the same period. Although the booksellers who published the dictionary paid him what was then the large sum of £1575, it was not enough to enable him to support his household, buy materials, and pay the wages of the six assistants whom he employed year by year until the task was accomplished. He therefore had to earn more money by writing. In 1749, his early tragedy *Irene* was produced at long last by his old friend Garrick, by then the manager of Drury Lane. The play was not a success, although Johnson made some profit from it. In the same year appeared his finest poem, *The Vanity of Human Wishes*. With the *Rambler* (1750—1752) and the *Idler* (1758—1760), two series of periodical essays, Johnson found a devoted audience, but his pleasure was tempered by the death of his wife in 1752. He never remarried.

About the Work

Lord Chesterfield, to whom Johnson had paid the high compliment of addressing to his Lordship the plan of his dictionary, had behaved to him in such a manner as to excite his contempt and indignation. The world has been for many years amused with a story confidently told, and as confidently repeated with additional circumstances, that a sudden disgust was taken by Johnson upon occasion of his having been one day kept long in waiting in his Lordship's antechamber, for which the reason assigned was that he had company with him; and that at last, when the door opened, out walked Colley Cibber; and that Johnson was so violently provoked when he found for whom he had been so long excluded, that he went away in a passion, and never would return. I remember having mentioned this story to George Lord Lyttelton, who told me he was very intimate with Lord Chesterfield; and holding it as a well known truth, defended Lord Chesterfield, by saying, that Cibber, who had been introduced familiarly by the back stairs, had probably not been there above ten minutes. It may seem strange even to entertain a doubt concerning a story so long and so widely current, and thus implicitly adopted, if not sanctioned, by the authority which I have mentioned; but Johnson himself assured me that there was not the least foundation for it. He told me that there never was any particular incident which produced a quarrel between Lord Chesterfield and him; but that his Lordship's continued neglect was the reason why he resolved to have no connection with him. When the dictionary was upon the eve of publication, Lord Chesterfield, who, it is said, had flattered himself with expectations that Johnson would dedicate the work to him, attempted, in a courtly manner, to soothe, and insinuate himself with the sage, conscious, as it should seem, of the cold indifference with which he had treated its learned author; and further attempted to conciliate him, by writing two papers in *The World*, in recommendation of the work; and it must be confessed that they contain some studied compliments, so finely turned, that if there had been no previous offense, it is probable that Johnson would have been highly delighted. Praise, in general, was pleasing to him; but by praise from a man of rank and elegant accomplishments, he was peculiarly gratified.

This courtly device failed of its effect. Johnson, who thought that "all was false and hollow," despised the honeyed words, and was even indignant that Lord Chesterfield should, for a moment, imagine that he could be dupe of such an artifice. His expression to me concerning Lord Chesterfield, upon this occasion, was, "Sir, after making great professions, he had, for many years, taken no notice of me; but when my dictionary was coming out, he fell a scribbling in *The World* about it. Upon which, I wrote him a letter expressed in civil terms, but such as might show him that I did not mind what he said or wrote, and that I had done with him."

This is that celebrated letter of which so much has been said, and about which curiosity has been so long excited, without being gratified. I for many years solicited Johnson to favor me with a copy of it, that so excellent a composition might not be lost to posterity. He delayed from time to time to give it me; till at last in 1781, when we were on a visit at Mr. Dilly's, at Southill in Bedfordshire, he was pleased to dictate it to me from memory. He afterwards found among his papers a copy of it, which he had dictated to Mr. Baretti, with its title and corrections, in his own handwriting. This he gave to Mr. Langton; adding that if it were to come into print, he wished it to be from that copy. By Mr. Langton's kindness, I am enabled to enrich my work with a perfect transcript of what the world has so eagerly desired to see.

The Idea of a University

John Henry Cardinal Newman

Discourse 5. Knowledge Its Own End

Now bear with me, gentlemen, if what I am about to say has at first sight a fanciful appearance. Philosophy, then, or science, is related to knowledge in this way: knowledge is called by the name of science or philosophy, when it is acted upon, informed, or if I may use a strong figure, impregnated by reason. Reason is the principle of that intrinsic fecundity of knowledge, which, to those who possess it, is its especial value, and which dispenses with the necessity of their looking abroad for any end to rest upon external to itself. Knowledge, indeed, when thus exalted into a scientific form, is also power; not only is it excellent in itself, but whatever such excellence may be, it is something more, it has a result beyond itself. Doubtless; but that is a further consideration, with which I am not concerned. I only say that, prior to its being a power, it is a good; that it is, not only an instrument, but an end. I know well it may resolve itself into an art, and terminate in a mechanical process, and in tangible fruit; but it also may fall back upon that reason which informs it, and resolve itself into philosophy. In one case it is called useful knowledge, in the other liberal. The same person may cultivate it in both ways at once; but this again is a matter foreign to my subject; here I do but say that there are two ways of using knowledge, and in matter of fact those who use it in one way are not likely to use it in the other, or at least in a very limited measure. You see, then, here are two methods of education; the end of the one is to be philosophical, of the other to be mechanical; the one rises towards general ideas, the other is exhausted upon what is particular and external. Let me not be thought to deny the necessity, or to decry the benefit, of such attention to what is particular and practical, as belongs to the useful or mechanical arts; life could not go on without them; we owe our daily welfare to them; their exercise is the duty of the many, and we owe to the many a debt of gratitude for fulfilling that duty. I only say that knowledge, in proportion as it tends more and more to be particular, ceases to be knowledge. It is a question whether knowledge can in any proper sense be predicated of the brute creation; without pretending to metaphysical exactness of phraseology, which would be unsuitable to an occasion like this, I say, it seems to me improper to call that passive sensation, or perception of things, which brutes seem to possess, by the name of knowledge. When I speak of knowledge, I mean something intellectual, something which grasps what it perceives through the senses; something which takes a view of things; which sees more than the senses convey; which reasons upon what it sees, and while it sees; which invests it with an idea. It expresses itself, not in a mere enunciation, but by an enthymeme: it is of the nature of science from the first, and in this consists its dignity. The principle of real dignity in knowledge, its worth, its desirableness, considered irrespectively of its results, is this germ within it of a scientific or a philosophical process. This is how it comes to be an end in itself; this is why it admits of being called liberal. Not to know the relative disposition of things is the state of slaves or children; to have mapped out the universe is the boast, or at least the ambition, of philosophy.

Moreover, such knowledge is not a mere extrinsic or accidental advantage, which is ours today and another's tomorrow, which may be got up from a book, and easily forgotten again, which we can command or communicate at our pleasure, which we can borrow for the occasion, carry about in our hand, and take into the market; it is an acquired illumination, it is a habit, a personal possession, and an inward endowment. And this is the reason why it is more correct, as well as more usual, to speak of a university as a place of education than of instruction, though, when knowledge is concerned, instruction would at first sight have seemed the more appropriate word. We are instructed, for instance, in manual exercises, in the fine and useful arts, in trades, and in ways of business; for these are methods, which have little or no effect upon the mind itself, are contained in rules committed to memory, to tradition, or to use, and bear upon an end external to themselves. But education is a higher word; it implies an action upon our mental nature, and the formation of a character; it is something individual and permanent, and is commonly spoken of in connection with religion and virtue. When, then, we speak of the communication of knowledge as being education, we thereby really imply that that knowledge is a state or condition of mind; and since cultivation of mind is surely worth seeking for its own sake, we are thus brought once more to the conclusion, which the word "liberal" and the word "philosophy" have already suggested, that there is a knowledge, which is desirable, though nothing come of it, as being of itself a treasure, and a sufficient remuneration of years of labor.

Discourse 7. Knowledge Viewed in Relation to Professional Skill

I have been insisting, in my two preceding discourses, first, on the cultivation of the intellect, as an end which may reasonably be pursued for its own sake; and next, on the nature of that cultivation, or what that cultivation con sists in. Truth of whatever kind is the proper object of the intellect; its cultivation then lies in fitting it to apprehend and contemplate truth. Now the intellect in its present state, with exceptions which need not here be specified, does not discern truth intuitively, or as a whole. We know, not by a direct and simple vision, not at a glance, but, as it were, by piecemeal and accumulation, by a mental process, by going round an object, by the comparison, the combination, the mutual correction, the continual adaptation, of many partial notions, by the employment, concentration, and joint action of many faculties and exercises of mind. Such a union and concert of the intellectual powers, such an enlargement and development, such a comprehensiveness, is neces sarily a matter of training. And again, such a training is a matter of rule; it is not mere application, however exemplary, which introduces the mind to truth, nor the reading many books, nor the getting up many subjects, nor the witnessing many experiments, nor the attending many lectures. All this is short of enough; a man may have done it all, yet be lingering in the vestibule of knowledge: he may not realize what his mouth utters; he may not see with his mental eye what confronts him; he may have no grasp of things as they are; or at least he may have no power at all of advancing one step forward of himself, in consequence of what he has already acquired, no power of discriminating between truth and falsehood, of sifting out the grains of truth from the mass, of arranging things according to their real value, and, if I may use the phrase, of building up ideas. Such a power is the result of a scientific formation of mind; it is an acquired faculty of judgment, of clearsightedness, of sagacity, of wisdom, of philosophical reach of mind, and of intellectual self possession and repose—qualities which do not come of mere acquirement. The bodily eye, the organ for apprehending material objects, is provided by nature; the eye of the mind, of which the object is truth, is the work of discipline and habit.

This process of training, by which the intellect, instead of being formed or sacrificed to some particular or accidental purpose, some specific trade or profession, or study or science, is disciplined for its own sake, for the perception of its own proper object, and for its own highest culture, is called "Liberal Education"; and though there is no one in whom it is carried as far as is conceivable, or whose intellect would be a pattern of what intellects should be made, yet there is scarcely anyone but may gain an idea of what real training is, and at least look towards it, and make its true scope and result, not some thing else, his standard of excellence; and numbers there are who may submit themselves to it, and secure it to themselves in good measure. And to set forth the right standard, and to train according to it, and to help forward all students toward it according to their various capacities, this I conceive to be the business of a university.

Now this is what some great men are very slow to allow; they insist that education should be confined to some particular and narrow end, and should issue in some definite work, which can be weighed and measured. They argue as if every thing, as well as every person, had its price; and that where there has been a great outlay, they have a right to expect a return in kind. This they call making education and instruction "useful," and "utility" becomes their watchword. With a fundamental principle of this nature, they very naturally go on to ask what there is to show for the expense of a university; what is the real worth in the market of the article called "a liberal education," on the supposition that it does not teach us definitely how to advance our manufactures, or to improve our lands, or to better our civil economy; or again, if it does not at once make this man a lawyer, that an engineer, and that a surgeon; or at least if it does not lead to discoveries in chemistry, astronomy, geology, magnetism, and science of every kind.

Questions for Discussion

1. Check resources on the Internet and make a presentation of Newman's influence on today's education.
2. What is the differences in Newman's idea of a university education with the kind of education that you have been receiving in your university?

About the Author

John Henry Cardinal Newman was born in London, the son (like Robert

Browning) of a banker. In his spiritual autobiography, *Apologia Pro Vita Sua* (in effect, his vindication of his life, 1864—1865), he traces the principal stages of his religious development from the strongly Protestant period of his youth to his conversion to Roman Catholicism in 1845. Along the way, after being elected to a fellowship at Oriel College in Oxford and becoming an Anglican clergyman, he was attracted briefly into the orbit of religious liberalism. Gradually coming to realize, however, that liberalism, with its reliance on human reason, would be powerless to defend traditional religion from attack, Newman shifted over into the new High Church wing of the Anglican Church and soon was recognized as the leading figure of what was known as the Oxford movement. During the 1830s he built up a large and influential following by his sermons at Oxford and also by his writing of tracts—that is, appeals, in pamphlet form, on behalf of a cause. In these publications he developed arguments about the powers of church versus state and other issues of deep concern to his High Church colleagues—or Tractarians, as they were also called. Newman's own efforts to demonstrate the true catholicity of the Church of England provoked increasing opposition as his position grew closer to Roman Catholicism. Distressed by constant denunciations, he with drew into isolation and silence. After much reflection he took the final step. At the age of forty-four he entered the Roman Catholic priesthood and moved to Birmingham, where he spent the rest of his life. In 1879 he was created cardinal. In 1991, at the instigation of Pope John Paul II, his title became The Venerable John Henry Cardinal Newman, marking the first of three stages toward sainthood.

Part One　British Literature

Tradition and the Individual Talent

T. S. Eliot

In English writing we seldom speak of tradition, though we occasionally apply its name in deploring its absence. We cannot refer to "the tradition" or to "a tradition"; at most, we employ the adjective in saying that the poetry of So-and-so is "traditional" or even "too traditional". Seldom, perhaps, does the word appear except in a phrase of censure. If otherwise, it is vaguely approbative, with the implication, as to the work approved, of some pleasing archaeological reconstruction. You can hardly make the word agreeable to English ears without this comfortable reference to the reassuring science of archaeology.

Certainly the word is not likely to appear in our appreciations of living or dead writers. Every nation, every race, has not only its own creative, but its own critical turn of mind; and is even more oblivious of the shortcomings and limitations of its critical habits than of those of its creative genius. We know, or think we know, from the enormous mass of critical writing that has appeared in the French language the critical method or habit of the French; we only conclude (we are such unconscious people) that the French are "more critical" than we, and sometimes even plume ourselves a little with the fact, as if the French were the less spontaneous. Perhaps they are; but we might remind ourselves that criticism is as inevitable as breathing, and that we should be none the worse for articulating what passes in our minds when we read a book and feel an emotion about it, for criticizing our own minds in their work of criticism. One of the facts that might come to light in this process is our tendency to insist, when we praise a poet, upon those aspects of his work in which he least resembles anyone else. In these aspects or parts of his work we pretend to find what is individual, what is the peculiar essence of the man. We dwell with satisfaction upon the poet's difference from his predecessors, especially his immediate predecessors; we endeavour to find something that can be isolated in order to be enjoyed. Whereas if we approach a poet without this prejudice we shall often find that not only the best, but the most individual parts of his work may be those in which the dead poets, his ancestors, assert their immortality most vigorously. And I do not mean the impressionable period of adolescence, but the period of full maturity.

Yet if the only form of tradition, of handing down, consisted in following the ways of the immediate generation before us in a blind or timid adherence to its successes, "tradition" should positively be discouraged. We have seen many such simple currents soon lost in the sand; and novelty is better than repetition. Tradition is a matter of much wider significance. It cannot be inherited, and if you want it you must obtain it by great labour. It involves, in the first place, the historical sense, which we may call nearly indispensable to any one who would continue to be a poet beyond his twenty-fifth year; and the historical sense involves a perception, not only of the pastness of the past, but of its presence; the historical sense compels a man to write not merely with his own generation in his bones, but with a feeling that the whole of the literature of Europe from Homer and within it the whole of the literature of his own country has a simultaneous existence and composes a simultaneous order. This historical sense, which is a sense of the timeless as well as of the temporal and of the timeless and of the temporal together, is what makes a writer traditional. And it is at the same time what makes a writer most acutely conscious of his place in time, of his own contemporaneity.

No poet, no artist of any art, has his complete meaning alone. His significance, his appreciation is the appreciation of his relation to the dead poets and artists. You cannot value him alone; you must set him, for contrast and comparison, among the dead. I mean this as a principle of aesthetic, not merely historical, criticism. The necessity that he shall conform, that he shall cohere, is not one-sided; what happens when a new work of art is created is something that happens simultaneously to all the works of art which preceded it. The existing monuments form an ideal order among themselves, which is modified by the introduction of the new (the really new) work of art among them. The existing order is complete before the new work arrives; for order to persist after the supervention of novelty, the whole existing order must be, if ever so slightly, altered; and so the relations, proportions, values of each work of art toward the whole are readjusted; and this is conformity between the old and the new. Whoever has approved this idea of order, of the form of European, of English literature will not find it preposterous that the past should be altered by the present as much as the present is directed by the past. And the poet who is aware of this will be aware of great difficulties and responsibilities.

In a peculiar sense he will be aware also that he must inevitably be judged by the standards of the past. I say judged, not amputated, by them; not judged to be as good as, or worse or better than, the dead; and certainly not judged by the canons of dead critics. It is a judgment, a comparison, in which two things are measured by each other. To conform merely would be for the new work not really to conform at all; it would not be new, and would therefore not be a work of art. And we do not quite say that the new is more valuable because it fits in; but its fitting in is a test of its value—a test, it is true, which can only be slowly and cautiously applied, for we are none of us infallible judges of conformity. We say: it appears to conform, and is perhaps individual, or it appears individual, and may conform; but we are hardly likely to find that it is one and not the other. To proceed to a more intelligible exposition of the relation of the poet to the past: he can neither take the past as a lump, an indiscriminate bolus,① nor can he form himself wholly on one or two private admirations, nor can he form himself wholly upon one preferred period. The first course is inadmissible, the second is an important experience of youth, and the third is a pleas ant and highly desirable supplement. The poet must be very conscious of the main current, which does not at all flow invariably through the most distinguished reputations. He must be quite aware of the obvious fact that art never improves, but that the material of art is never quite the same. He must be aware that the mind of Europe—the mind of his own country—a mind which he learns in time to be much more important than his own private mind—is a mind which changes, and that this change is a development which abandons nothing en route, which does not superannuate either Shakespeare, or Homer, or the rock drawing of the Magdalenian② draftsmen. That this development, refinement perhaps, complication certainly, is not, from the point of view of the artist, any improvement. Perhaps not even an improvement from the point of view of the psychologist or not to the extent which we imagine; perhaps only in the end based upon a complication in economics and machinery. But the difference between the present and the past is that the conscious present is an awareness of the past in a way and to an extent which the past's awareness of itself cannot show.

Someone said: "The dead writers are remote from us because we know so much more than they did." Precisely, and they are that which we know. I am

---

① A round mass of anything; a large pill.
② The most advanced culture of the European Paleolithic period.

alive to a usual objection to what is clearly part of my program for the metier1 of poetry. The objection is that the doctrine requires a ridiculous amount of erudition (pedantry), a claim which can be rejected by appeal to the lives of poets in any pantheon. It will even be affirmed that much learning deadens or perverts poetic sensibility. While, however, we persist in believing that a poet ought to know as much as will not encroach upon his necessary receptivity and necessary laziness, it is not desirable to confine knowledge to whatever can be put into a useful shape for examinations, drawing-rooms, or the still more pretentious modes of publicity. Some can absorb knowledge, the more tardy must sweat for it. Shakespeare acquired more essential history from Plutarch than most men could from the whole British Museum. What is to be insisted upon is that the poet must develop or procure the consciousness of the past and that he should continue to develop this consciousness throughout his career. What happens is a continual surrender of himself as he is at the moment to something which is more valuable. The progress of an artist is a continual self-sacrifice, a continual extinction of personality. There remains to define this process of depersonalisation and its relation to the sense of tradition. It is in this depersonalization that art may be said to approach the condition of science. I, therefore, invite you to consider, as a suggestive analogy, the action which takes place when a bit of finely filiated platinum is introduced into a chamber containing oxygen and sulphur dioxide.

Questions for Discussion

1. What's Eliot's opinion on the relationship between tradition and the individual?
2. In what kind of context did Eliot write down this essay?

About the Author

Thomas Stearns Eliot (1888—1965) was born in St. Louis, Missouri, of New England stock. He entered Harvard in 1906 and was influenced there by the anti-Romanticism of Irving Babbitt and the philosophical and critical interests of George Santayana, as well as by the enthusiastic study of Renaissance literature and of South Asian religions. He wrote his Harvard dissertation on the English idealist philosopher F. H. Bradley, whose emphasis on the private nature of individual experience, "a circle enclosed on the outside," influenced Eliot's poetry considerably. He also studied literature and philosophy in France and Germany, before going to England shortly after the out break of World War I in 1914. He studied Greek philosophy at Oxford, taught school in London, and then obtained a position with Lloyd's Bank. In 1915 he married an English writer, Vivienne Haigh-Wood, but the marriage was not a success. She suffered from poor emotional and physical health. The strain told on Eliot, too. By November 1921 distress and worry had brought him to the verge of a nervous break down, and on medical advice he went to recuperate in a Swiss sanitorium. Two months later he returned, pausing in Paris long enough to give his early supporter and adviser Ezra Pound the manuscript of *The Waste Land*. Eliot left his wife in 1933, and she was eventually committed to a mental home, where she died in 1947. Ten years later he was happily remarried to his secretary, Valerie Fletcher.

Part Two American Literature

Poetry

To a Waterfowl

Whither, 'midst falling dew,
While glow the heavens with the last steps of day,
Far, through their rosy depths, dost thou pursue
Thy solitary way?

Vainly the fowler's eye
Might mark thy distant flight to do thee wrong,
As, darkly painted on the crimson sky,
Thy figure floats along.

Seek'st thou the plashy① brink
Of weedy lake, or marge of river wide,
Or where the rocking billows rise and sink
On the chafed② ocean side?

There is a Power whose care
Teaches thy way along that pathless coast,—
The desert and illimitable air,—
Lone wandering, but not lost.

All day thy wings have fanned
At that far height, the cold thin atmosphere;
Yet stoop not, weary, to the welcome land,
Though the dark night is near.

And soon that toil shall end,
Soon shalt thou find a summer home, and rest,
And scream among thy fellows; reeds shall bend
Soon o'er thy sheltered nest.

---

① Marshy; a plash is a pool.
② To wear away or irritate by rubbing.

Thou'rt gone, the abyss of heaven
Hath swallowed up thy form; yet, on my heart
Deeply hath sunk the lesson thou hast given,
And shall not soon depart.

He, who, from zone to zone,
Guides through the boundless sky thy certain flight,
In the long way that I must tread alone,
Will lead my steps aright.

Questions for Discussion

1. Please describe the waterfowl's flight.
2. Who is the guide of waterfowl? How?
3. Try to figure out Bryant's conception of God.

About the Author

William Cullen Bryant (1794—1878) is an American romantic poet, journalist, and long-time editor of the *New York Evening Post*. He was born at Cummington, Mass. His fame rose after the printing of his *Thanatopsis*, a meditation on nature and death that remains his best-known poem, and he gradually became a leading poet. Admitted to the bar at 21, he spent nearly 10 years as an attorney, a profession he hated. His *Poems* (1821), including *To a Waterfowl*, secured his reputation. He was a poet of nature, and his work is often compared with that of Wordsworth. Nature is simply the visible token of God's transcendent beauty and awful power, and thus nature influences man for good.

Annabel Lee

It was many and many a year ago,
  In a kingdom by the sea
That a maiden there lived whom you may know.
  By the name of Annabel Lee;
And this maiden she lived with no other thought

Than to love and be loved by me.

I was a child and she was a child,
    In this kingdom by the sea;
But we loved with a love that was more than love—
    I and my Annabel Lee—
With a love that the winged seraphs① of heaven
    Coveted her and me.

And this was the reason that, long ago,
    In this kingdom by the sea,
A wind blew out of a cloud, chilling
    My beautiful Annabel Lee;
So that her highborn kinsmen came
    And bore her away from me,
To shut her up in a sepulcher②
    In this kingdom by the sea.
The angels, not half so happy in heaven,
    Went envying her and me—
Yes!—that was the reason (as all men know,
    In this kingdom by the sea)
That the wind came out of the cloud by night,
    Chilling and killing my Annabel Lee.

But our love it was stronger by far than the love
    Of those who were older than we—
    Of many far wiser than we—
And neither the angels in heaven above,
    Nor the demons down under the sea,
Can ever dissever my soul from the soul
    Of the beautiful Annabel Lee.

---

① A celestial being having three pairs of wings.
② A burial vault.

For the moon never beams, without bringing me dreams
　　Of the beautiful Annabel Lee;
And the stars never rise, but I feel the bright eyes
　　Of the beautiful Annabel Lee;
And so, all the night tide, I lie down by the side
Of my darling—my darling—my life and my bride,
　　In hersepulcher there by the sea—
　　In her tomb by the sounding sea.

Questions for Discussion

1. What are the images in the poem?
2. What is the musical/sound effect of the lines?
3. What kind of idea do you think Poe is trying to convey to us?

About the Author

Edgar Allan Poe(1809—1849) is a U. S. poet, critic, and short-story writer. Poe is famous for his short poems. *The Raven* brought him international celebrity, and poems like *Ulalume* and *The Bells* soon enhanced that fame among Poe's constantly enlarging posthumous audience. He thought poetry should appeal only to the sense of beauty, not truth; informational poetry, poetry of ideas, or any sort of didactic poetry was illegitimate. In this aspect, Poe is the forerunner of the "art for art's sake" movement at the end of the century in Britain. Holding that the true poetic emotion was a vague sensory state, he set himself against realistic details in poetry, although the prose tale, with truth as one object, could profit from the discreet use of specifics. Both poems and tales should be short enough to be read in one sitting; otherwise the unity of effect would be dissipated. Poe's principles of writing poetry are expressed in his *The Philosophy of Composition*.

Beat! Beat! Drums!

Beat! beat! drums! —blow! bugles! blow!
Through the windows—through doors—burst like a ruthless force,
Into the solemn church, and scatter the congregation,

Into the school where the scholar is studying;
Leave not the bridegroom quiet—no happiness must he have now
 with his bride,
Nor the peaceful farmer any peace, ploughing his field or gathering
 his grain,
So fierce you whirr and pound you drums—so shrill you bugles blow.

Beat! beat! drums!—blow! bugles! blow!
Over the traffic of cities—over the rumble of wheels in the streets;
Are beds prepared for sleepers at night in the houses? no sleepers
 must sleep in those beds,
Nor bargainers' bargains by day—no brokers or speculators—
 would they continue?
Would the talkers be talking? would the singer attempt to sing?
Would the lawyer rise in the court to state his case before his judge?
Then rattle quicker, heavier drums—you bugles wilder blow.

Beat! beat! drums!—blow! bugles! blow!
Make no parley—stop for no expostulation,
Mind not the timid—mind not the weeper or prayer,
Mind not the old man beseeching the young man,
Let not the child's voice be heard, nor the mother's entreaties,
Make even the trestle to shake the dead where they lie awaiting the
 hearse,
So strong you thump O terrible drums—so loud you bugles blow.

Questions for Discussion

1. Read the poem aloud and find out its rhythm.
2. Discuss how the vocal characteristics of Whitman's words help to express the theme.
3. Explain the organization of the poem.

About the Author

Walt Whitman (1819—1892) is a U. S. poet, journalist, and essayist. He was born on Long Island, New York, and raised in Brooklyn. He left school early and had tried several jobs. His revolutionary poetry dealt with extremely private experiences (including sexuality) while celebrating the collective experience of an idealized democratic American life. His *Leaves of Grass* (first ed., 1855), revised and much expanded in successive editions that incorporated his subsequent poetry, was too frank and unconventional to win wide acceptance in its day, but was hailed by such figures as R. W. Emerson and exerted a strong influence on American and foreign literature. Individual poems in the collection that celebrated the body and sexuality opened him up to charges of obscenity. His prosody proved as controversial as his subject matter. In fact, Whitman is one of the most pioneering figures in American poetry; he experimented on the poetic form and subject matter and had deep influence for many other poets.

Because I Could Not Stop for Death

Because I could not stop for Death—
He kindly stopped for me—
The Carriage held but just Ourselves—
And Immortality.

We slowly drove—He knew no haste
And I had put away
My labor and my leisure too,
For His Civility—

We passed the School, where Children strove
At Recess—in the Ring—
We passed the Fields of Gazing Grain—
We passed the Setting Sun—

Or rather—He passed Us—
The Dews drew quivering and chill—

For only Gossamer①, my Gown—
My Tippet②—only Tulle③—

We paused before a House that seemed
A Swelling of the Ground—
The Roof was scarcely visible—
The Cornice④—in the Ground—

Since then—'tis Centuries—and yet
Feels shorter than the Day
I first surmised the Horses' Heads
Were toward Eternity—

Questions for Discussion

1. What is the image of death in this poem?
2. What is the speaker's attitude toward death?
3. What is the relationship between death and eternity?

Hope Is the Thing with Feathers

Hope is the thing with feathers—
That perches in the soul—
And sings the tune without the words—
And never stops— at all—

And sweetest— in the Gale— is heard—
And sore must be the storm—
That could abash the little Bird
That kept so many warm—

---

① A soft sheer gauzy fabric.
② A covering for the shoulders, as of fur, with long ends that hang in front.
③ A fine, often starched net of silk, rayon, or nylon, used especially for veils, tutus, or gowns.
④ A horizontal molded projection that crowns or completes a building or wall.

I've heard it in the chillest land—
And on the strangest sea—
Yet, never, in extremity,
It asked a crumb of ME.

Questions for Discussion

1. Why does Dickinson use so many dashes here?
2. Find out the images in this poem.
3. What literary devicesdoes Dickinson use in this poem?

I'm Nobody

I'm Nobody! Who are you?
Are you—Nobody—too?
Then there is a pair of us!
Don't tell! they'd advertise—you know!

How dreary—to be—Somebody!
How public—like a frog—
To tell one's name—the living June—
To an admiring Bog!

Questions for Discussion

1. What is the relationship between the speaker and the addresser?
2. Do they really not care about fame? Why?

About the Author

Emily Dickinson (1830—1886), U. S. poet. Granddaughter of the cofounder of Amherst College and daughter of a respected lawyer and one-term congressman, she was educated at Amherst (Mass.) Academy and Mount Holyoke Female Seminary. She subsequently spent virtually all her life, increasingly reclusive, in her family home in Amherst. She began writing in the 1850s; by 1860 she was boldly experimenting with language and prosody, striving for vivid, exact words and epigrammatic concision, while adhering to the basic quatrains and meters of the Protestant hymn. The subjects of her deceptively simple lyrics, whose depth and intensity contrast with the apparent quiet of her life, include love, death, and nature. Her numerous letters are sometimes equal in artistry to her poems. By 1870 she was dressing only in white and declining to see most visitors, and she never again left the boundaries of the house. Of her 1775 poems, only seven were published during her lifetime. After posthumous publications (some rather inaccurate), her reputation and readership grew.

Stopping by Woods on a Snowy Evening

Whose woods these are I think I know,
His house is in the village though;
He will not see me stopping here
To watch his woods fill up with snow.

My little horse must think it queer
To stop without a farmhouse near
Between the woods and frozen lake
The darkest evening of the year.

He gives his harness bells a shake
To ask if there is some mistake.
The only other sound's the sweep
Of easy wind and downy flake.

The woods are lovely, dark and deep,
But I have promises to keep,
And miles to go before I sleep,
And miles to go before I sleep.

Questions for Discussion

1. What is the darkest evening of the year?
2. What do the woods symbolize? And what is the speaker's final decision?
3. Explain the meaning of the poem in light of Frost's life.

Part Two   American Literature

The Road Not Taken

Two roads diverged in a yellow wood,
And sorry I could not travel both
And be one traveler, long I stood
And looked down one as far as I could
To where it bent in the undergrowth;

Then took the other, as just as fair,
And having perhaps the better claim,
Because it was grassy and wanted wear;
Though as for that the passing there
Had worn them really about the same,

And both that morning equally lay
In leaves no step had trodden black.
Oh, I kept the first for another day!
Yet knowing how way leads on to way,
I doubted if I should ever come back.

I shall be telling this with a sigh
Somewhere ages and ages hence:
Two roads diverged in a wood, and I—
I took the one less traveled by,
And that has made all the difference.

Questions for Discussion

1. In what way are the two roads different?
2. What is the consequence of the choice?
3. Discuss in class if you have similar experiences.

About the Author

Robert Frost (1874—1963) was born in San Francisco, but his family soon moved to New England. After stints at Dartmouth and Harvard colleges and a difficult period as a teacher and farmer, he moved to England and published his first collections, *A Boy's Will* (1913) and *North of Boston* (1914). At the outbreak of war he returned to New England to farm and to pursue a distinguished teaching career at Amherst and Dartmouth colleges and elsewhere. He acutely observed the details of rural life and in his poetry endowed them with universal, even metaphysical, meaning, using colloquial language, familiar rhythms, and symbols taken from common life to express both the pastoral ideals and the dark complexities of New England life.

Anecdote of the Jar

I placed a jar in Tennessee,
And round it was, upon a hill.
It made the slovenly wilderness
Surround that hill.

The wilderness rose up to it,
And sprawled around, no longer wild.
The jar was round upon the ground
And tall and of a port in air.

It took dominion everywhere.
The jar was gray and bare.
It did not give of bird or bush,
Like nothing else in Tennessee.

Questions for Discussion

1. Please explain the meaning of the title.
2. Please discuss the importance of the jar, esp. in relation to its surroundings.
3. What does the jar symbolize?

About the Author

Wallace Stevens (1879—1955) was born and raised in Reading,

Pennsylvania. He practiced law in New York City before joining an insurance firm in Hartford in 1916; he rose to vice president, a position he held until his death. His poems began appearing in literary magazines in 1914. In *Harmonium* (1923), his first and most verbally brilliant book, he introduced the theme that occupied his creative lifetime and unified his thought: the relationship between imagination and reality. His later poetry, in such collections as *Ideas of Order* (1936), *The Man with the Blue Guitar* (1937), and *The Auroras of Autumn* (1950), continued to explore this theme with greater depth and rigor. His life was almost completely uneventful, and not until his late years was he widely read or recognized as a major poet by more than a few; he received a Pulitzer Prize only with his *Collected Poems* in 1955. He is now often considered America's greatest 20th-century poet.

The Red Wheelbarrow

so much depends
upon

a red wheel
barrow

glazed with rain
water

beside the white
chickens.

Questions for Discussion

1. What depends on the red wheelbarrow?
2. Please describe the scene in the poem.
3. Discuss the significance of the scene.

About the Author

William Carlos Williams (1883—1963) was an American poet closely associated with modernism and Imagism. He was also a pediatrician and general practitioner of medicine. Williams "worked harder at being a writer than he did at being a physician," wrote biographer Linda Wagner-Martin. During his long lifetime, Williams excelled both as a poet and a physician. He wrote poetry, fiction, drama and essays. In his early years, he was influenced by Ezra Pound and was a proponent of imagism, which focused on the direct treatment of things. Later he regretted that imagism had "dribbled off into so called 'free verse'" and declared himself an objectivist, valuing the rigor of form. His poetry treats the particulars, which can be illustrated by his saying: "No ideas but in things."

In a Station of the Metro

The apparition[①] of these faces in the crowd;
Petals on a wet, black bough.

Questions for Discussion

1. What is the image in the poem?
2. What are the characteristics of the image?
3. What meaning do you think Pound is trying to convey?

About the Author

Ezra Pound (1885—1972) is a quite unique figure in the American history. He was born in Hailey, Idaho, educated at Hamilton College and at the University of Pennsylvania, where he studied languages. He was associated with or influenced many poets as W. B. Yeats, Robert Frost, T. S. Eliot, and James Joyce. Pound led his later life as an expatriate. During World War II he made a series of pro-Fascist broadcasts and was tried for treason. He was adjudged mentally unfit and sentenced to St. Elizabeth's Hospital. In 1912, Pound, H. D., and Richard Aldington had launched imagism, a literary movement which proposed: 1. Direct treatment of the "thing" whether subjective or objective. 2. To use absolutely no word that does not contribute to the presentation. 3. As

---

① Apparition: 1. A ghostly figure; a specter. 2. The act of appearing; appearance.

regarding rhythm: to compose in the sequence of a musical phrase.

Journey of the Magi

"A cold coming we had of it,
Just the worst time of the year
For the journey, and such a long journey:
The ways deep and the weather sharp,
The very dead of winter."
And the camels galled①, sore-footed, refractory②,
Lying down in the melting snow.
There were times we regretted
The summer palaces on slopes, the terraces,
And the silken girls bringing sherbet③.
Then the camel men cursing and grumbling④
And running away, and wanting their liquor and women,
And the night-fires going out, and the lack of shelters,
And the cities hostile and the towns unfriendly
And the villages dirty and charging high prices:
A hard time we had of it.
At the end we preferred to travel all night,
Sleeping in snatches⑤,
With the voices singing in our ears, saying
That this was all folly.

Then at dawn we came down to a temperate valley,
Wet, below the snow line, smelling of vegetation,
With a running stream and a water-mill beating the darkness,
And three trees on the low sky,
And an old white horse galloped away in the meadow.

---

① Cause pain to (an animal, part of the body, etc) by rubbing; chafe.
② Difficult to control or discipline.
③ Refreshing drink of weak sweet fruit-juice.
④ Complain or protest in a bad-tempered way.
⑤ Not continuously.

Then we came to a tavern with vine-leaves over the lintel①,
Six hands at an open door dicing for pieces of silver,
And feet kicking the empty wine-skins,
But there was no information, and so we continued
And arrived at evening, not a moment too soon
Finding the place; it was (you may say) satisfactory

All this was a long time ago, I remember,
And I would do it again, but set down
This set down
This: were we led all that way for
Birth or Death? There was a Birth, certainly,
We had evidence and no doubt. I had seen birth and death,
But had thought they were different; this Birth was
Hard and bitter agony for us, like Death, our death,
We returned to our places, these Kingdoms,
But no longer at ease here, in the old dispensation,
With an alien people clutching their gods.
I should be glad of another death.

Questions for Discussion

1. Please retell the story and compare it to the story in the Bible.
2. What is the difference between the two?
3. In retelling the story, what is Eliot trying to convey to the reader?

About the Author

Thomas Stearns Eliot (1888—1965), U. S.-British poet, playwright, and critic. Born in St. Louis, he studied at Harvard University before moving to England in 1914, where he would work as an editor from the early 1920s until his death. He moved to the United Kingdom in 1914 (at age 25), and became a British subject in 1927 at the age of 39. *The Waste Land* (1922), which expresses with startling power the disillusionment of the postwar years, made

---

① Horizontal piece of wood or stone over a door or window, forming part of the frame.

his international reputation. From the 1920s on he was the most influential English-language modernist poet. He won the Nobel Prize in 1948; from then until his death he achieved public adulation unequaled by any other 20th-century poet.

l(a

l(a

le
af
fa

ll

s)
one
l

iness

Questions for Discussion

1. Try to work out the meaning of the poem.
2. Try to work out the visual image of the poem.
3. How does the form of the poem reinforce the theme?

in Just—

in Just—
spring   when the world is mud—
luscious the little
lame balloonman

whistles   far   and wee

and eddieandbill come
running from marbles and
piracies and it's
spring

when the world is puddle-wonderful

the queer
old balloonman whistles
far   and   wee
and bettyandisbel come dancing

from hop-scotch and jump-rope and

it's
spring
and
  the

       goat-footed

balloonMan   whistles
far
and
wee

Questions for Discussion

1. What is the poem about?
2. Explain what effects the telescoped words "eddieandbill" and "bettyandisbel" can achieve?
3. How does the typographical design of poem reinforce the theme?

About the Author

    E. E. Cummings (1894—1962) is an American poet, painter, essayist, and playwright. He was born in Cambridge, Massachusetts, and educated at Harvard University. He belonged to the avant-garde artists: he was influenced by the impressionist and cubist movements in the visual arts and by imagism, vorticism, and futurism in literature. Cummings' publishers and others have sometimes echoed the unconventional orthography in his poetry by writing his name in lower case and without periods. Through his radical experiments with syntax, typography, and lines, he defamiliarized common subject. His body of work encompasses more than 900 poems, several plays and essays, numerous drawings, sketches, and paintings, as well as two novels. He is remembered as a preeminent voice of 20th century poetry, as well as one of the most popular.

I, Too

I, too, sing America.

I am the darker brother.
They send me to eat in the kitchen
When company comes,
But I laugh,
And eat well,
And grow strong.

Tomorrow,
I'll sit at the table
When company comes.
Nobody'll dare
Say to me:
"Eat in the kitchen"
Then.

Besides,
They'll see how beautiful I am
And be ashamed—

I, too, am America.

Questions for Discussion

1. What kind of faith is shown in the poem?
2. What is the style of language? Colloquial or formal?
3. Explain how strong the structure of the poem is.

Dreams

Hold fast to dreams,
For if dreams die,
Life is a broken-winged bird
That cannot fly.

Hold fast to dreams,
For when dreams go,
Life is a barren field
Frozen with snow.

Questions for Discussion

1. What is the point the author tries to make?
2. How are the images created in the poem? What effects do they have?

About the Author

Langston Hughes (1902—1967) is an American poet, novelist, playwright, short story writer, and columnist. Born in Joplin, Mo., he published the poem *The Negro Speaks of Rivers* when he was 19, briefly attended Columbia Univ., and worked on an Africa-bound freighter. His career was dramatically launched when Hughes, working as a busboy, presented his poems to V. Lindsay as he dined. From 1928 to 1930 he lived in New York City and was a prominent figure in the Harlem Renaissance. In addition to poetry, he wrote fiction, drama, screenplays, essays, and autobiography. His poems are concerned with Negro life in America, and he drew his meters and moods from street language, jazz, and the blues.

Drama

A Streetcar Named Desire

Tennessee Williams

Scene 4

It is early the following morning. There is a confusion of street cries like a choral chant.

STELLA *is lying down in the bedroom. Her face is serene in the early morning sunlight. One hand rests on her belly, rounding slightly with new maternity. From the other dangles a book of colored comics. Her eyes and lips have that almost narcotized tranquility that is in the faces of Eastern idols.*

The table is sloppy with remains of breakfast and the debris of the preceding night, and STANLEY'*s gaudy pyjamas lie across the threshold of the bathroom. The outside door is slightly ajar on a sky of summer brilliance.*

BLANCHE *appears at this door. She has spent a sleepless night and her appearance entirely contrasts with* STELLA'*s. She presses her knuckles nervously to her lips as she looks through the door, before entering.*

BLANCHE Stella?

STELLA (*Stirring lazily.*) Hmmh?

(*Blanche utters a moaning cry and runs into the bedroom, throwing herself down besides in a rush of hysterical tenderness.*)

BLANCHE Baby, my baby sister!

STELLA (*Drawing away from her.*) Blanche, what is the matter with you?

(*Blanche straightens up slowly and stands beside the bed looking down at her sister with knuckles pressed to her lips.*)

BLANCHE He's left?

STELLA Stan? Yes.

BLANCHE Will he be back?

STELLA He's gone to get the car greased. Why?

BLANCHE Why! I've been half crazy, Stella! When I found out you'd been insane enough to come back in here after what happened—I started to rush in after you!

STELLA I'm glad you didn't.

BLANCHE What were you thinking of? (*Stella makes an indefinite gesture.*) Answer me! What? What!

STELLA Please, Blanche! Sit down and stop yelling.

BLANCHE All right, Stella. I will repeat the question quietly now. How could you come back in this place last night? Why, you must have slept with him!

(*Stella gets up in a calm and leisurely way.*)

STELLA Blanche, I'd forgotten how excitable you are. You're making much too much fuss about this.

BLANCHE Am I?

STELLA Yes, you are, Blanche. I know how it must have seemed to you and I'm awful sorry it had to happen, but it wasn't anything as anything as serious as you seem to take it. In the first place, when men are drinking and playing poker anything can happen. It's always a powder-keg. He didn't know what he was doing.... He was as good as a lamb when I came back and he's really very, very ashamed of himself.

BLANCHE And that—that makes it all right?

STELLA No, it isn't all right for anybody to make such a terrible row, but—people do sometimes. Stanley's always smashed things. Why, on our wedding night—soon as we came in here—he snatched off one of my slippers and rushed about the places smashing light bulbs with it.

BLANCHE He did—*what*?

STELLA He smashed all the lightbulbs with the heel of my slipper! (*She laughs.*)

BLANCHE And you—you *let* him? Didn't *run*, didn't *scream*?

STELLA I was—sort of—thrilled by it. (*She waits for a moment.*) Eunice and you had breakfast?

BLANCHE Do you suppose I wanted any breakfast?

STELLA There's some coffee left on the stove.

BLANCHE You're so—matter-of-fact about it, Stella.

STELLA What other can I be? He's taken the radio to get it fixed. It didn't land on the pavement so only one tube was smashed.

BLANCHE And you are standing there smiling!

STELLA What do you want me to do?

BLANCHE Pull yourself together and face the facts.

STELLA What are they, in your opinion?

BLANCHE In my opinion? You're married to a madman!

STELLA No!

BLANCHE Yes, you are, your fix is worse than mine is! Only you're not being sensible about it. I'm going to *do* something. Get hold of myself and make myself a new life!

STELLA Yes?

BLANCHE But you've given in. And that isn't right, you're not old! You can get out.

STELLA (*Slowly and emphatically.*) I'm not in anything I want to get out of.

BLANCHE (*Incredulously.*) What—Stella?

STELLA I said I am not in anything that I have a desire to get out of. Look at the mess in this room! And those empty bottles! They went through two cases last night! He promised this morning that he was going to quit having these poker parties, but you know how long such a promise is going to keep. Oh, well, it's his pleasure, like mine is movies and bridge. People have got to tolerate each other's habits, I guess.

BLANCHE I don't understand you. (*Stella turns toward her.*) I don't understand your indifference. Is this a Chinese philosophy you've—cultivated?

STELLA Is what—what?

BLANCHE This—shuffling about and mumbling—"One tube smashed—beer bottles—mess in the kitchen!" —as if nothing out of the ordinary has happened! (*Stella laughs uncertainly and picking up the broom, twirls it in her hands.*) Are you deliberately shaking that thing in my face?

STELLA No.

BLANCHE Stop it. Let go of that broom. I won't have you cleaning up for him!

STELLA Then who's going to do it? Are you?

BLANCHE I? I!

STELLA No, I didn't think so.

BLANCHE Oh, let me think, if only my mind would function! We've got to get hold of some money, that's the way out!

STELLA I guess that money is always nice to get hold of.

BLANCHE Listen to me. I have an idea of some kind. (*Shakily she twists a cigarette into her holder.*) Do you remember Shep Huntleigh? (*Stella shakes her head.*) Of course you remember Shep Huntleigh. I went out with him at college and wore his pin for a while. Well—

STELLA   Well?

BLANCHE   I ran into him last winter. You know I went to Miami during the Christmas holidays?

STELLA   No.

BLANCHE   Well, I did. I took the trip as an investment, thinking I'd meet someone with a million dollars.

STELLA   Did you?

BLANCHE   Yes. I ran into Shep Huntleigh—I ran into him on Biscayne Boulevard, on Christmas Eve, about dusk... getting into his car—Cadillac convertible; must have been a block long!

STELLA   I should think it would have been—inconvenient in traffic!

BLANCHE   You've heard of oil well?

STELLA   Yes—remotely.

BLANCHE   He has them, all over Texas. Texas is literally spouting gold in his pockets.

STELLA   My, my.

BLANCHE   Y'know how indifferent I am to money. I think of money in terms of what it does for you. But he could do it, he could certainly do it!

STELLA   Do what, Blanche?

BLANCHE   Why—set us up in a—shop!

STELLA   What kind of shop?

BLANCHE   Oh, a—shop of some kind! He could do it with half what his wife throws away at the races.

STELLA   He's married?

BLANCHE   Honey, would I be here if the man weren't married? (*Stella laughs a little, Blanche suddenly springs up and crosses to phone. She speaks shrilly.*) How do I get Western Union? —Operator! Western Union!

STELLA   That's a dial phone, honey.

BLANCHE   I can't dial, I'm too—

STELLA   Just dial O.

BLANCHE   O?

STELLA   Yes, "O" for operator!

(*Blanche considers a moment; then she puts the phone down.*)

BLANCHE　Give me a pencil. Where is a slip of paper? I've got to write it down first—the message, I mean... (*She goes to the dressing table, and grabs up a sheet of Kleenex and an eyebrow pencil for writing equipment.*) Let me see now... (*She bites the pencil.*) "Darling Shep. Sister and I in desperate situation."

STELLA　I beg your pardon!

BLANCHE　"Sister and I in desperate situation. Will explain details later. Would you be interested in—?" (*She bites the pencil again.*) "Would you be—interested—in..." (*She smashed the pencil on the table and springs up.*) You never get anywhere with direct appeals!

STELLA　(*With a laugh.*) Don't be so ridiculous, darling!

BLANCHE　But I'll think of something, I've *got* to think of—something! Don't laugh at me, Stella! Please, please don't-I-I want you to look at the contents of my purse! Here's what's in it! (*She snatches her purse open.*) Sixty-five measly cents in coin of the realm!

STELLA　(*Crossing to bureau.*) Stanley doesn't give me a regular allowance, he likes to pay bills himself, but—this morning he gave me ten dollars to smooth things over. You take five of it, Blanche, and I'll keep the rest.

BLANCHE　Oh, no. No, Stella.

STELLA　(*Insisting.*) I know how it helps your morale just having a little pocket-money on you.

BLANCHE　No, thank you—I'll take to the streets!

STELLA　Talk sense! How did you happen to get so low on funds?

BLANCHE　Money just goes—it goes places. (*She rubs her forehead.*) Sometime today I've got to get hold of a Bromo[①]!

STELLA　I'll fix you one now.

BLANCHE　Not yet—I've got to keep thinking!

STELLA　I wish you'd just let things go, at least for a—while.

BLANCHE　Stella, I can't live with him! You can, he's your husband. But how could I stay here with him, after last night, with just those curtains between us?

STELLA　Blanche, you saw him at his worst last night.

---

①　Short for "Bromo Seltzer," a headache remedy.

BLANCHE On the contrary, I aw him at his best! What such a man has to offer is animal force and he gave a wonderful exhibition of that! But the only way to live with such a man is to—go to bed with him! And that's your job—not mine!

STELLA After you've rested a little, you'll see it's going to work out. You don't have to worry about anything while you're here. I mean—expenses...

BLANCHE I have to plan for us both, to get us both—out!

STELLA You take it for granted that I am in something that I want to get out of.

BLANCHE I take it for granted that you still have sufficient memory of Belle Reve to find this place and these poker players impossible to live with.

STELLA Well, you're taking entirely too much for granted.

BLANCHE I can't believe you're in earnest.

STELLA No?

BLANCHE I understand how it happened—a little. You saw him in uniform, an officer, not here but—

STELLA I'm not sure it would have made any difference where I saw him.

BLANCHE Now don't say it was one of those mysterious electric things between people! If you do I'll laugh in your face.

STELLA I am not going to say anything more at all about it!

BLANCHE All right, then, don't!

STELLA But there are things that happen between a man and a woman in the dark—that sort of make everything else seem—unimportant. (*Pause.*)

BLANCHE What you are talking about is brutal desire—just—Desire! —the name of that rattle-rap streetcar that bangs through the Quarter, up one old narrow street and down another...

STELLA Haven't you ever ridden on that streetcar?

BLANCHE It brought me here. —Where I'm not wanted and where I'm ashamed to be...

STELLA Then don't you think your superior attitude is a bit out of place?

BLANCHE I am not being or feeling at all superior, Stella. Believe me I'm not! It's just this. This is how I look at it. A man like that is someone to go out with—once—twice—three times when the devil is in you. But live with? Have a child by?

STELLA I have told you I love him.

BLANCHE Then I *tremble* for you! I just—*tremble* for you...

STELLA I can't help your trembling if you insist on trembling!

(*There is a pause.*)

BLANCHE May I—speak—*plainly*?

STELLA Yes, do. Go ahead. As plainly as you want to.

(*Outside, a train approaches. They are silent till the noise subsides. They are both in the bedroom. Under cover of the train's noise* STANLEY *enters from outside. He stands unseen by the women, holding some packages in his arms, and overhears their following conversation. He wears an undershirt and grease-stained seersucker pants.*)

BLANCHE Well—if you'll forgive me—he's *common*!

STELLA Why, yes, I suppose he is.

BLANCHE Suppose! You can't have forgotten that much of our bringing up, Stella, that you just *suppose* that any part of a gentleman's in his nature! *Not one particle, no*! Oh, if he was just—*ordinary*! Just *plain*—but good and wholesome, but—*no*. There's something downright—*bestial*—about him! You're hating me saying this, aren't you?

STELLA (*Coldly.*) Go on and say it all, Blanche.

BLANCHE He acts like an animal, has an animal's habits! Eats like one, moves like one, talks like one! There's even something—sub-human—something not quite to the stage of humanity yet! Yes, something—ape-like about him, like one of those pictures I've seen in—anthropological studies! Thousands and thousands of years have passed him right by, and there he is—Stanley Kowalski—survivor of the Stone Age! Bearing the raw meat home from the kill in the jungle! And you—*you* here—*waiting* for him! Maybe he'll strike you or maybe grunt and kiss you! That is, if kisses have been discovered yet! Night falls and the other apes gather! There in the front of the cave, all grunting like him, and swilling and gnawing and hulking! His poker night! You call it—this party of apes! Somebody growls—some creature snatches at something—the fight is on! *God*! Maybe we are a long way from being made in God's image, but Stella—my sister—there has been *some* progress since then! Such things as art—as poetry and music—such kinds of new light have come into the world since then! In some kinds of people some tenderer feelings have had some little beginning! That we have got to make *grow*! And *cling* to, and hold as our flag! In this dark march toward whatever it is we're approaching... *Don't*—*don't hang back with the brutes*!

(*Another train passes outside. Stanley hesitates, licking his lips. Then suddenly he turns stealthily about and withdraws through front door. The women are still unaware of his presence. When the train has passed he calls through the closed front door.*)

STANLEY   Hey! Hey, Stella!

STELLA   (*Who has listened gravely to Blanche.*) Stanley!

BLANCHE   Stell, I—

(*But Stella has gone to the front door. Stanley enters casually with his packages.*)

STANLEY   Hiyuh, Stella. Blanche back?

STELLA   Yes, she's back.

STANLEY   Hiyuh, Blanche. (*He grins at her.*)

STELLA   You must've got under the car.

STANLEY   Them darn mechanics at Fritz's don't know their ass fr'm—*Hey*!

(*Stella has embraced him with both arms, fiercely, and full in the view of Blanche. He laughs and clasps her head to him. Over her head he grins through the curtains at Blanche. As the lights fade away, with a lingering brightness on their embrace, the music of the "Blue Piano" and trumpet and drums is heard.*)

Questions for Discussion

1. What does Blanche stand for in the play?
2. What is Blanche's attitude towards Stanley?
3. Can Blanche really rely on Shep Huntleigh for help? Why or why not?
4. Please tell something about the culture Blanche comes from.
5. What is the conflict between the two cultures?

About the Author

Tennessee Williams (1911—1983), U. S. playwright. The son of a traveling salesman and a clergyman's daughter, he was born in Columbus, Miss., and lived in St. Louis from age 12. He attended several colleges, graduating from the University of Iowa. He moved to New Orleans in 1939 and changed his name to "Tennessee," the state of his father's birth. He won recognition by the Group Theatre for his one-act plays *American Blues* (1939). Wider success came with The *Glass Menagerie* (1944) and mounted with *Summer and Smoke* (1948), *A Streetcar Named Desire* (1947, Pulitzer Prize; film, 1951), *Camino Real* (1953), and *Cat on a Hot Tin Roof* (1955, Pulitzer Prize; film, 1958). His plays, which also included *Suddenly Last Summer* (1958; film, 1959), *Sweet Bird of Youth* (1959; film, 1962), and *The Night of the Iguana* (1961; film, 1964), described a world of repressed sexuality and violence thinly veiled by gentility. A clear-sighted chronicler of fragile illusions, he is regarded as one of the greatest American playwrights.

A Streetcar Named Desire is widely considered Williams' landmark play. It deals with a culture clash between two symbolic characters, Blanche DuBois, a pretentious, fading relic of the Old South, and Stanley Kowalski, a rising member of the industrial, urban immigrant class.

The play is set in the French Quarter of New Orleans. As the play opens, Blanche DuBois has arrived at the home of her sister, Stella, and Stella's husband, Stanley Kowalski. Blanche and Stanley represent the polarities of human existence that Williams often explored in his drama. The play presents Blanche DuBois, a fading but still attractive Southern belle whose pretensions to virtue and culture only thinly mask delusions of grandeur and alcoholism. Her poise is an illusion she presents to shield others, but most of all herself, from her reality, and an attempt to make herself still attractive to new male suitors. Stanley is a crude but vigorous figure, sexually dynamic and brutally honest. He sees Blanche as a threat to his relationship with Stella, whom he loves.

Death of a Salesman

Arthur Miller

Act I

...

Light has risen on the boys' room. Unseen, Willy is heard talking to himself, "Eight thousand miles," and a little laugh. Biff gets out of bed, comes downstage a bit, and stands attentively. Biff is two years older than his brother Happy, well built, but in these days bears a worn air and seems less self-assured. He has succeeded less, and his dreams are stronger and less acceptable than Happy's. Happy is tall, powerfully made. Sexuality is like a visible color on him, or a scent that many women have discovered. He, like his brother, is lost, but in a different way, for he has never allowed himself to turn his face toward defeat and is thus more confused and hard-skinned, although seemingly more content.

HAPPY (*getting out of bed*) He's going to get his license taken away if he keeps that up. I'm getting nervous about him, y'know, Biff?

BIFF His eyes are going.

HAPPY No, I've driven with him. He sees all right. He just doesn't keep his mind on it. I drove into the city with him last week. Eh stops at a green light and then it turns red and he goes. (*He laughs.*)

BIFF Maybe he's color-blind.

HAPPY Pop? Why he's got the finest eye for color in the business. You know that.

BIFF (*sitting down on his bed*) I'm going to sleep.

HAPPY You're not still sour on Dad, are you, Biff?

BIFF He's all right, I guess.

WILLY (*underneath them, in the living-room*) Yes, sir, eighty thousand miles—eighty-two thousand!

BIFF You smoking?

HAPPY (*holding out a packet of cigarettes*) Want one?

BIFF (*taking a cigarette*) I can never sleep when I smell it.

WILLY What a simonizing job, heh!

HAPPY (*with deep sentiment*) Funny, Biff, y'know? Us sleeping in here again? The old beds. (*He pats his bed affectionately.*) All the talk that went across those two beds, huh? Our whole lives.

BIFF Yeah. Lotta dreams and plans.

HAPPY (*with a deep and masculine laugh*) About five hundred women would like to know what was said in this room.

They share a soft laugh.

BIFF Remember that big Betsy something—what the hell was her name—over on Bushwick Avenue?

HAPPY (*combing his hair*) With the collie dog!

BIFF That's the one. I got you in there, remember?

HAPPY Yeah, that was my first time—I think. Boy, there was a pig! (*They laugh, almost crudely.*) You taught me everything I know about women. Don't forget that.

BIFF I bet you forgot how bashful you used to be. Especially with girls.

HAPPY Oh, I still am, Biff.

BIFF Oh, go on.

HAPPY I just control it, that's all. I think I got less bashful and you got more so. What happened, Biff? Where's the old humor, the old confidence? (*He shakes Biff's knee. Biff gets up and moves restlessly about the room.*) What's the matter?

BIFF Why does Dad mock me all the time?

HAPPY He's not mocking you, he—

BIFF Everything I say there's a twist of mockery on his face. I can't get near him.

HAPPY He just wants you to make good, that's all. I wanted to talk to you about Dad for a long time, Biff. Something's—happening to him. He—talks to himself.

BIFF I noticed that this morning. But he always mumbled.

HAPPY But not so noticeable. It got so embarrassing I sent him to Florida. And you know something? Most of the time he's talking to you.

BIFF What's he say about me?

HAPPY I can't make it out.

BIFF What's he say about me?

HAPPY I think the fact that you're not settled, that you're still kind of up in the air...

BIFF   There's one or two other things depressing him, Happy.

HAPPY   What do you mean?

BIFF   Never mind. Just don't lay it all to me.

HAPPY   But I think if you just got started—I mean—is there any future for you out there?

BIFF   I tell ya, Hap, I don't know what the future is. I don't know—what I'm supposed to want.

HAPPY   What do you mean?

BIFF   Well, I spent six or seven years after high school trying to work myself up. Shipping clerk, salesman, business of one kind or another. And it's a measly manner of existence. To get on that subway on the hot mornings in summer. To devote your whole life to keeping stock, or making phone calls, or selling or buying. To suffer fifty weeks of the year for the sake of a two-week vacation, when all you really desire is to be outdoors, with your shirt off. And always to have to get ahead of the next fella. And still—that's how your build a future.

HAPPY   Well, you really enjoy it on a farm? Are you content out there?

BIFF   (*with rising agitation*) Hap, I've had twenty or thirty different kinds of jobs since I left home before the war, and it always turns out the same. I just realized it lately. In Nebraska when I herded cattle, and the Dakotas, and Arizona, and now in Texas. It's why I came home now, I guess, because I realized it. This farm I work on, it's spring there now, see? And they've got about fifteen new colts. There's nothing more inspiring or—beautiful than the sight of a mare and a new colt. And it's cool there now, see? Texas is cool now, and it's spring. And whenever spring comes to where I am, I suddenly get the feeling, my God, I'm not getting' anywhere! What the hell am I doing, playing around with horses, twenty-eight dollars a week! I'm thirty-four years old, I oughta be makin' my future. That's when I come running home. And now, I get here, and I don't know what to do with myself. (*After a pause.*) I've always made a point of not wasting my life, and every time I come back here I know that all I've done is to waste my life.

HAPPY   You're a poet, you know that, Biff? You're a—you're an idealist!

BIFF   No, I'm mixed up very bad. Maybe I oughta get married. Maybe I oughta get stuck into something. Maybe that's my trouble. I'm like a boy. I'm not married, I'm not in business, I just—I'm like a boy. Are you content, Hap? You're a success, aren't you? Are you content?

HAPPY   Hell, no!

BIFF   Why? You're making money, aren't you?

HAPPY   (*moving about with energy, expressiveness*) All I can do now is wait for the merchandise manager to die. And suppose I get to be merchandise manager? He's a good friend of mine, and he just built a terrific estate on Long Island. And he lived there about two months and sold it, and now he's building another one. He can't enjoy it once it's finished. And I know that's just what I would do. I don't know what the hell I'm workin' for. Sometimes I sit in my apartment—all alone. And I think of the rent I'm paying. And it's crazy. But then, it's what I always wanted. My own apartment, a car, and plenty of women. And still, goddammit, I'm lonely.

BIFF   (*with enthusiasm*) Listen, why don't you come out West with me?

HAPPY   You and I, heh?

BIFF   Sure, maybe we could buy a ranch. Raise cattle, use our muscles. Men built like we are should be working out in the open.

HAPPY   (*avidly*) The Loman Brothers, heh?

BIFF   (*with vast affection*) Sure, we'd be known all over the countries!

HAPPY   (*enthralled*) That's what I dream about, Biff. Sometimes I want to just rip my clothes off in the middle of the store and outbox that goddam merchandise manager. I mean I can outbox, outrun, and outlift anybody in that store, and I have to take orders from those common, petty sons-of-bitches till I can't stand it any more.

BIFF   I'm tellin' you, kid, if you were with me I'd be happy out there.

HAPPY   (*enthused*) See, Biff, everybody around me is so false that I'm constantly lowering my ideals...

BIFF   Baby, together we'd stand up for one another, we'd have someone to trust.

HAPPY   If I were around you—

BIFF   Hap, the trouble is we weren't brought up to grub for money. I don't know how to do it.

HAPPY   Neither can I!

BIFF   Then let's go!

HAPPY The only thing is—what can you make out there?

BIFF But look at your friend. Builds an estate and then hasn't the peace of mind to live in it.

HAPPY Yeah, but when he walks into the store the waves part in front of him. That's fifty-two thousand dollars a year coming through the revolving door, and I got more in my pinky finger than he's got in his head.

BIFF Yeah, but you just said—

HAPPY I gotta show some of those pompous, self-important executives over there that Hap Loman can make the grade. I want to walk into the store the way he walks in. Then I'll go with you, Biff. We'll be together yet, I swear. But take those two we had tonight. Now weren't they gorgeous creatures?

BIFF Yeah, yeah, most gorgeous I've had in years.

HAPPY I get that any time I want, Biff. Whenever I feel disgusted. The only trouble is, it gets like bowling or something. If just keep knockin' them over and it doesn't mean anything. You still run around a lot?

BIFF Naa. I'd like to find a girl—steady, somebody with substance.

HAPPY That's what I long for.

BIFF Go on You'd never come home.

HAPPY I would! Somebody with character, with resistance! Like Mom, y'know? You're gonna call me a bastard when I tell you this. That girl Charlotte I was with tonight is engaged to be married in five weeks. (*He tries on his new hat.*)

BIFF No kiddin'!

HAPPY Sure, the guy's in line for the vice-presidency of the store. I don't know what gets into me, maybe I just have an overdeveloped sense of competition or something, but I went and ruined her, and furthermore I can't get rid of her. And he's the third executive I've done that to. Isn't that a crummy characteristic? And to top it all, I go to their weddings! (*Indignantly, but laughing.*) Like I'm not supposed to take bribes. Manufacturers offer me a hundred-dollar bill now and then to throw an order their way. You know how honest I am, but it's like this girl, see. I hate myself for it. Because I don't want the girl, and, still, I take it and— I love it!

BIFF Let's go to sleep.

HAPPY I guess we didn't settle anything, heh?

BIFF I just got one idea that I think I'm going to try.

HAPPY What's that?

BIFF Remember Bill Oliver?

HAPPY Sure, Oliver is very big now. You want to work for him again?

BIFF No, but when I quit he said something to me. He put his arm on my shoulder, and he said, "Biff, if you ever need anything, come to me."

HAPPY I remember that. That sounds good.

BIFF I think I'll go to see him. If I could get ten thousand or even seven or eight thousand dollars I could buy a beautiful ranch.

HAPPY I bet he'd back you. 'Cause he thought highly of you, Biff, I mean, they all do. You're well liked, Biff. That's why I say to come back here, and we both have the apartment. And I'm tellin' you, Biff, any babe you want...

BIFF No, with a ranch I could do the work I like and still be something. I just wonder though. I wonder if Oliver still thinks I stole that carton of basketballs.

HAPPY Oh, he probably forgot that long ago. It's almost ten years. You're too sensitive. Anyway, he didn't really fire you.

BIFF Well, I think he was going to. I think that's why I quit. I was never sure whether he knew or now. I know he thought the world of me, though. I was the only one he'd let lock up the place.

WILLY (*below*) You gonna wash the engine, Biff?

HAPPY Shh!

(*Biff looks at Happy, who is gazing down, listening. Willy is mumbling in the parlor.*)

HAPPY You hear that?

(*They listen. Willy laughs warmly.*)

BIFF (*growing angry*) Doesn't he know Mom can hear that?

WILLY Don't get your sweater dirty, Biff!

(*A look of pain crosses Biff's face.*)

HAPPY Isn't that terrible? Don't leave again, will you? You'll find a job here. You gotta stick around. I don't know what to do about him, it's getting embarrassing.

WILLY What a simonizing job!

BIFF   Mom's hearing that!

WILLY   No kiddin', Billy, you got a date? Wonderful!

HAPPY   Go on to sleep. But talk to him in the morning, will you?

BIFF   (*reluctantly getting into bed*) With her in the house. Brother!

HAPPY   (*getting into bed*) I wish you'd have a good talk with him.

(*The light on their room begins to fade.*)

BIFF   (*to himself in bed*) That selfish, stupid...

HAPPY   Sh... Sleep, Biff.

(*Their light is out. Well before they have finished speaking, Willy's form is dimly seen below in the darkened kitchen. HE opens the refrigerator, searches in there, and takes out a bottle of milk. The apartment houses are fading out, and the entire house and surroundings become covered with leaves. Music insinuates itself as the leaves appear.*)

WILLY   Just wanna be care with those girls, Biff, that's all. Don't' make any promises. No promises of any kind. Because a girl, y'know, they always believe what you tell'em, and you're very young, Biff, you're too young to be talking seriously to girls.

Questions for Discussion

1. According to the selection, what kind of people are Biff and Happy?
2. What are the causes of their failure?
3. What is the relationship between the brothers and their father?
4. What do you think have caused the failures of the brothers and the illusion of the father?
5. Please explain the theme of the play in its historical context.

About the Author

Arthur Miller (1915—2005) was born in New York. He graduated from the University of Michigan, where he began to write plays. He was a prominent figure in American literature and cinema for over 61 years, writing a wide variety of plays, including celebrated plays such as *The Crucible*, *A View from the Bridge*, *All My Sons*, and *Death of a Salesman*, which are still studied and performed worldwide.

Miller was often in the public eye, most famously for refusing to give evidence against others to the House Un-American Activities Committee, being the recipient of the Pulitzer Prize for Drama among countless other awards, and for his marriage to Marilyn Monroe. Miller is considered by audiences and scholars as one of America's greatest playwrights, and his plays are lauded throughout the world.

In the selection, Willy Loman is a salesman whose career is nearly over. He is a man whose life has been devoted to the dream of success. His boys, Biff Loman and Happy Loman, are the objects of his unbridled adoration, and it had always been his intent to leave them with enough money to begin their own business. Yet Willy's dreams and his life itself are based on self-deception. Despite the flamboyant, exaggerated stories of his successes, his career as a salesman has been mediocre, and he is fired from his position early in the play.

His sons have never fulfilled their father's dreams of achievement. Biff, who had been a high school athlete, cheated on exams to get through school and is refused admission to a good college for failing a math class. Happy is a salesman like his father, and, like his father, a failure and a womanizer. Both of the boys engage in petty thefts in their jobs, furthering the undercurrent of deception in the play.

True West

Sam Shepard

Scene 4

Night. Coyotes in distance, fade, sound of typewriter in dark, crickets, candlelight in alcove, dim light in kitchen, lights reveal Austin at glass table typing, Lee sits across from him, foot on table, drinking beer and whiskey, the T. V. is still on sink counter, Austin types for a while, then stops.

LEE   All right, now read it back to me.

AUSTIN   I'm not reading it back to you, Lee. Yu can read it when we're finished. I can't spend all night on this.

LEE   You got better things to do?

AUSTIN   Let's just go ahead. Now what happens when he leaves Texas?

LEE   (*Sitting up.*) No, see this is one a' the crucial parts. Right here. (*Taps paper with beer can.*) We can't rush through this. He's not right at the border. He's a good fifty miles from the border. A lot can happen in fifty miles.

AUSTIN   It's only an outline. We're not writing an entire script now.

LEE   Well ya' can't leave things out even if it is an outline. It's one a' the most important parts. Ya' can't go leavin' it out.

AUSTIN   Okay, okay. Let's just—get it done.

LEE   All right. Now. He's in the truck and he's got his horse trailer and his horse.

AUSTIN   We've already established that.

LEE   And he sees this other guy comin' up behind him in another truck. And that truck is pullin' a gooseneck.

AUSTIN   What's a gooseneck?

LEET   Cattle trailer. You know the kind with a gooseneck, goes right down in the bed a' the pick-up.

AUSTIN   Oh. All right. (*Types.*)

LEE   It's important.

AUSTIN   Okay. I got it.

LEE All these details are important.

(*Austin types as they talk.*)

AUSTIN I've got it.

LEE And this other guy's got his horse all saddled up in the back a' the gooseneck.

AUSTIN Right.

LEE So both these guys have got their horses right along with 'em, see.

AUSTIN I understand.

LEE Then this first guy suddenly realizes two things.

AUSTIN The guy in front?

LEE Right. The guy in front realizes two things almost at the same time. Simultaneous.

AUSTIN What were the two things?

LEE Number one, he realizes that the guy behind him is the husband of the woman he's been—

(*Lee makes gesture of screwing by pumping his arm.*)

AUSTIN (*Sees Lee's gesture.*) Oh, Yeah.

LEE And number two, he realizes he's in the middle of Tornado Country.

AUSTIN What's "Tornado Country"?

LEE Panhandle.

AUSTIN Panhandle?

LEE Sweetwater. Around in that area. Nothin'. Nowhere. And number three—

AUSTIN I thought there was only two.

LEE There's three. There's a third unforeseen realization.

AUSTIN And what's that?

LEE That he's runnin' outa' gas.

AUSTIN (*Stops typing.*) Come on, Lee.

(*Austin gets up, moves to kitchen, gets a glass of water.*)

LEE Whadya' mean, "come on"? That's what it is. Write it down! He's runnin' outa' gas.

AUSTIN Its too—

LEE What? It's too what? It's too real! That's what ya' mean isn't it? It's too much like real life!

AUSTIN It's not like real life! It's not enough like real life. Things don't happen like that.

LEE   What! Men don't fuck other men's women?

AUSTIN   Yes. But they don't end up chasing each other across the Panhandle. Through "Tornado Country."

LEE   They do in this movie!

AUSTIN   And they don't have horses conveniently along with them when they run out of gas! And they don't run out of gas either!

LEE   These guys run outa' gas! This is my story and one a' these guys runs outa' gas!

AUSTIN   It's just a dumb excuse to get them into a chase scene. It's contrived.

LEE   It is a chase scene! It's already a chase scene. They been chasin' each other fer days.

AUSTIN   So now they're supposed to abandon their trucks, climb on their horses and chase each other into the mountains?

LEE   (*Standing suddenly.*) There aren't any mountains in Panhandle! It's flat!

(*Lee turns violently toward windows in alcove and throws beer can at them.*)

LEE   Goddamn these crickets! (*Yells at crickets.*) Shut up out there! (*Pause, turns back toward table.*) This place is like a fuckin' rest home here. How're you supposed to think!

AUSTIN   You wanna' take a break?

LEE   No, I don't wann' take a break! I wanna' get this done! This is my last chance to get this done.

AUSTIN   (*Moves back into alcove.*) All right. Take it easy.

LEE   I'm gonna' be leavin' this area. I don't have time to mess around here.

AUSTIN   Where are you going?

LEE   Never mind where I'm goin'! That's got nothin' to do with you. I just gotta' get this done. I'm not like you. Hangin' around bein' a parasite offa' other fools. I gotta' do this thing and get out.

(*Pause*)

AUSTIN   A parasite? Me?

LEE   Yeah, you!

AUSTIN   After you break into people's houses and take their televisions?

LEE   They don't need their televisions! I'm doin' them a service.

AUSTIN Give me back my keys, Lee.

LEE Not until you write this thing! You're gonna' write this outline thing for me or that car's gonna' wind up in Arizona with a different paint job.

AUSTIN You think you can force me to write this? I was doing you a favor.

LEE Git off yer high horse will ya'! Favor! Big favor. Handin' down favors from the mountain top.

AUSTIN Let's just write it, okay? Let sit down and not get upset and see if we can just get through this.

(*Austin sits at typewriter.*)

(*Long pause.*)

LEE Yer not gonna' even show it to him, are ya?

AUSTIN What?

LEE This outline. You got no intention of showin' it to him. Yer just doin' this 'cause yer afaid a' me.

AUSTIN You can show it to him youself.

LEE I will, boy! I'm gonna' read it to him on the golf course.

AUSTIN And I'm not afaid of you either.

LEE Then how come yer doin' it?

AUSTIN (*Pause.*) So I can get my keys back.

(*Pause as Lee takes keys out of his pocket slowly and throws them on table, long pause, Austin stare at keys.*)

LEE There. Now you got yer keys back.

(*Austin slowly takes keys off table and puts them back in his own pocket.*)

Now what're you gonna' do? Kick me out?

AUSTIN I'm not going to kick you out, Lee.

LEE You couldn't kick me out, boy.

AUSTIN I know.

LEE So you can't even consider that one. (*Pause.*) You could call the police. That'd be the obvious thing.

AUSTIN You're my brother.

LEE That don't mean a thing. You go down to the L. A. Police Department there and ask them what kina' people kill each other the most. What do you think they'd say?

AUSTIN Who said anything about killing?

LEE Family people. Brothers. Brothers-in-law. Cousins, Real American-type people. They kill each other in the heat mostly. In the Smog-Alerts. In the Brush Fire Season. Right about this time a' year.

AUSTIN This isn't the same.

LEE Oh no? What makes it different?

AUSTIN We're not insane. We're not driven to acts of violence like that. Not over a dumb movie script. Now sit down.

(*Long pause, Lee considers which way to go with it.*)

LEE Maybe not. (*He sits back down at table across from Austin.*) Maybe you're right. Maybe we're too intelligent, huh? (*Pause.*) We got our heads on our shoulders. One of us has even got a Ivy League diploma. Now that means somethi' don't it? Doesn't that mean sometin'?

AUSTIN Look, I'll write this thing for you, Lee. I don't mind writing it. I just don't want to get all worked up about it. It's not worth it. Now, come on. Let's just get through it, okay?

LEE Nah. I think there's easier money. Lotsa' places I could pick up thousands. Maybe millions. I don't need this shit. I could go up to Sacramento Valley, and steal me a diesel. Ten thousand a week dismantling one a' those suckers. Ten thousand a week!

(*Lee opens another beer, puts his foot back up on table.*)

AUSTIN No, really, look, I'll write it out for you. I think it's a great idea.

LEE Nah, you got yer own work to do I don't wanna' interfere with yer life.

AUSTIN I mean it'd be really fantastic if you could sell this. Turn it into a movie. I mean it.

(*Pause*)

LEE Ya' think so huh?

AUSTIN Absolutely. You could really turn your life around, you know. Change thins.

LEE I could get me a house maybe.

AUSTIN Sure you could get a house. You could get a whole ranch if you wanted to.

LEE (*Laughs*) A ranch? I could get a ranch?

AUSTIN 'Course you could. You know what a screenplay sells for these days?

LEE No. What's it sell for?

AUSTIN A lot. A whole lot of money.

LEE Thousands?

AUSTIN Yeah. Thousands.

LEE Millions?

AUSTIN Well—

LEE We could get the old man outa' hock then.

AUSTIN Maybe.

LEE Maybe? Whadya' mean, maybe?

AUSTIN I mean it might take more than money.

LEE You were just tellin' me it'd change my whole life around. Why wouldn't it change his?

AUSTIN He's different.

LEE Oh, he's of a different ilk huh?

AUSTIN He's not gonna' change. Let's leave the old man out of it.

LEE That's right. He's not gonna' change but I will. I'll just turn myself right inside out. I could be just like you then, huh? Sittin' around dreamin' stuff up. Gettin' paid to dream. Ridn' back and forth on the freeway just dreamin' my fool head off.

AUSTIN It's not all that easy.

LEE It's not, huh?

AUSTIN No. There's a lot of work involved.

LEE What's the toughest part? Deciding whether to jog or play tennis?

(*Long pause.*)

AUSTIN Well, look. You can stay here—do whatever you want to. Borrow the car. Come in and out. Doesn't matter to me. It's not my house. I'll help you write this thing or—not. Just let me know what you want. You tell me.

LEE Oh. So now suddenly you're at my service. Is that it?

AUSTIN What do you want to do Lee?

(*Long pause, Lee stares at him then turns and dreams at windows.*)

LEE I tell ya' what I'd do if I still had that dog. Ya' wanna' know what I'd do?

AUSTIN What?

LEE Head out to Ventura. Cook up a little match. God that little dog could bear down. Lota' money in dog fightin'. Big money.

(*Pause*)

AUSTIN Why don't we try to see this through, Lee. Just for the hell of it.

Maybe you've really got something here. What do you think?

(*Pause, Lee considers.*)

LEE   Maybe so. No harm in tryin' I guess. You think it's such a hot idea. Besides, I always wondered what'd be like to be you.

AUSTIN   You did?

LEE   Yeah, sure. I used to picture you walkin' around some campus with yer arms fulla' books. Blondes chasin' after ya'.

AUSTIN   Blondes? Thats funny.

LEE   What's funny about it?

AUSTIN   Because I always used to picture you somewhere.

LEE   Where'd you picture me?

AUSTIN   Oh, I don't know. Different places. Adventures. You were always on some adventure.

LEE   Yeah.

AUSTIN   And I used to say to myself, "LEE's got the right idea. He's out there in the world and here I am. What am I doing?"

LEE   Well you were settin' yourself up for somethin'.

AUSTIN   I guess.

LEE   We better get started on this thing then.

AUSTIN   Okay.

(*Austin sits up at typewriter, puts new paper in.*)

LEE   Oh. Can I get the keys back before I forget?

(*Austin hesitates.*)

You said I could borrow the car if I wanted, right? Isn't that what you said?

AUSTIN   Yeah. Right.

(*Austin takes keys out of his pocket, sets them on table, Lee takes keys slowly, plays with them in his hand.*)

LEE   I could get a ranch, huh?

AUSTIN   Yeah. We have to write it first though.

LEE   Okay. Let's write it.

(*Lights start dimming slowly to end as Austin types, Lee speaks.*)

So they take off after each other straight into an endless black prairie. The sun is just comin' down and they can feel the night on their backs. What they don't know is that each one of 'em is afraid, see. Each one separately thinks that he's the only one that's afraid. And they keep ridin' like that straight into the night. Not knowing. And the one who's chasin' doesn't know where the other one is taking him. And the one who's being chased doesn't know where he's going.

(*Light to black, typing stops in the dark, crickets fade.*)

Questions for Discussion

1. What are the two brothers like?
2. What is the relation between them?
3. What are their different attitudes toward the project they are working on?
4. What do you think the two brothers represent?
5. What is the implication or the meaning of "true west"?

About the Author

Sam Shepard (1943—), U.S. playwright and actor. Born in Ft. Sheridan, Ill., he worked as an actor and rock musician before writing the early one-act dramas and experimental plays that were performed off-Broadway in the 1960s, winning several Obie awards.

Shepard became very much involved in New York's off-off-Broadway theater scene, beginning at the age of nineteen. Although his plays were staged at several off-off-Broadway venues, he was most closely connected with Theatre Genesis, housed at St. Mark's Church in the East Village. He acted occasionally in those days, but his interests were almost strictly confined to writing, up until the late 1970s. After three years of living in England, in 1976 Shepard relocated to the San Francisco Bay Area and was named playwright in residence at the Magic Theatre where many of his works received their premier productions. Throughout the years, Shepard has done a considerable amount of teaching on playwriting and other aspects of theatre. His classes and seminars have occurred at various theatre workshops, festivals, and universities. During the 1970s he served a stint as a Regents Professor at the University of California, Davis. In 1986, Shepard was elected to The American Academy of Arts and Letters. In 2000, Shepard decided to repay a debt of gratitude to the Magic Theatre by staging his play *The Late Henry Moss* as a benefit in San Francisco.

Shepard is an American artist who worked as an award-winning playwright, writer and actor. His many written works are known for being frank and often absurd, as well as for having an authentic sense of the style and sensibility of the gritty modern American west.

The selected play is about two brothers: Austin is an ambitious Hollywood screenwriter working on a potential million-dollar deal when an ill wind off the desert blows in Lee, a hobo thief with a six-pack and a case of sibling rivalry. The conflict arises when a film producer offers Lee to write a "true" west. In a role reversal as intricate as it is riveting, the brothers head toward Shepard's outrageous version of the Western movie showdown.

Fiction

The Tell-Tale Heart

Edgar Allan Poe

True! —Nervous—very, very dreadfully nervous I had been and am; but why *will* you say that I am mad? The disease had sharpened my senses—not destroyed —not dulled them. Above all was the sense of hearing acute. I heard all things in the heaven and in the earth. I heard many things in hell[①]. How, then, am I mad? Hearken! and observe how healthily—how calmly I can tell you the whole story.

It is impossible to say how first the idea entered my brain; but once conceived, it haunted me day and night. Object there was none. Passion there was none. I loved the old man. He had never wronged me. He had never given me insult. For his gold I had no desire. I think it was his eye! Yes, it was this! One of his eyes resembled that of a vulture—a pale blue eye, with a film over it. Whenever it fell upon me, my blood ran cold; and so by degrees—very gradually—I made up my mind to take the life of the old man, and thus rid myself of the eye forever.

Now this is the point. You fancy me mad. Madmen know nothing. But you should have seen *me*. You should have seen how wisely I proceeded—with what caution—with what foresight—with what dissimulation I went to work! I was never kinder to the old man than during the whole week before I killed him. And every night, about midnight, I turned the latch of his door and opened it—oh, so gently! And then, when I had made an opening sufficient for my head, I put in a dark lantern, all closed, closed, so that no light shone out, and then I thrust in my head. Oh, you would have laughed to see how cunningly I thrust it in! I moved it slowly—very, very slowly, so that I might not disturb the old man's sleep. It took me an hour to place my whole head within the opening so far that I could see him as he lay upon his bed. Ha! —Would a madman have been so wise as this? And then, when my head was well in the room, I undid the lantern cautiously—oh, so cautiously—cautiously (for the hinges creaked) —I undid it

---

① Philippians 2:10, "That at the name of Jesus every knee should bow, of things in heaven, and things in earth, and things under the earth."

just so much that a single thin ray fell upon the vulture eye. And this I did for seven long nights—every night just at midnight—but I found the eye always closed; and so it was impossible to do the work; for it was not the old man who vexed me, but his Evil Eye. And every morning, when the day broke, I went boldly into the chamber, and spoke courageously to him, calling him by name in a hearty tone, and inquiring how he had passed the night. So you see he would have been a very profound old man, indeed, to suspect that every night, just at twelve, I looked in upon him while he slept.

Upon the eighth night I was more than usually cautious in opening the door. A watch's minute hand moves more quickly than did mine. Never, before that night, had I *felt* the extent of my own powers—of my sagacity. I could scarcely contain my feelings of triumph. To think that there I was, opening the door, little by little, and he not even to dream of my secret deeds or thoughts. I fairly chuckled at the idea; and perhaps he heard me; for he moved on the bed suddenly, as if startled. Now you may think that I drew back—but no. His room was as black as pitch with the thick darkness, (for the shutters were close fastened, through fear of robbers,) and so I knew that he could not see the opening of the door, and I kept pushing it on steadily, steadily.

I had my head in, and was about to open the lantern, when my thumb slipped upon the tin fastening, and the old man sprang up in the bed, crying out—"Who's there?"

I kept quite still and said nothing. For a whole hour I did not move a muscle, and in the meantime I did not hear him lie down. He was still sitting up in the bed, listening; —just as I have done, night after night, hearkening to the death watches① in the wall.

Presently I heard a slight groan, and I knew it was the groan of mortal terror. It was not a groan of pain or of grief—oh, no! —It was the low stifled sound that arises from the bottom of the soul when overcharged with awe. I knew the sound well. Many a night, just at midnight, when all the world slept, it has welled up from my own bosom, deepening, with its dreadful echo, the terrors that distracted me. I say I knew it well. I knew what the old man felt, and pitied him, although I chuckled at heart. I knew that he had been lying awake ever since the first slight noise, when he had turned in the bed. His fears had been ever

---

① A beetle.

since growing upon him. He had been trying to fancy them causeless, but could not. He had been saying to himself—"It is nothing but the wind in the chimney—it is only a mouse crossing the floor," or "it is merely a cricket which has made a single chirp." Yes, he had been trying to comfort himself with these suppositions: but he had found all in vain. *All in vain*; because Death, in approaching him, had stalked with his black shadow before him, and enveloped the victim. And it was the mournful influence of the unperceived shadow that caused him to feel—although he neither saw nor heard—to *feel* the presence of my head within the room.

When I had waited a long time, very patiently, without hearing him lie down, I resolved to open a little—a very, very little crevice in the lantern. So I opened it—you cannot imagine how stealthily, stealthily—until, at length, a simple dim ray, like the thread of the spider, shot from out the crevice and fell full upon the vulture eye.

It was open—wide, wide open—and I grew furious as I gazed upon it. I saw it with perfect distinctness—all a dull blue, with a hideous veil over it that chilled the very marrow in my bones; but I could see nothing else of the old man's face or person[①]: for I had directed the ray as if by instinct, precisely upon the damned spot.

And now—have I not told you that what you mistake for madness is but over acuteness of the sense? —Now, I say, there came to my ears a low, dull, quick sound, such as a watch makes when enveloped in cotton. I knew *that* sound well, too. It was the beating of the old man's heart. It increased my fury, as the beating of a drum stimulates the soldier into courage.

But even yet I refrained and kept still. I scarcely breathed. I held the lantern motionless. I tried how steadily I could maintain the ray upon the eye. Meantime the hellish tattoo of the heart increased. It grew quicker and quicker, and louder and louder every instant. The old man's terror *must* have been extreme! It grew louder, I say, louder every moment! —Do you mark me well? I have told you that I am nervous: so I am. And now at the dead hour of the night, amid the dreadful silence of that old house, so strange a noise as this excited me to uncontrollable terror. Yet, for some minutes longer I refrained and stood still. But the beating grew louder, louder! I thought the heart must burst. And now a new anxiety

---

① Body.

seized me—the sound would be heard by a neighbour! The old man's hour had come! With a loud yell, I threw open the lantern and leaped into the room. He shrieked once—once only. In an instant I dragged him to the floor, and pulled the heavy bed over him. I then smiled gaily, to find the deed so far done. But, for many minutes, the heart beat on with a muffled sound. This, however, did not vex me; it would not be heard through the wall. At length it ceased. The old man was dead. I removed the bed and examined the corpse. Yes, he was stone, stone dead. I placed my hand upon the heart and held it there many minutes. There was no pulsation. He was stone dead. His eye would trouble me no more.

If still you think me mad, you will think so no longer when I describe the wise precautions I took for the concealment of the body. The night waned, and I worked hastily, but in silence. First of all I dismembered the corpse. I cut off the head and the arms and the legs.

I then took up three planks from the flooring of the chamber, and deposited all between the scantlings. I then replaced the boards so cleverly, so cunningly, that no human eye—not even *his*—could have detected any thing wrong. There was nothing to wash out—no stain of any kind—no blood-spot whatever. I had been too wary for that. A tub had caught all—ha! ha!

When I had made an end of these labors, it was four o'clock—still dark as midnight. As the bell sounded the hour, there came a knocking at the street door. I went down to open it with a light heart,—for what had I *now* to fear? There entered three men, who introduced themselves, with perfect suavity, as officers of the police. A shriek had been heard by a neighbour during the night; suspicion of foul play had been aroused; information had been lodged at the police office, and they (the officers) had been deputed to search the premises.

I smiled,—for *what* had I to fear? I bade the gentlemen welcome. The shriek, I said, was my own in a dream. The old man, I mentioned, was absent in the country. I took my visitors all over the house. I bade them search—search *well*. I led them, at length, to *his* chamber. I showed them his treasures, secure, undisturbed. In the enthusiasm of my confidence, I brought chairs into the room, and desired them *here* to rest from their fatigues, while I myself, in the wild audacity of my perfect triumph, placed my own seat upon the very spot beneath which reposed the corpse of the victim.

The officers were satisfied. My *manner* had convinced them. I was singularly at ease. They sat, and while I answered cheerily, they chatted of familiar things. But, ere long, I felt myself getting pale and wished them gone. My head ached, and I fancied a ringing in my ears: but still they sat and still chatted. The ringing became more distinct:—it continued and became more distinct: I talked more freely to get rid of the feeling: but it continued and gained definiteness—until, at length, I found that the noise was not within my ears.

No doubt I now grew *very* pale; —but I talked more fluently, and with a heightened voice. Yet the sound increased—and what could I do? It was a *low, dull, quick sound—much such a sound as a watch makes when enveloped in cotton*. I gasped for breath—and yet the officers heard it not. I talked more quickly—more vehemently; but the noise steadily increased. I arose and argued about trifles, in a high key and with violent gesticulations; but the noise steadily increased. Why would they not be gone? I paced the floor to and fro with heavy strides, as if excited to fury by the observations of the men—but the noise steadily increased. Oh God! what *could* I do? I foamed—I raved—I swore! I swung the chair upon which I had been sitting, and grated it upon the boards, but the noise arose over all and continually increased. It grew louder—louder—louder! And still the men chatted pleasantly, and smiled. Was it possible they heard not? Almighty God! —No, no! They heard! —They suspected! —They knew! —They were making a mockery of my horror! —This I thought, and this I think. But anything was better than this agony! Anything was more tolerable than this derision! I could bear those hypocritical smiles no longer! I felt that I must scream or die! —And now—again! —Hark! Louder! Louder! Louder! Louder! —

"Villains!" I shrieked, "dissemble no more! I admit the deed! —Tear up the planks! Here, here! —It is the beating of his hideous heart!"

Questions for Discussion

1. This story seems to be a murderer's confession of his guilt. To whom is he confessing and why does he confess it?
2. What is the murderer's motive to kill the old man?
3. Do you think Poe's description of the murderer's psychology believable?
4. What is the advantage of the first-person narrator in this story?

About the Author

Edgar Allan Poe (1809—1849) is known as a poet, critic, short story writer and perhaps the world's master of the macabre.

Born in Boston, on January 19, 1809, he was taken care of by John and Frances Allan after his parents died. After spending a short period at the University of Virginia and briefly attempting a military career, Poe left the Allans, and then moved into the home of his aunt, and her daughter Virginia, whom he married later.

He began to publish poems at the age of 15. In 1835, he became the editor of the *Southern Literary Messenger* in Richmond. Over the next ten years, Poe would edit a number of literary journals. It was during these years that he established himself as a poet, a short-story writer, and an editor. He published some of his best-known stories and poems including *The Fall of the House of Usher*, *The Tell-Tale Heart*, *The Murders in the Rue Morgue*, and *The Raven*. Poe died in 1849.

His stories mark him as one of the originators of both horror and detective fiction. Many anthologies credit him as the "architect" of the modern short story. He was also one of the first critics to focus primarily on the effect of the style and of the structure in a literary work; as such, he has been seen as a forerunner to the "art for art's sake" movement. French Symbolists such as Mallarmé and Rimbaud claimed him as a literary precursor.

The Tell-Tale Heart, first published in 1843, is widely considered a classic of the Gothic fiction genre and one of Poe's most famous short stories. It follows an unnamed narrator who insists on his sanity after murdering an old man with a "vulture eye".

The Egg

Sherwood Anderson

My father was, I am sure, intended by nature to be a cheerful, kindly man. Until he was thirty-four years old he worked as a farm-hand for a man named Thomas Butterworth whose place lay near the town of Bidwell, Ohio. He had then a horse of his own and on Saturday evenings drove into town to spend a few hours in social intercourse with other farm-hands. In town he drank several glasses of beer and stood about in Ben Head's saloon—crowded on Saturday evenings with visiting farm-hands. Songs were sung and glasses thumped on the bar. At ten o'clock father drove home along a lonely country road, made his horse comfortable for the night, and himself went to bed, quite happy in his position in life. He had at that time no notion of trying to rise in the world.

It was in the spring of his thirty-fifth year that father married my mother, then a country school-teacher, and in the following spring I came wriggling and crying into the world. Something happened to the two people. They became ambitious. The American passion for getting up in the world took possession of them.

It may have been that mother was responsible. Being a school-teacher she had no doubt read books and magazines. She had, I presume, read of how Garfield①, Lincoln, and other Americans rose from poverty to fame and greatness and as I lay beside her—in the days of her lying-in—she may have dreamed that I would some day rule men and cities. At any rate she induced father to give up his place as a farm-hand, sell his horse and embark on an independent enterprise of his own. She was a tall silent woman with a long nose and troubled gray eyes. For herself she wanted nothing. For father and myself she was incurably ambitious.

The first venture into which the two people went turned out badly. They rented ten acres of poor stony land on Grigg's Road, eight miles from Bidwell, and launched into chicken raising. I grew into boyhood on the place and got my

---

① James A. Garfield (1831—1881) was the twentieth president of the United States. Like the narrator, he was born on an Ohio farm and grew up in poverty.

first impressions of life there. From the beginning they were impressions of disaster and if, in my turn, I am a gloomy man inclined to see the darker side of life, I attribute it to the fact that what should have been for me the happy joyous days of childhood were spent on a chicken farm.

One unversed in such matters can have no notion of the many and tragic things that can happen to a chicken. It is born out of an egg, lives for a few weeks as a tiny fluffy thing such as you will see pictured on Easter cards①, then becomes hideously naked, eats quantities of corn and meal bought by the sweat of your father's brow, gets diseases called pip, cholera, and other names, stands looking with stupid eyes at the sun, becomes sick and dies. A few hens and now and then a rooster, intended to serve God's mysterious ends②, struggle through to maturity. The hens lay eggs out of which come other chickens and the dreadful cycle is thus made complete. It is all unbelievably complex. Most philosophers must have been raised on chicken farms. One hopes for so much from a chicken and is so dreadfully disillusioned. Small chickens, just setting out on the journey of life, look so bright and alert and they are in fact so dreadfully stupid. They are so much like people they mix one up in one's judgments of life. If disease does not kill them, they wait until your expectations are thoroughly aroused and then walk under the wheels of a wagon—to go squashed and dead back to their maker. Vermin infest their youth, and fortunes must be spent for curative powders. In later life I have seen how a literature has been built up on the subject of fortunes to be made out of the raising of chickens. It is intended to be read by the gods who have just eaten of the tree of the knowledge of good and evil③. It is a hopeful literature and declares that much may be done by simple ambitious people who own a few hens. Do not be led astray by it. It was not written for you. Go hunt for gold on the frozen hills of Alaska, put your faith in the honesty of a politician, believe if you will that the world is daily growing better and that good will triumph over evil, but do not read and believe the literature that is written concerning the hen. It was not written for you.

---

① Cards of greetings for Easter, an annual Christian festival held on the first Sunday after the date of the first full moon that occurs on or after March 21.
② According to the Bible, everything on earth was created by God. God first made man and woman, and then other things to accompany them. So the phrase here means to live on as God meant.
③ Originally it refers to Adam and Eve who, after eating from the tree of knowledge in the Garden of Eden, were sent down to earth. Here it means by those who are ambitious in life and will suffer from it.

I, however, digress. My tale does not primarily concern itself with the hen. If correctly told it will center on the egg. For ten years my father and mother struggled to make our chicken farm pay and then they gave up that struggle and began another. They moved into the town of Bidwell, Ohio and embarked in the restaurant business. After ten years of worry with incubators that did not hatch, and with tiny—and in their own way lovely—balls of fluff that passed on into semi-naked pullethood and from that into dead henhood, we threw all aside and packing our belongings on a wagon drove down Grigg's Road toward Bidwell, a tiny caravan of hope looking for a new place from which to start on our upward journey through life.

We must have been a sad looking lot, not, I fancy, unlike refugees fleeing from a battlefield. Mother and I walked in the road. The wagon that contained our goods had been borrowed for the day from Mr. Albert Griggs, a neighbor. Out of its side stuck the legs of cheap chairs and at the back of the pile of beds, tables, and boxes filled with kitchen utensils was a crate of live chickens, and on top of that the baby carriage in which I had been wheeled about in my infancy. Why we stuck to the baby carriage I don't know. It was unlikely other children would be born and the wheels were broken. People who have few possessions cling tightly to those they have. That is one of the facts that make life so discouraging.

Father rode on top of the wagon. He was then a baldheaded man of forty-five, a little fat, and from long association with mother and the chickens he had become habitually silent and discouraged. All during our ten years on the chicken farm he had worked as a laborer on neighboring farms and most of the money he had earned had been spent for remedies to cure chicken diseases, on Wilmer's White Wonder Cholera Cure or Professor Bidlow's Egg Producer or some other preparations that mother found advertised in the poultry papers. There were two little patches of hair on father's head just above his ears. I remember that as a child I used to sit looking at him when he had gone to sleep in a chair before the stove on Sunday afternoons in the winter. I had at that time already begun to read books and have notions of my own, and the bald path that led over the top of his head was, I fancied, some thing like a broad road, such a road as Caesar[①] might have made on which to lead his legions out of Rome and into the wonders

---

① Julius G. Caesar, ancient Roman general, statesman and dictator of the Roman Empire.

of an unknown world. The tufts of hair that grew above father's ears were, I thought, like forests. I fell into a half sleeping, half waking state and dreamed I was a tiny thing going along the road into a far beautiful place where there were no chicken farms and where life was a happy eggless affair.

One might write a book concerning our flight from the chicken farm into town. Mother and I walked the entire eight miles—she to be sure that nothing fell from the wagon and I to see the wonders of the world. On the seat of the wagon beside father was his greatest treasure. I will tell you of that.

On a chicken farm where hundreds and even thousands of chickens come out of eggs surprising things sometimes happen. Grotesques are born out of eggs as out of people. The accident does not often occur—perhaps once in a thousand births. A chicken is, you see, born that has four legs, two pairs of wings, two heads, or what not. The things do not live. They go quickly back to the hand of their maker that has for a moment trembled. The fact that the poor little things could not live was one of the tragedies of life to father. He had some sort of notion that if he could but bring into henhood or roosterhood a five-legged hen or a two-headed rooster his fortune would be made. He dreamed of taking the wonder about to the county fairs and of growing rich by exhibiting it to other farm-hands.

At any rate he saved all the little monstrous things that had been born on our chicken farm. They were preserved in alcohol and put each in its own glass bottle. These he had carefully put into a box and on our journey into town it was carried on the wagon seat beside him. He drove the horses with one hand and with the other clung to the box. When we got to our destination the box was taken down at once and the bottles removed. All during our days as keepers of a restaurant in the town of Bidwell, Ohio, the grotesques in their little glass bottles sat on a shelf back of the counter. Mother sometimes protested but father was a rock on the subject of his treasure. The grotesques were, he declared, valuable. People, he said, liked to look at strange and wonderful things.

Did I say that we embarked in the restaurant business in the town of Bidwell, Ohio? I exaggerated a little. The town itself lay at the foot of a low hill and on the shore of a small river. The railroad did not run through the town and the station was a mile away to the north at a place called Pickleville. There had been a cider mill and pickle factory at the station, but before the time of our coming they had both gone out of business. In the morning and in the evening buses came down to the station along a road called Turner's Pike from the hotel on the main street of Bidwell. Our going to the out of the way place to embark in the restaurant business was mother's idea. She talked of it for a year and then one day went off and rented an empty store building opposite the railroad station. It was her idea that the restaurant would be profitable. Traveling men, she said, would be always waiting around to take trains out of town and town people would come to the station to await incoming trains. They would come to the restaurant to buy pieces of pie and drink coffee. Now that I am older I know that she had another motive in going. She was ambitious for me. She wanted me to rise in the world, to get into a town school and become a man of the towns.

At Pickleville father and mother worked hard as they always had done. At first there was the necessity of putting our place into shape to be a restaurant. That took a month. Father built a shelf on which he put tins of vegetables. He painted a sign on which he put his name in large red letters. Below his name was the sharp command—"EAT HERE"—that was so seldom obeyed. A showcase was bought and filled with cigars and tobacco. Mother scrubbed the floors and the walls of the room. I went to school in the town and was glad to be away from the farm, and from the presence of the discouraged, sad-looking chickens. Still I was not very joyous. In the evening I walked home from school along Turner's Pike and remembered the children I had seen playing in the town school yard. A troop of little girls had gone hopping about and singing. I tried that. Down along the frozen road I went hopping solemnly on one leg. "Hippity Hop To the Barber Shop," I sang shrilly. Then I stopped and looked doubtfully about. I was afraid of being seen in my gay mood. It must have seemed to me that I was doing a thing that should not be done by one who, like myself, had been raised on a chicken farm where death was a daily visitor.

Mother decided that our restaurant should remain open at night. At ten in the evening a passenger train went north past our door followed by a local freight. The freight crew had switching to do in Pickleville and when the work was done they came to our restaurant for hot coffee and food. Sometimes one of them ordered a fried egg. In the morning at four they resumed north-bound and again visited us. A little trade began to grow up. Mother slept at night and during the day tended the restaurant and fed our boarders while father slept. He slept in the same bed mother had occupied during the night and I went off to the town of Bidwell and to school. During the long nights, while mother and I slept, father cooked meats that were to go into sandwiches for the lunch baskets of our boarders. Then an idea in regard to getting up in the world came into his head. The American spirit took hold of him. He also became ambitious.

In the long nights when there was little to do father had time to think. That was his undoing. He decided that he had in the past been an unsuccessful man because he had not been cheerful enough and that in the future he would adopt a cheerful outlook on life. In the early morning he came upstairs and got into bed with mother. She woke and the two talked. From my bed in the corner I listened.

It was father's idea that both he and mother should try to entertain the people who came to eat at our restaurant. I cannot now remember his words, but he gave the impression of one about to become in some obscure way a kind of public entertainer. When people, particularly young people from the town of Bidwell, came into our place, as on very rare occasions they did, bright entertaining conversation was to be made. From father's words I gathered that something of the jolly innkeeper effect was to be sought. Mother must have been doubtful from the first, but she said nothing discouraging. It was father's notion that a passion for the company of himself and mother would spring up in the breasts of the younger people of the town of Bidwell. In the evening bright happy groups would come singing down Turner's Pike. They would troop shouting with joy and laughter into our place. There would be song and festivity. I do not mean to give the impression that father spoke so elaborately of the matter. He was as I have said an uncommunicative man. "They want some place to go. I tell you they want some place to go," he said over and over. That was as far as he got. My own imagination has filled in the blanks.

For two or three weeks this notion of father's invaded our house. We did not talk much, but in our daily lives tried earnestly to make smiles take the place of glum looks. Mother smiled at the boarders and I, catching the infection, smiled at our cat. Father became a little feverish in his anxiety to please. There was no doubt, lurking somewhere in him, a touch of the spirit of the showman. He did not waste much of his ammunition on the railroad men he served at night but seemed to be waiting for a young man or woman from Bidwell to come in to show what he could do. On the counter in the restaurant there was a wire basket kept always filled with eggs, and it must have been before his eyes when the idea of being entertaining was born in his brain. There was something pre-natal about the way eggs kept themselves connected with the development of his idea. At any rate an egg ruined his new impulse in life. Late one night I was awakened by a roar of anger coming from father's throat. Both mother and I sat upright in our beds. With trembling hands she lighted a lamp that stood on a table by her head. Downstairs the front door of our restaurant went shut with a bang and in a few minutes father tramped up the stairs. He held an egg in his hand and his hand trembled as though he were having a chill. There was a half insane light in his eyes. As he stood glaring at us I was sure he intended throwing the egg at either mother or me. Then he laid it gently on the table beside the lamp and dropped on his knees beside mother's bed. He began to cry like a boy and I, carried away by his grief, cried with him. The two of us filled the little upstairs room with our wailing voices. It is ridiculous, but of the picture we made I can remember only the fact that mother's hand continually stroked the bald path that ran across the top of his head. I have forgotten what mother said to him and how she induced him to tell her of what had happened downstairs. His explanation also has gone out of my mind. I remember only my own grief and fright and the shiny path over father's head glowing in the lamp light as he knelt by the bed.

As to what happened downstairs. For some unexplainable reason I know the story as well as though I had been a witness to my father's discomfiture. One in time gets to know many unexplainable things. On that evening young Joe Kane, son of a merchant of Bidwell, came to Pickleville to meet his father, who was expected on the ten o'clock evening train from the South. The train was three hours late and Joe came into our place to loaf about and to wait for its arrival. The local freight train came in and the freight crew were fed. Joe was left alone in the restaurant with father.

From the moment he came into our place the Bidwell young man must have been puzzled by my father's actions. It was his notion that father was angry at him for hanging around. He noticed that the restaurant keeper was apparently disturbed by his presence and he thought of going out. However, it began to rain and he did not fancy the long walk to town and back. He bought a five-cent cigar and ordered a cup of coffee. He had a newspaper in his pocket and took it out and began to read. "I'm waiting for the evening train. It's late," he said apologetically.

For a long time father, whom Joe Kane had never seen before, remained silently gazing at his visitor. He was no doubt suffering from an attack of stage fright. As so often happens in life he had thought so much and so often of the situation that now confronted him that he was somewhat nervous in its presence.

For one thing, he did not know what to do with his hands. He thrust one of them nervously over the counter and shook hands with Joe Kane. "How-de-do," he said. Joe Kane put his newspaper down and stared at him. Father's eyes lighted on the basket of eggs that sat on the counter and he began to talk. "Well," he began hesitatingly, "well, you have heard of Christopher Columbus, eh?" He seemed to be angry. "That Christopher Columbus was a cheat," he declared emphatically. "He talked of making an egg stand on its end. He talked, he did, and then he went and broke the end of the egg."

My father seemed to his visitor to be beside himself at the duplicity of Christopher Columbus. He muttered and swore. He declared it was wrong to teach children that Christopher Columbus was a great man when, after all, he cheated at the critical moment. He had declared he would make an egg stand on end and then when his bluff had been called he had done a trick. Still grumbling at Columbus, father took an egg from the basket on the counter and began to walk up and down. He rolled the egg between the palms of his hands. He smiled genially. He began to mumble words regarding the effect to be produced on an egg by the electricity that comes out of the human body. He declared that without breaking its shell and by virtue of rolling back and forth in his hands he could stand the egg on its end. He explained that the warmth of his hands and the gentle rolling movement he gave the egg created a new center of gravity, and Joe Kane was mildly interested. "I have handled thousands of eggs," father said. "No one knows more about eggs than I do."

He stood the egg on the counter and it fell on its side. He tried the trick again and again, each time rolling the egg between the palms of his hands and saying the words regarding the wonders of electricity and the laws of gravity. When after a half hour's effort he did succeed in making the egg stand for a moment he looked up to find that his visitor was no longer watching. By the time he had succeeded in calling Joe Kane's attention to the success of his effort, the egg had again rolled over and lay on its side.

Afire with the showman's passion and at the same time a good deal disconcerted by the failure of his first effort, father now took the bottles containing the poultry monstrosities down from their place on the shelf and began to show them to his visitor. "How would you like to have seven legs and two heads like this fellow?" he asked, exhibiting the most remarkable of his treasures. A cheerful smile played over his face. He reached over the counter and tried to slap Joe Kane on the shoulder as he had seen men do in Ben Head's saloon when he was a young farm-hand and drove to town on Saturday evenings. His visitor was made a little ill by the sight of the body of the terribly deformed bird floating in the alcohol in the bottle and got up to go. Coming from behind the counter father took hold of the young man's arm and led him back to his seat. He grew a little angry and for a moment had to turn his face away and force himself to smile. Then he put the bottles back on the shelf. In an outburst of generosity he fairly compelled Joe Kane to have a fresh cup of coffee and another cigar at his expense. Then he took a pan and filling it with vinegar, taken from a jug that sat beneath the counter, he declared himself about to do a new trick. "I will heat this egg in this pan of vinegar," he said. "Then I will put it through the neck of a bottle without breaking the shell. When the egg is in side the bottle it will resume its normal shape and the shell will become hard again. Then I will give the bottle with the egg in it to you. You can take it about with you wherever you go. People will want to know how you got the egg in the bottle. Don't tell them. Keep them guessing. That is the way to have fun with this trick."

Father grinned and winked at his visitor. Joe Kane decided that the man who confronted him was mildly insane but harmless. He drank the cup of coffee that had been given him and began to read his paper again. When the egg had been heated in vinegar father carried it on a spoon to the counter and going into a back room got an empty bottle. He was angry because his visitor did not watch him as he began to do his trick, but nevertheless went cheerfully to work. For a long time he struggled, trying to get the egg to go through the neck of the bottle. He put the pan of vinegar back on the stove, intending to reheat the egg, then picked it up and burned his fingers. After a second bath in the hot vinegar the shell of the egg had been softened a little but not enough for his purpose. He worked and worked and a spirit of desperate determination took possession of him. When he thought that at last the trick was about to be consummated the delayed train came in at the station and Joe Kane started to go nonchalantly out at the door. Father made a last desperate effort to conquer the egg and make it do the thing that would establish his reputation as one who knew how to entertain guests who came into his restaurant. He worried the egg. He attempted to be somewhat rough with it. He swore and the sweat stood out on his forehead. The egg broke under his hand. When the contents spurted over his clothes, Joe Kane, who had stopped at the door, turned and laughed.

A roar of anger rose from my father's throat. He danced and shouted a string of inarticulate words. Grabbing another egg from the basket on the counter, he threw it, just missing the head of the young man as he dodged through the door and escaped.

Father came upstairs to mother and me with an egg in his hand. I do not know what he intended to do. I imagine he had some idea of destroying it, of destroying all eggs, and that he intended to let mother and me see him begin. When, however, he got into the presence of mother something happened to him. He laid the egg gently on the table and dropped on his knees by the bed as I have already explained. He later decided to close the restaurant for the night and to come upstairs and get into bed. When he did so, he blew out the light and after much muttered conversation both he and mother went to sleep. I suppose I went to sleep also, but my sleep was troubled. I awoke at dawn and for a long time looked at the egg that lay on the table. I wondered why eggs had to be and why from the egg came the hen who again laid the egg. The question got into my blood. It has stayed there. I imagine because I am the son of my father. At any rate, the problem remains unsolved in my mind. And that, I conclude, is but another evidence of the complete and final triumph of the egg—at least as far as my family is concerned.

Questions for Discussion

1. What kind of man was the narrator's father before he married? What changes did he undergo after marriage?
2. How does the narrator feel about and view chickens?
3. What role does the father's collection of "grotesques" play in the story?
4. What is the meaning of the narrator's statement at the end of the story about "the complete and final triumph of the egg"?
5. Why is the story entitled "The Egg"? What does the egg symbolize in this story?

About the Author

Sherwood Anderson (1876—1941) is an American writer, mainly of short stories. The influence of his book *Winesburg, Ohio* on American fiction was profound, and its literary voice can be heard in Ernest Hemingway, William Faulkner, Thomas Wolfe, John Steinbeck, Erskine Caldwell and others.

Born of a poor family in a small town in Ohio, he had a few years of schooling. At the age of 14, he began his restless career, drifting from job to job. For a time he settled in his native state, was married, and became the manager of a paint factory. But without explanations, he suddenly left his home, abandoning his wife and children, and went to Chicago to become a writer.

His *Winesburg, Ohio*, was published in 1919 and attracted wide attention. Thus he was widely hailed as a writer of genius. *The Triumph of the Egg* (1921), a collection of short stories was almost as successful as *Winesburg, Ohio*. But most of his subsequent works were not as well received as these two books.

Anderson's works record America's transition from a rural society into an industrial one, and show that with industrialization, village peace and stability have departed. He wrote about lonely, sad people, deformed in their characters by frustrations imposed by their societies and environment and felt compassion for such emotionally twisted grotesques, because they were the victims of modern existence.

Strongly influenced by Mark Twain's "colloquial tradition", Anderson's style of writing appears simple, easy, almost conversational. In fact, his stories were very carefully constructed, closer to real life than to literary art.

The Egg, taken from Sherwood Anderson's second short story collection, *The Triumph of the Egg* (New York: Huebsch, 1921) is a humorous tale about a farmer who, "intended by nature to be a cheerful, kindly man" becomes infected with the American passion for "success" and turns into a grotesque.

Part Two American Literature

Rip Van Winkle

Washington Irving

    Whoever has made a voyage up the Hudson must remember the Kaatskill mountains. They are a dismembered branch of the great Appalachian family, and are seen away to the west of the river, swelling up to a noble height, and lording it over the surrounding country. Every change of season, every change of weather, indeed, every hour of the day produces some change in the magical hues and shapes of these mountains; and they are regarded by all the good wives, far and near, as perfect barometers. When the weather is fair and settled, they are clothed in blue and purple, and print their bold outlines on the clear evening sky; but sometimes, when the rest of the landscape is cloudless, they will gather a hood of gray vapors about their summits, which, in the last rays of the setting sun, will glow and light up like a crown of glory.

    At the foot of these fairy mountains, the voyager may have descried the light smoke curling up from a Village, whose shingle roofs gleam among the trees, just where the blue tints of the upland melt away into the fresh green of the nearer landscape. It is a little village of great antiquity, having been founded by some of the Dutch colonists, in the early times of the province, just about the beginning of the government of the good Peter Stuyvesant (may he rest in peace!), and there were some of the houses of the original settlers standing within a few years, built of small yellow bricks, brought from Holland, having latticed windows and gable fronts, surmounted with weathercocks.

    In that same village, and in one of these very houses (which, to tell the precise truth, was sadly time-worn and weather-beaten), there lived, many years since, while the country was yet a province of Great Britain, a simple, good-natured fellow, of the name of Rip Van Winkle. He was a descendant of the Van Winkles who figured so gallantly in the chivalrous days of Peter Stuyvesant, and accompanied him to the siege of Fort Christina. He inherited, however, but little of the martial character of his ancestors. I have observed that he was a simple, good-natured man; he was, moreover, a kind neighbor, and an obedient henpecked husband. Indeed, to the latter circumstance might be owing that meekness of spirit which gained him such universal popularity; for those men are apt to be obsequious and conciliating abroad, who are under the discipline of shrews at home. Their tempers, doubtless, are rendered pliant and malleable in the fiery furnace of domestic tribulation, and a curtain-lecture is worth all the sermons in the world for teaching the virtues of patience and long-suffering. A termagant wife may, therefore, in some respects, be considered a tolerable blessing, and if so, Rip Van Winkle was thrice blessed.

Certain it is, that he was a great favorite among all the good wives of the village, who, as usual with the amiable sex, took his part in all family squabbles, and never failed, whenever they talked those matters over in their evening gossipings, to lay all the blame on Dame Van Winkle. The children of the village, too, would shout with joy whenever he approached. He assisted at their sports, made their playthings, taught them to fly kites and shoot marbles, and told them long stories of ghosts, witches, and Indians. Whenever he went dodging about the village, he was surrounded by a troop of them hanging on his skirts, clambering on his back, and playing a thousand tricks on him with impunity; and not a dog would bark at him throughout the neighborhood.

The great error in Rip's composition was an insuperable aversion to all kinds of profitable labor. It could not be for want of assiduity or perseverance; for he would sit on a wet rock, with a rod as long and heavy as a Tartar's lance, and fish all day without a murmur, even though he should not be encouraged by a single nibble. He would carry a fowling-piece on his shoulder, for hours together, trudging through woods and swamps, and up hill and down dale, to shoot a few squirrels or wild pigeons. He would never refuse to assist a neighbor even in the roughest toil, and was a foremost man in all country frolics for husking Indian corn, or building stone fences; the women of the village, too, used to employ him to run their errands, and to do such little odd jobs as their less obliging husbands would not do for them. In a word, Rip was ready to attend to anybody's business but his own; but as to doing family duty, and keeping his farm in order, he found it impossible.

In fact, he declared it was of no use to work on his farm; it was the most pestilent little piece of ground in the whole country; everything about it went wrong, in spite of him. His fences were continually falling to pieces; his cow would either go astray, or get among the cabbages; weeds were sure to grow quicker in his fields than anywhere else; the rain always made a point of setting in just as he had some out-door work to do; so that though his patrimonial estate had dwindled away under his management, acre by acre, until there was little more left than a mere patch of Indian corn and potatoes, yet it was the worst-conditioned farm in the neighborhood.

His children, too, were as ragged and wild as if they belonged to nobody. His son Rip, an urchin begotten in his own likeness, promised to inherit the habits, with the old clothes, of his father. He was generally seen trooping like a colt at his mother's heels, equipped in a pair of his father's cast-off galligaskins, which he had much ado to hold up with one hand, as a fine lady does her train in bad weather.

Rip Van Winkle, however, was one of those happy mortals, of foolish, well-oiled dispositions, who take the world easy, eat white bread or brown, whichever can be got with least thought or trouble, and would rather starve on a penny than work for a pound. If left to himself, he would have whistled life away, in perfect contentment; but his wife kept continually dinning in his ears about his idleness, his carelessness, and the ruin he was bringing on his family. Morning, noon, and night, her tongue was incessantly going, and every thing he said or did was sure to produce a torrent of household eloquence. Rip had but one way of replying to all lectures of the kind, and that, by frequent use, had grown into a habit. He shrugged his shoulders, shook his head, cast up his eyes, but said nothing. This, however, always provoked a fresh volley from his wife, so that he was fain to draw off his forces, and take to the outside of the house—the only side which, in truth, belongs to a henpecked husband.

Rip's sole domestic adherent was his dog Wolf, who was as much henpecked as his master; for Dame Van Winkle regarded them as companions in idleness, and even looked upon Wolf with an evil eye, as the cause of his master's going so often astray. True it is, in all points of spirit befitting in honorable dog, he was as courageous an animal as ever scoured the woods—but what courage can withstand the evil-doing and all-besetting terrors of a woman's tongue? The moment Wolf entered the house, his crest fell, his tail drooped to the ground, or curled between his legs, he sneaked about with a gallows air, casting many a sidelong glance at Dame Van Winkle, and at the least flourish of a broomstick or ladle, he would fly to the door with yelping precipitation.

Times grew worse and worse with Rip Van Winkle as years of matrimony rolled on; a tart temper never mellows with age, and a sharp tongue is the only edged tool that grows keener with constant use. For a long while he used to console himself, when driven from home, by frequenting a kind of perpetual club of the sages, philosophers, and other idle personages of the village, which held its sessions on a bench before a small inn, designated by a rubicund portrait of his Majesty George the Third. Here they used to sit in the shade through a long, lazy summer's day, talking listlessly over village gossip, or telling endless, sleepy stories about nothing. But it would have been worth any statesman's money to have heard the profound discussions which sometimes took place, when by chance an old newspaper fell into their hands from some passing traveller. How solemnly they would listen to the contents, as drawled out by Derrick Van Bummel, the school-master, a dapper learned little man, who was not to be daunted by the most gigantic word in the dictionary; and how sagely they would deliberate upon public events some months after they had taken place.

The opinions of this junto were completely controlled by Nicholas Vedder, a patriarch of the village, and landlord of the inn, at the door of which he took his seat from morning till night, just moving sufficiently to avoid the sun, and keep in the shade of a large tree; so that the neighbors could tell the hour by his movements as accurately as by a sun-dial. It is true, he was rarely heard to speak, but smoked his pipe incessantly. His adherents, however (for every great man has his adherents), perfectly understood him, and knew how to gather his opinions. When any thing that was read or related displeased him, he was observed to smoke his pipe vehemently, and to send forth, frequent, and angry puffs; but when pleased, he would inhale the smoke slowly and tranquilly, and emit it in light and placid clouds, and sometimes, taking the pipe from his mouth, and letting the fragrant vapor curl about his nose, would gravely nod his head in token of perfect approbation.

From even this stronghold the unlucky Rip was at length routed by his termagant wife, who would suddenly break in upon the tranquillity of the assemblage, and call the members all to nought; nor was that august personage, Nicholas Vedder himself, sacred from the daring tongue of this terrible virago, who charged him outright with encouraging her husband in habits of idleness.

Poor Rip was at last reduced almost to despair; and his only alternative, to escape from the labor of the farm and the clamor of his wife, was to take gun in hand, and stroll away into the woods. Here he would sometimes seat himself at the foot of a tree, and share the contents of his wallet with Wolf, with whom he sympathized as a fellow-sufferer in persecution. "Poor Wolf," he would say, "thy mistress leads thee a dog's life of it; but never mind, my lad, whilst I live thou shalt never want a friend to stand by thee!" Wolf would wag his tail, look wistfully in his master's face, and if dogs can feel pity, I verily believe he reciprocated the sentiment with all his heart.

In a long ramble of the kind, on a fine autumnal day, Rip had unconsciously scrambled to one of the highest parts of the Kaatskill mountains. He was after his favorite sport of squirrel-shooting, and the still solitudes had echoed and reechoed with the reports of his gun. Panting and fatigued, he threw himself, late in the afternoon, on a green knoll, covered with mountain herbage, that crowned the brow of a precipice. From an opening between the trees, he could overlook all the lower country for many a mile of rich woodland. He saw at a distance the lordly Hudson, far, far below him, moving on its silent but majestic course, with the reflection of a purple cloud, or the sail of a lagging bark, here and there sleeping on its glassy bosom and at last losing itself in the blue highlands.

On the other side he looked down into a deep mountain glen, wild, lonely, and shagged, the bottom filled with fragments from the impending cliffs, and scarcely lighted by the reflected rays of the setting sun. For some time Rip lay musing on this scene; evening was gradually advancing; the mountains began to throw their long blue shadows over the valleys; he saw that it would be dark long before he could reach the village; and he heaved a heavy sigh when he thought of encountering the terrors of Dame Van Winkle.

As he was about to descend, he heard a voice from a distance hallooing: "Rip Van Winkle! Rip Van Winkle!" He looked around, but could see nothing but a crow winging its solitary flight across the mountain. He thought his fancy must have deceived him, and turned again to descend, when he heard the same cry ring through the still evening air, "Rip Van Winkle! Rip Van Winkle!"—at the same time Wolf bristled up his back, and giving a low growl, skulked to his master's side, looking fearfully down into the glen. Rip now felt a vague apprehension stealing over him; he looked anxiously in the same direction, and perceived a strange figure slowly toiling up the rocks, and bending under the weight of something he carried on his back. He was surprised to see any human being in this lonely and unfrequented place, but supposing it to be some one of the neighborhood in need of his assistance, he hastened down to yield it.

On nearer approach, he was still more surprised at the singularity of the stranger's appearance. He was a short, square-built old fellow, with thick bushy hair, and a grizzled beard. His dress was of the antique Dutch fashion—a cloth jerkin strapped round the waist—several pairs of breeches, the outer one of ample volume, decorated with rows of buttons down the sides, and bunches at the knees. He bore on his shoulders a stout keg, that seemed full of liquor, and made signs for Rip to approach and assist him with the load. Though rather shy and distrustful of this new acquaintance, Rip complied with his usual alacrity; and mutually relieving each other, they clambered up a narrow gully, apparently the dry bed of a mountain torrent. As they ascended, Rip every now and then heard long rolling peals, like distant thunder, that seemed to issue out of a deep ravine, or rather cleft between lofty rocks, toward which their rugged path conducted. He paused for an instant, but supposing it to be the muttering of one of those transient thunder-showers which often take place in the mountain heights, he proceeded. Passing through the ravine, they came to a hollow, like a small amphitheatre, surrounded by perpendicular precipices, over the brinks of which impending trees shot their branches, so that you only caught glimpses of the azure sky, and the bright evening cloud. During the whole time Rip and his companion had labored on in silence; for though the former marvelled greatly what could be the object of carrying a keg of liquor up this wild mountain, yet there was something strange and incomprehensible about the unknown, that inspired awe, and checked familiarity.

On entering the amphitheatre, new objects of wonder presented themselves. On a level spot in the centre was a company of odd-looking personages playing at ninepins. They were dressed in quaint outlandish fashion; some wore short doublets, others jerkins, with long knives in their belts, and most of them had enormous breeches, of similar style with that of the guide's. Their visages, too, were peculiar; one had a large head, broad face, and small piggish eyes; the face of another seemed to consist entirely of nose, and was surmounted by a white sugar-loaf hat, set off with a little red cock's tail. They all had beards, of various shapes and colors. There was one who seemed to be the commander. He was a stout old gentleman, with a weather-beaten countenance; he wore a laced doublet, broad belt and hanger, high-crowned hat and feather, red stockings, and high-heeled shoes, with roses in them. The whole group reminded Rip of the figures in an old Flemish painting, in the parlor of Dominie Van Schaick, the village parson, and which had been brought over from Holland at the time of the settlement.

What seemed particularly odd to Rip was, that though these folks were evidently amusing themselves, yet they maintained the gravest faces, the most mysterious silence, and were, withal, the most melancholy party of pleasure he had ever witnessed. Nothing interrupted the stillness of the scene but the noise of the balls, which, whenever they were rolled, echoed along the mountains like rumbling peals of thunder.

As Rip and his companion approached them, they suddenly desisted from their play, and stared at him with such a fixed statue-like gaze, and such strange uncouth, lack-lustre countenances, that his heart turned within him, and his knees smote together. His companion now emptied the contents of the keg into large flagons, and made signs to him to wait upon the company. He obeyed with fear and trembling; they quaffed the liquor in profound silence, and then returned to their game.

By degrees, Rip's awe and apprehension subsided. He even ventured, when no eye was fixed upon him, to taste the beverage which he found had much of the flavor of excellent Hollands. He was naturally a thirsty soul, and was soon tempted to repeat the draught. One taste provoked another; and he reiterated his visits to the flagon so often, that at length his senses were overpowered, his eyes swam in his head, his head gradually declined, and he fell into a deep sleep.

On waking, he found himself on the green knoll whence he had first seen the old man of the glen. He rubbed his eyes—it was a bright sunny morning. The birds were hopping and twittering among the bushes, and the eagle was wheeling aloft, and breasting the pure mountain breeze. "Surely," thought Rip, "I have not slept here all night." He recalled the occurrences before he fell asleep. The strange man with the keg of liquor—the mountain ravine—the wild retreat among the rocks—the woe-begone party at ninepins—the flagon—"Oh! that flagon! that wicked flagon!" thought Rip—"what excuse shall I make to Dame Van Winkle?"

He looked round for his gun, but in place of the clean well-oiled fowling-piece, he found an old firelock lying by him, the barrel encrusted with rust, the lock falling off, and the stock worm-eaten. He now suspected that the grave roysterers of the mountains had put a trick upon him, and, having dosed him with liquor, had robbed him of his gun. Wolf, too, had disappeared, but he might have strayed away after a squirrel or partridge. He whistled after him and shouted his name, but all in vain; the echoes repeated his whistle and shout, but no dog was to be seen.

He determined to revisit the scene of the last evening's gambol, and if he met with any of the party, to demand his dog and gun. As he rose to walk, he found himself stiff in the joints, and wanting in his usual activity. "These mountain beds do not agree with me," thought Rip, "and if this frolic, should lay me up with a fit of the rheumatism, I shall have a blessed time with Dame Van Winkle." With some difficulty he got down into the glen: he found the gully up which he and his companion had ascended the preceding evening; but to his astonishment a mountain stream was now foaming down it, leaping from rock to rock, and filling the glen with babbling murmurs. He, however, made shift to scramble up its sides, working his toilsome way through thickets of birch, sassafras, and witch-hazel; and sometimes tripped up or entangled by the wild grape vines that twisted their coils and tendrils from tree to tree, and spread a kind of network in his path.

At length he reached to where the ravine had opened through the cliffs to the amphitheatre; but no traces of such opening remained. The rocks presented a high impenetrable wall, over which the torrent came tumbling in a sheet of feathery foam, and fell into a broad deep basin, black from the shadows of the surrounding forest. Here, then, poor Rip was brought to a stand. He again called and whistled after his dog; he was only answered by the cawing of a flock of idle crows, sporting high in the air about a dry tree that overhung a sunny precipice; and who, secure in their elevation, seemed to look down and scoff at the poor man's perplexities. What was to be done? The morning was passing away, and Rip felt famished for want of his breakfast. He grieved to give up his dog and gun; he dreaded to meet his wife; but it would not do to starve among the mountains. He shook his head, shouldered the rusty firelock, and, with a heart full of trouble and anxiety, turned his steps homeward.

As he approached the village, he met a number of people, but none whom he knew, which somewhat surprised him, for he had thought himself acquainted with every one in the country round. Their dress, too, was of a different fashion from that to which he was accustomed. They all stared at him with equal marks of surprise, and whenever they cast eyes upon him, invariably stroked their chins. The constant recurrence of this gesture, induced Rip, involuntarily, to do, the same, when, to his astonishment, he found his beard had grown a foot long!

He had now entered the skirts of the village. A troop of strange children ran at his heels, hooting after him, and pointing at his gray beard. The dogs, too, not one of which he recognized for an old acquaintance, barked at him as he passed. The very village was altered: it was larger and more populous. There were rows of houses which he had never seen before, and those which had been his familiar haunts had disappeared. Strange names were over the doors—strange faces at the windows—everything was strange. His mind now misgave him; he began to doubt whether both he and the world around him were not bewitched. Surely this was his native village, which he had left but a day before. There stood the Kaatskill mountains—there ran the silver Hudson at a distance—there was every hill and dale precisely as it had always been—Rip was sorely perplexed—"That flagon last night," thought he, "has addled my poor head sadly!"

It was with some difficulty that he found the way to his own house, which he approached with silent awe, expecting every moment to hear the shrill voice of Dame Van Winkle. He found the house gone to decay—the roof had fallen in, the windows shattered, and the doors off the hinges. A half-starved dog, that looked like Wolf, was skulking about it. Rip called him by name, but the cur snarled, showed his teeth, and passed on. This was an unkind cut indeed. —"My very dog," sighed poor Rip, " has forgotten me!"

He entered the house, which, to tell the truth, Dame Van Winkle had always kept in neat order. It was empty, forlorn, and apparently abandoned. This desolateness overcame all his connubial fears—he called loudly for his wife and children—the lonely chambers rang for a moment with his voice, and then all again was silence.

He now hurried forth, and hastened to his old resort, the village inn—but it too was gone. A large rickety wooden building stood in its place, with great gaping windows, some of them broken, and mended with old hats and petticoats, and over the door was painted, "The Union Hotel, by Jonathan Doolittle." Instead of the great tree that used to shelter the quiet little Dutch inn of yore, there now was reared a tall naked pole, with something on the top that looked like a red nightcap, and from it was fluttering a flag, on which was a singular assemblage of stars and stripes—all this was strange and incomprehensible. He recognized on the sign, however, the ruby face of King George, under which he had smoked so many a peaceful pipe, but even this was singularly metamorphosed. The red coat was changed for one of blue and buff, a sword was held in the hand instead of a sceptre, the head was decorated with a cocked hat, and underneath was painted in large characters, "GENERAL WASHINGTON."

There was, as usual, a crowd of folk about the door, but none that Rip recollected. The very character of the people seemed changed. There was a busy, bustling, disputatious tone about it, instead of the accustomed phlegm and drowsy tranquillity. He looked in vain for the sage Nicholas Vedder, with his broad face, double chin, and fair long pipe, uttering clouds of tobacco-smoke, instead of idle speeches; or Van Bummel, the schoolmaster, doling forth the contents of an ancient newspaper. In place of these, a lean, bilious-looking fellow, with his pockets full of handbills, was haranguing, vehemently about rights of citizens-elections—members of Congress—liberty—Bunker's hill—heroes of seventy-six-and other words, which were a perfect Babylonish jargon to the bewildered Van Winkle.

The appearance of Rip, with his long, grizzled beard, his rusty fowling-piece, his uncouth dress, and the army of women and children at his heels, soon attracted the attention of the tavern politicians. They crowded round him, eying him from head to foot, with great curiosity. The orator bustled up to him, and, drawing him partly aside, inquired, "on which side he voted?" Rip stared in vacant stupidity. Another short but busy little fellow pulled him by the arm, and rising on tiptoe, inquired in his ear, "whether he was Federal or Democrat." Rip was equally at a loss to comprehend the question; when a knowing, self-important old gentleman, in a sharp cocked hat, made his way through the crowd, putting them to the right and left with his elbows as he passed, and planting himself before Van Winkle, with one arm akimbo, the other resting on his cane, his keen eyes and sharp hat penetrating, as it were, into his very soul, demanded in an austere tone, "What brought him to the election with a gun on his shoulder, and a mob at his heels; and whether he meant to breed a riot in the village?"

"Alas! gentlemen," cried Rip, somewhat dismayed, "I am a poor, quiet man, a native of the place, and a loyal subject of the King, God bless him!"

Here a general shout burst from the bystanders—"a tory! A tory! A spy! A refugee! Hustle him! Away with him!" It was with great difficulty that the self-important man in the cocked hat restored order; and having assumed a tenfold austerity of brow, demanded again of the unknown culprit, what he came there for, and whom he was seeking. The poor man humbly assured him that he meant no harm, but merely came there in search of some of his neighbors, who used to keep about the tavern.

"Well—who are they? —Name them."

Rip bethought himself a moment, and inquired, Where's Nicholas Vedder?

There was a silence for a little while, when an old man replied, in a thin, piping voice, "Nicholas Vedder? why, he is dead and gone these eighteen years! There was a wooden tombstone in the churchyard that used to tell all about him, but that's rotten and gone too."

"Where's Brom Dutcher?"

"Oh, he went off to the army in the beginning of the war; some say he was killed at the storming of Stony-Point—others say he was drowned in a squall at the foot of Antony's Nose. I don't know —he never came back again."

"Where's Van Bummel, the schoolmaster?"

"He went off to the wars, too; was a great militia general, and is now in Congress."

Rip's heart died away, at hearing of these sad changes in his home and friends, and finding himself thus alone in the world. Every answer puzzled him too, by treating of such enormous lapses of time, and of matters which he could not understand: war—Congress-Stony-Point;—he had no courage to ask after any more friends, but cried out in despair, "Does nobody here know Rip Van Winkle?"

"Oh, Rip Van Winkle!" exclaimed two or three. "Oh, to be sure! That's Rip Van Winkle yonder, leaning against the tree."

Rip looked, and beheld a precise counterpart of himself as he went up the mountain; apparently as lazy, and certainly as ragged. The poor fellow was now completely confounded. He doubted his own identity, and whether he was himself or another man. In the midst of his bewilderment, the man in the cocked hat demanded who he was, and what was his name?

"God knows!" exclaimed he at his wit's end; "I'm not myself—I'm somebody else—that's me yonder-no—that's somebody else, got into my shoes—I was myself last night, but I fell asleep on the mountain, and they've changed my gun, and everything's changed, and I'm changed, and I can't tell what's my name, or who I am!"

The by-standers began now to look at each other, nod, wink significantly, and tap their fingers against their foreheads. There was a whisper, also, about securing the gun, and keeping the old fellow from doing mischief; at the very suggestion of which, the self-important man with the cocked hat retired with some precipitation. At this critical moment a fresh, comely woman pressed through the throng to get a peep at the gray-bearded man. She had a chubby child in her arms, which, frightened at his looks, began to cry. "Hush, Rip," cried she, "hush, you little fool; the old man won't hurt you." The name of the child, the air of the mother, the tone of her voice, all awakened a train of recollections in his mind.

"What is your name, my good woman?" asked he.

"Judith Gardenier."

"And your father's name?"

"Ah, poor man, Rip Van Winkle was his name, but it's twenty years since he went away from home with his gun, and never has been heard of since,—his dog came home without him; but whether he shot himself, or was carried away by the Indians, nobody can tell. I was then but a little girl."

Rip had but one more question to ask; but he put it with a faltering voice:

"Where's your mother?"

Oh, she too had died but a short time since; she broke a blood-vessel in a fit of passion at a New-England pedler.

There was a drop of comfort, at least, in this intelligence. The honest man could contain himself no longer. He caught his daughter and her child in his arms. "I am your father!" cried he—"Young Rip Van Winkle once-old Rip Van Winkle now—Does nobody know poor Rip Van Winkle!"

All stood amazed, until an old woman, tottering out from among the crowd, put her hand to her brow, and peering under it in his face for a moment exclaimed, "sure enough! It is Rip Van Winkle—it is himself. Welcome home again, old neighbor. Why, where have you been these twenty long years?"

Rip's story was soon told, for the whole twenty years had been to him but as one night. The neighbors stared when they heard it; some were seen to wink at each other, and put their tongues in their cheeks; and the self-important man in the cocked hat, who, when the alarm was over, had returned to the field, screwed down the corners of his mouth, and shook his head—upon which there was a general shaking of the head throughout the assemblage.

It was determined, however, to take the opinion of old Peter Vanderdonk, who was seen slowly advancing up the road. He was a descendant of the historian of that name, who wrote one of the earliest accounts of the province.

Peter was the most ancient inhabitant of the village, and well versed in all the wonderful events and traditions of the neighborhood. He recollected Rip at once, and corroborated his story in the most satisfactory manner. He assured the company that it was a fact, handed down from his ancestor, the historian, that the Kaatskill mountains had always been haunted by strange beings. That it was affirmed that the great Hendrick Hudson, the first discoverer of the river and country, kept a kind of vigil there every twenty years, with his crew of the Half-moon; being permitted in this way to revisit the scenes of his enterprise, and keep a guardian eye upon the river and the great city called by his name. That his father had once seen them in their old Dutch dresses playing at ninepins in the hollow of the mountain; and that he himself had heard, one summer afternoon, the sound of their balls, like distant peals of thunder.

To make a long story short, the company broke up, and returned to the more important concerns of the election. Rip's daughter took him home to live with her; she had a snug, well-furnished house, and a stout cheery farmer for a husband, whom Rip recollected for one of the urchins that used to climb upon his back. As to Rip's son and heir, who was the ditto of himself, seen leaning against the tree, he was employed to work on the farm; but evinced an hereditary disposition to attend to anything else but his business.

Rip now resumed his old walks and habits; he soon found many of his former cronies, though all rather the worse for the wear and tear of time; and preferred making friends among the rising generation, with whom be soon grew into great favor.

Having nothing to do at home, and being arrived at that happy age when a man can be idle with impunity, he took his place once more on the bench, at the inn door, and was reverenced as one of the patriarchs of the village, and a chronicle of the old times "before the war." It was some time before he could get into the regular track of gossip, or could be made to comprehend the strange events that had taken place during his torpor. How that there had been a revolutionary war—that the country had thrown off the yoke of old England—and that, instead of being a subject to his Majesty George the Third, he was now a free citizen of the United States. Rip, in fact, was no politician; the changes of states and empires made but little impression on him; but there was one species of despotism under which he had long groaned, and that was—petticoat government. Happily, that was at an end; he had got his neck out of the yoke of matrimony, and could go in and out whenever he pleased, without dreading the tyranny of Dame Van Winkle. Whenever her name was mentioned, however, he shook his head, shrugged his shoulders, and cast up his eyes; which might pass either for an expression of resignation to his fate, or joy at his deliverance.

He used to tell his story to every stranger that arrived at Mr. Doolittle's hotel. He was observed, at first, to vary on some points every time he told it, which was, doubtless, owing to his having so recently awaked. It at last settled down precisely to the tale I have related, and not a man, woman, or child in the neighborhood, but knew it by heart. Some always pretended to doubt the reality of it, and insisted that Rip had been out of his head, and that this was one point on which he always remained flighty. The old Dutch inhabitants, however, almost universally gave it full credit. Even to this day, they never hear a thunder-storm of a summer afternoon about the Kaatskill, but they say Hendrick Hudson and his crew are at their game of ninepins; and it is a common wish of all henpecked husbands in the neighborhood, when life hangs heavy on their hands, that they might have a quieting draught out of Rip Van Winkle's flagon.

Questions for Discussion

1. Have you found anything similar in the story's treatment of time with any Chinese story? What are they?
2. What kind of people is Rip Van Winkle?

About the Author

Washington Irving (1783—1859) is called the "first *American.* man of letters." Born in New York City, he began his career as a lawyer but soon became a leader of the group that published Salmagundi (1807—1808), a periodical containing whimsical essays and poems. After his comic *Knickerbocker's History of New York* (1809), he wrote little until his very successful *The Sketch Book* (1819—1820), containing his best-known stories, *The Legend of Sleepy Hollow* and *Rip Van Winkle*. It was followed by a sequel, *Bracebridge Hall* (1822). He held diplomatic positions in Madrid, where his writings (including *The Alhambra*, 1832) reflected his interest in Spain's past, then spent most of his later life at his Hudson River home, "Sunnyside."

A Clean, Well-Lighted Place

Ernest Hemingway

It was very late and everyone had left the cafe except an old man who sat in the shadow the leaves of the tree made against the electric light. In the day time the street was dusty, but at night the dew settled the dust and the old man liked to sit late because he was deaf and now at night it was quiet and he felt the difference. The two waiters inside the cafe knew that the old man was a little drunk, and while he was a good client they knew that if he became too drunk he would leave without paying, so they kept watch on him.

"Last week he tried to commit suicide," one waiter said.

"Why?"

"He was in despair."

"What about?"

"Nothing."

"How do you know it was nothing?"

"He has plenty of money."

They sat together at a table that was close against the wall near the door of the cafe and looked at the terrace where the tables were all empty except where the old man sat in the shadow of the leaves of the tree that moved slightly in the wind. A girl and a soldier went by in the street. The street light shone on the brass number on his collar. The girl wore no head covering and hurried beside him.

"The guard will pick him up," one waiter said.

"What does it matter if he gets what he's after?"

"He had better get off the street now. The guard will get him. They went by five minutes ago."

The old man sitting in the shadow rapped on his saucer with his glass. The younger waiter went over to him.

"What do you want?"

The old man looked at him. "Another brandy," he said.

"You'll be drunk," the waiter said. The old man looked at him. The waiter went away.

"He'll stay all night," he said to his colleague. "I'm sleepy now. I never get into bed before three o'clock. He should have killed himself last week."

The waiter took the brandy bottle and another saucer from the counter inside the cafe and marched out to the old man's table. He put down the saucer and poured the glass full of brandy.

"You should have killed yourself last week," he said to the deafman. The old man motioned with his finger. "A little more," he said. The waiter poured on into the glass so that the brandy slopped over and ran down the stem into the top saucer of the pile. "Thank you," the old man said. The waiter took the bottle back inside the cafe. He sat down at the table with his colleague again.

"He's drunk now," he said.

"He's drunk every night."

"What did he want to kill himself for?"

"How should I know."

"How did he do it?"

"He hung himself with a rope."

"Who cut him down?"

"His niece."

"Why did they do it?"

"Fear for his soul."

"How much money has he got?" "He's got plenty."

"He must be eighty years old."

"Anyway I should say he was eighty."

"I wish he would go home. I never get to bed before three o'clock. What kind of hour is that to go to bed?"

"He stays up because he likes it."

"He's lonely. I'm not lonely. I have a wife waiting in bed for me."

"He had a wife once too."

"A wife would be no good to him now."

"You can't tell. He might be better with a wife."

"His niece looks after him. You said she cut him down."

"I know." "I wouldn't want to be that old. An old man is a nasty thing."

"Not always. This old man is clean. He drinks without spilling. Even now, drunk. Look at him."

"I don't want to look at him. I wish he would go home. He has no regard for those who must work."

The old man looked from his glass across the square, then over at the waiters.

"Another brandy," he said, pointing to his glass. The waiter who was in a hurry came over.

"Finished," he said, speaking with that omission of syntax stupid people employ when talking to drunken people or foreigners. "No more tonight. Close now."

"Another," said the old man.

"No. Finished." The waiter wiped the edge of the table with a towel and shook his head.

The old man stood up, slowly counted the saucers, took a leather coin purse from his pocket and paid for the drinks, leaving half a peseta tip. The waiter watched him go down the street, a very oldman walking unsteadily but with dignity.

"Why didn't you let him stay and drink?" the unhurried waiter asked. They were putting up the shutters. "It is not half-past two."

"I want to go home to bed."

"What is an hour?"

"More to me than to him."

"An hour is the same."

"You talk like an old man yourself. He can buy a bottle and drink at home."

"It's not the same."

"No, it is not," agreed the waiter with a wife. He did not wish to be unjust. He was only in a hurry.

"And you? You have no fear of going home before your usual hour?"

"Are you trying to insult me?"

"No, hombre, only to make a joke."

"No," the waiter who was in a hurry said, rising from pulling down the metal shutters. "I have confidence. I am all confidence."

"You have youth, confidence, and a job," the older waiter said. "You have everything."

"And what do you lack?"

"Everything but work."

"You have everything I have."

"No. I have never had confidence and I am not young."

"Come on. Stop talking nonsense and lock up."

"I am of those who like to stay late at the cafe," the older waiter said.

"With all those who do not want to go to bed. With all those who need a light for the night."

"I want to go home and into bed."

"We are of two different kinds," the older waiter said. He was now dressed to go home. "It is not only a question of youth and confidence although those things are very beautiful. Each night I am reluctant to close up because there may be some one who needs the cafe."

"Hombre, there are bodegas open all night long."

"You do not understand. This is a clean and pleasant cafe. It is well lighted. The light is very good and also, now, there are shadows of the leaves."

"Good night," said the younger waiter.

"Good night," the other said. Turning off the electric light he continued the conversation with himself. It was the light of course but it is necessary that the place be clean and pleasant. You do not want music. Certainly you do not want music. Nor can you stand before a bar with dignity although that is all that is provided for these hours. What did he fear? It was not a fear or dread. It was a nothing that he knew too well. It was all a nothing and a man was a nothing too. It was only that and light was all it needed and a certain cleanness and order. Some lived in it and never felt it but he knew it all was nada y pues nada y nada y pues nada. Our nada who art in nada, nada be thy name thy kingdom nada thy will be nada in nada as it is in nada. Give us this nada our daily nada and nada us our nada as we nada our nadas and nada us not into nada but deliver us from nada; pues nada. Hail nothing full of nothing, nothing is with thee. He smiled and stood before a bar with a shining steam pressure coffee machine.

"What's yours?" asked the barman.

"Nada."

"Otro loco mas," said the barman and turned away.

"A little cup," said the waiter.

The barman poured it for him.

"The light is very bright and pleasant but the bar is unpolished," the waiter said.

The barman looked at him but did not answer. It was too late at night for conversation.

"You want another copita?" the barman asked.

"No, thank you," said the waiter and went out. He disliked bars and bodegas. A clean, well-lighted cafe was a very different thing. Now, without thinking further, he would go home to his room. He would lie in the bed and finally, with daylight, he would go to sleep. After all, he said to himself, it's probably only insomnia. Many must have it.

Questions for Discussion

1. What is the significance of the clean well-lighted place in the development of the story?
2. How do you judge the old man?

About the Author

Ernest Hemingway (1899—1961) is an American novelist and short story writer. He was regarded as a representative of "the Lost Generation." His distinctive writing style, characterized by economy and understatement, had a significant influence on the development of twentieth-century fiction writing.

He was born in Oak Park, Illinois, started his career as a writer in a newspaper office in Kansas City at the age of seventeen. After the United States entered the First World War, he joined a volunteer ambulance unit in the Italian army. Serving at the front, he was wounded, was decorated by the Italian Government, and spent considerable time in hospitals. After his return to the United States, he became a reporter for Canadian and American newspapers and was soon sent back to Europe to cover such events as the Greek Revolution.

During the twenties, Hemingway became a member of the group of expatriate Americans in Paris, which he described in his first important work, *The Sun Also Rises* (1926). Equally successful was *A Farewell to Arms* (1929), the study of an American ambulance officer's disillusionment in the war and his role as a deserter. Hemingway used his experiences as a reporter during the civil war in Spain as the background for his most ambitious novel, *For Whom the Bell Tolls* (1940). Among his later works, the most outstanding is the short novel, *The Old Man and the Sea* (1952), the story of an old fisherman's journey, his long and lonely struggle with a fish and the sea, and his victory in defeat.

Hemingway—himself a great sportsman—liked to portray soldiers, hunters, bullfighters—tough, at times primitive people whose courage and honesty are set against the brutal ways of modern society, and who in this confrontation lose hope and faith. His straightforward prose, his spare dialogue, and his predilection for understatement are particularly effective in his short stories, some of which are collected in *Men Without Women* (1927) and *The Fifth Column and the First Forty-Nine Stories* (1938). Hemingway received the Nobel Prize for literature in 1954 and killed himself in Idaho in 1961.

"Soldier's Home", first collected in *In Our Time* (1925), is a story about a soldier's life, before and after the First World War. Hemingway referred to it as "the best short story" he had ever written. It is clear that in one way or another, or perhaps in many ways, "Soldier's Home" is a tale that is heavily influenced by the life of its writer.

A Rose for Emily

William Faulkner

I

When Miss Emily Grierson died, our whole town went to her funeral: the men through a sort of respectful affection for a fallen monument, the women mostly out of curiosity to see the inside of her house, which no one save an old manservant—a combined gardener and cook—had seen in at least ten years.

It was a big, squarish frame house that had once been white, decorated with cupolas and spires and scrolled balconies in the heavily lightsome style of the seventies, set on what had once been our most select street. But garages and cotton gins had encroached and obliterated even the august names of that neighborhood; only Miss Emily's house was left, lifting its stubborn and coquettish decay above the cotton wagons and the gasoline pumps—an eyesore among eyesores. And now Miss Emily had gone to join the representatives of those august names where they lay in the cedar-bemused cemetery among the ranked and anonymous graves of Union and Confederate[①] soldiers who fell at the battle of Jefferson.

Alive, Miss Emily had been a tradition, a duty, and a care; a sort of hereditary obligation upon the town, dating from that day in 1894 when Colonel Sartoris[②], the mayor—he who fathered the edict that no Negro woman should appear on the streets without an apron—remitted her taxes, the dispensation dating from the death of her father on into perpetuity. Not that Miss Emily would have accepted charity. Colonel Sartoris invented an involved tale to the effect that Miss Emily's father had loaned money to the town, which the town, as a matter of business, preferred this way of repaying. Only a man of Colonel Sartoris' generation and thought could have invented it, and only a woman could have believed it.

When the next generation, with its more modern ideas, became mayors and aldermen, this arrangement created some little dissatisfaction. On the first of the

---

① This refers to the American Civil War, or the war between the South and the North.
② A famous character in many of Faulkner's stories.

year they mailed her a tax notice. February came, and there was no reply. They wrote her a formal letter, asking her to call at the sheriff's office at her convenience. A week later the mayor wrote her himself, offering to call or to send his car for her, and received in reply a note on paper of an archaic shape, in a thin, flowing calligraphy in faded ink, to the effect that she no longer went out at all. The tax notice was also enclosed, without comment.

They called a special meeting of the Board of Aldermen. A deputation waited upon her, knocked at the door through which no visitor had passed since she ceased giving china-painting lessons eight or ten years earlier. They were admitted by the old Negro into a dim hall from which a stairway mounted into still more shadow. It smelled of dust and disuse—a close, dank smell. The Negro led them into the parlor. It was furnished in heavy, leather-covered furniture. When the Negro opened the blinds of one window, they could see that the leather was cracked; and when they sat down, a faint dust rose sluggishly about their thighs, spinning with slow motes in the single sun-ray. On a tarnished gilt easel before the fireplace stood a crayon portrait of Miss Emily's father.

They rose when she entered—a small, fat woman in black, with a thin gold chain descending to her waist and vanishing into her belt, leaning on an ebony cane with a tarnished gold head. Her skeleton was small and spare; perhaps that was why what would have been merely plumpness in another was obesity in her. She looked bloated, like a body long submerged in motionless water, and of that pallid hue. Her eyes, lost in the fatty ridges of her face, looked like two small pieces of coal pressed into a lump of dough as they moved from one face to another while the visitors stated their errand.

She did not ask them to sit. She just stood in the door and listened quietly until the spokesman came to a stumbling halt. Then they could hear the invisible watch ticking at the end of the gold chain.

Her voice was dry and cold. "I have no taxes in Jefferson[①]. Colonel Sartoris explained it to me. Perhaps one of you can gain access to the city records and satisfy yourselves."

"But we have. We are the city authorities, Miss Emily. Didn't you get a

---

① The name for this fictitious town.

notice from the sheriff①, signed by him?"

"I received a paper, yes," Miss Emily said. "Perhaps he considers himself the sheriff... I have no taxes in Jefferson."

"But there is nothing on the books to show that, you see we must go by the—"

"See Colonel Sartoris. I have no taxes in Jefferson."

"But, Miss Emily—"

"See Colonel Sartoris." (Colonel Sartoris had been dead almost ten years.) "I have no taxes in Jefferson. To be!" The Negro appeared. "Show these gentlemen out."

II

So she vanquished them, horse and foot, just as she had vanquished their fathers thirty years before about the smell. That was two years after her father's death and a short time after her sweetheart—the one we believed would marry her—had deserted her. After her father's death she went out very little; after her sweetheart went away, people hardly saw her at all. A few of the ladies had the temerity to call, but were not received, and the only sign of life about the place was the Negro man—a young man then—going in and out with a market basket.

"Just as if a man—any man—could keep a kitchen properly, "the ladies said; so they were not surprised when the smell developed. It was another link between the gross, teeming world and the high and mighty Griersons.

A neighbor, a woman, complained to the mayor, Judge Stevens, eighty years old.

"But what will you have me do about it, madam?" he said.

"Why, send her word to stop it," the woman said. "Isn't there a law?"

"I'm sure that won't be necessary," Judge Stevens said. "It's probably just a snake or a rat that nigger of hers killed in the yard. I'll speak to him about it."

The next day he received two more complaints, one from a man who came in diffident deprecation. "We really must do something about it, Judge. I'd be the last one in the world to bother Miss Emily, but we've got to do something."

---

① (in the US) An elected officer in a local area (county) with duties including carrying out the orders of courts and preserving public order. 治安官员

That night the Board of Aldermen met—three gray-beards and one younger man, a member of the rising generation.

"It's simple enough," he said. "Send her word to have her place cleaned up. Give her a certain time to do it in, and if she don't..."

"Dammit, sir," Judge Stevens said, "will you accuse a lady to her face of smelling bad?"

So the next night, after midnight, four men crossed Miss Emily's lawn and slunk about the house like burglars, sniffing along the base of the brickwork and at the cellar openings while one of them performed a regular sowing motion with his hand out of a sack slung from his shoulder. They broke open the cellar door and sprinkled lime there, and in all the outbuildings. As they recrossed the lawn, a window that had been dark was lighted and Miss Emily sat in it, the light behind her, and her upright torso motionless as that of an idol. They crept quietly across the lawn and into the shadow of the locusts that lined the street. After a week or two the smell went away.

That was when people had begun to feel really sorry for her. People in our town, remembering how old lady Wyatt, her great-aunt, had gone completely crazy at last, believed that the Griersons held themselves a little too high for what they really were. None of the young men were quite good enough for Miss Emily and such. We had long thought of them as a tableau; Miss Emily a slender figure in white in the background, her father a spraddled silhouette① in the foreground, his back to her and clutching a horsewhip, the two of them framed by the back-flung front door. So when she got to be thirty and was still single, we were not pleased exactly, but vindicated; even with insanity in the family she wouldn't have turned down all of her chances if they had really materialized.

When her father died, it got about that the house was all that was left to her; and in a way, people were glad. At last they could pity Miss Emily. Being left alone, and a pauper, she had become humanized. Now she too would know the old thrill and the old despair of a penny more or less.

The day after his death all the ladies prepared to call at the house and offer condolence and aid, as is our custom. Miss Emily met them at the door, dressed as usual and with no trace of grief on her face. She told them that her father was

---

① A shadow-like representation of the shape of something, filled in with a solid colour, usually black. 黑色半面画像,侧面影像,剪影

not dead. She did that for three days, with the ministers calling on her, and the doctors, trying to persuade her to let them dispose of the body. Just as they were about to resort to law and force, she broke down, and they buried her father quickly.

We did not say she was crazy then. We believed she had to do that. We remembered all the young men her father had driven away, and we knew that with nothing left, she would have to cling to that which had robbed her, as people will.

III

She was sick for a long time. When we saw her again, her hair was cut short, making her look like a girl, with a vague resemblance to those angels in colored church windows—sort of tragic and serene.

The town had just let the contracts for paving the sidewalks, and in the summer after her father's death they began to work. The construction company came with niggers and mules and machinery, and a foreman named Homer Barron, a Yankee[①]—a big, dark, ready man, with a big voice and eyes lighter than his face. The little boys would follow in groups to hear him cuss the niggers, and the niggers singing in time to the rise and fall of picks. Pretty soon he knew everybody in town. Whenever you heard a lot of laughing anywhere about the square, Homer Barron would be in the center of the group. Presently we began to see him and Miss Emily on Sunday afternoons driving in the yellow-wheeled buggy and the matched team of bays from the livery stable.

At first we were glad that Miss Emily would have an interest, because the ladies all said, "Of course a Grierson would not think seriously of a Northerner, a day laborer." But there were still others, older people, who said that even grief could not cause a real lady to forget noblesse oblige—without calling it noblesse oblige. They just said, "Poor Emily. Her kinsfolk should come to her." She had some kin in Alabama; but years ago her father had fallen out with them over the estate of old lady Wyatt, the crazy woman, and there was no communication between the two families. They had not even been represented at the funeral.

---

① American English, a person born or living in the northern or north-eastern states of the USA. 北方佬

And as soon as the old people said, "Poor Emily," the whispering began. "Do you suppose it's really so?" they said to one another. "Of course it is. What else could..." This behind their hands; rustling of craned silk and satin behind jalousies closed upon the sun of Sunday afternoon as the thin, swift clop-clop-clop of the matched team passed: "Poor Emily."

She carried her head high enough—even when we believed that she was fallen. It was as if she demanded more than ever the recognition of her dignity as the last Grierson; as if it had wanted that touch of earthiness to reaffirm her imperviousness. Like when she bought the rat poison, the arsenic. That was over a year after they had begun to say "Poor Emily," and while the two female cousins were visiting her.

"I want some poison," she said to the druggist. She was over thirty then, still a slight woman, though thinner than usual, with cold, haughty black eyes in a face the flesh of which was strained across the temples and about the eyesockets as you imagine a lighthouse-keeper's face ought to look. "I want some poison," she said.

"Yes, Miss Emily. What kind? For rats and such? I'd recom—"

"I want the best you have. I don't care what kind."

The druggist named several. "They'll kill anything up to an elephant. But what you want is—"

"Arsenic[①]," Miss Emily said. "Is that a good one?"

"Is... arsenic? Yes, ma'am. But what you want—"

"I want arsenic."

The druggist looked down at her. She looked back at him, erect, her face like a strained flag. "Why, of course," the druggist said. "If that's what you want. But the law requires you to tell what you are going to use it for."

Miss Emily just stared at him, her head tilted back in order to look him eye for eye, until he looked away and went and got the arsenic and wrapped it up. The Negro delivery boy brought her the package; the druggist didn't come back. When she opened the package at home there was written on the box, under the skull and bones: "For rats."

---

① A chemical substance that is poisonous, used in medicine and for killing rats. 砒霜

IV

So the next day we all said, "She will kill herself"; and we said it would be the best thing. When she had first begun to be seen with Homer Barron, we had said, "She will marry him." Then we said, "She will persuade him yet," because Homer himself had remarked—he liked men, and it was known that he drank with the younger men in the Elks' Club—that he was not a marrying man. Later we said, "Poor Emily," behind the jalousies as they passed on Sunday afternoon in the glittering buggy, Miss Emily with her head high and Homer Barron with his hat cocked and a cigar in his teeth, reins and whip in a yellow glove.

Then some of the ladies began to say that it was a disgrace to the town and a bad example to the young people. The men did not want to interfere, but at last the ladies forced the Baptist minister—Miss Emily's people were Episcopal—to call upon her. He would never divulge what happened during that interview, but he refused to go back again. The next Sunday they again drove about the streets, and the following day the minister's wife wrote to Miss Emily's relations in Alabama.

So she had blood-kin under her roof again and we sat back to watch developments. At first nothing happened. Then we were sure that they were to be married. We learned that Miss Emily had been to the jeweler's and ordered a man's toilet set in silver, with the letters H. B. on each piece. Two days later we learned that she had bought a complete outfit of men's clothing, including a nightshirt, and we said, "They are married." We were really glad. We were glad because the two female cousins were even more Grierson than Miss Emily had ever been.

So we were not surprised when Homer Barron—the streets had been finished some time since—was gone. We were a little disappointed that there was not a public blowing-off, but we believed that he had gone on to prepare for Miss Emily's coming, or to give her a chance to get rid of the cousins. (By that time it was a cabal, and we were all Miss Emily's allies to help circumvent the cousins.) Sure enough, after another week they departed. And, as we had expected all along, within three days Homer Barron was back in town. A neighbor saw the Negro man admit him at the kitchen door at dusk one evening.

And that was the last we saw of Homer Barron. And of Miss Emily for some time. The Negro man went in and out with the market basket, but the front door remained closed. Now and then we would see her at a window for a moment, as the men did that night when they sprinkled the lime, but for almost six months she did not appear on the streets. Then we knew that this was to be expected too; as if that quality of her father which had thwarted her woman's life so many times had been too virulent and too furious to die.

When we next saw Miss Emily, she had grown fat and her hair was turning gray. During the next few years it grew grayer and grayer until it attained an even pepper-and-salt iron-gray, when it ceased turning. Up to the day of her death at seventy-four it was still that vigorous iron-gray, like the hair of an active man.

From that time on her front door remained closed, save for a period of six or seven years, when she was about forty, during which she gave lessons in china-painting. She fitted up a studio in one of the downstairs rooms, where the daughters and granddaughters of Colonel Sartoris' contemporaries were sent to her with the same regularity and in the same spirit that they were sent to church on Sundays with a twenty-five-cent piece for the collection plate. Meanwhile her taxes had been remitted.

Then the newer generation became the backbone and the spirit of the town, and the painting pupils grew up and fell away and did not send their children to her with boxes of color and tedious brushes and pictures cut from the ladies' magazines. The front door closed upon the last one and remained closed for good. When the town got free postal delivery, Miss Emily alone refused to let them fasten the metal numbers above her door and attach a mailbox to it. She would not listen to them.

Daily, monthly, yearly we watched the Negro grow grayer and more stooped, going in and out with the market basket. Each December we sent her a tax notice, which would be returned by the post office a week later, unclaimed. Now and then we would see her in one of the downstairs windows—she had evidently shut up the top floor of the house—like the carven torso of an idol in a niche, looking or not looking at us, we could never tell which. Thus she passed from generation to generation—dear, inescapable, impervious, tranquil, and perverse.

And so she died. Fell ill in the house filled with dust and shadows, with only a doddering Negro man to wait on her. We did not even know she was sick; we had long since given up trying to get any information from the Negro. He talked to no one, probably not even to her, for his voice had grown harsh and rusty, as if from disuse.

She died in one of the downstairs rooms, in a heavy walnut bed with a curtain, her gray head propped on a pillow yellow and moldy with age and lack of sunlight.

V

The Negro met the first of the ladies at the front door and let them in, with their hushed, sibilant voices and their quick, curious glances, and then he disappeared. He walked right through the house and out the back and was not seen again.

The two female cousins came at once. They held the funeral on the second day, with the town coming to look at Miss Emily beneath a mass of bought flowers, with the crayon face of her father musing profoundly above the bier and the ladies sibilant and macabre; and the very old men—some in their brushed Confederate uniforms—on the porch and the lawn, talking of Miss Emily as if she had been a contemporary of theirs, believing that they had danced with her and courted her perhaps, confusing time with its mathematical progression, as the old do, to whom all the past is not a diminishing road, but, instead, a huge meadow which no winter ever quite touches, divided from them now by the narrow bottleneck of the most recent decade of years.

Already we knew that there was one room in that region above stairs which no one had seen in forty years, and which would have to be forced. They waited until Miss Emily was decently in the ground before they opened it.

The violence of breaking down the door seemed to fill this room with pervading dust. A thin, acrid pall as of the tomb seemed to lie everywhere upon this room decked and furnished as for a bridal: upon the valance curtains of faded rose color, upon the rose-shaded lights, upon the dressing table, upon the delicate array of crystal and the man's toilet things backed with tarnished silver, silver so tarnished that the monogram was obscured. Among them lay a collar and tie, as if they had just been removed, which, lifted, left upon the surface a pale crescent in the dust. Upon a chair hung the suit, carefully folded; beneath it the two mute shoes and the discarded socks.

The man himself lay in the bed.

For a long while we just stood there, looking down at the profound and fleshless grin. The body had apparently once lain in the attitude of an embrace, but now the long sleep that outlasts love, that conquers even the grimace of love, had cuckolded him. What was left of him, rotted beneath what was left of the nightshirt, had become inextricable from the bed in which he lay; and upon him and upon the pillow beside him lay that even coating of the patient and biding dust.

Then we noticed that in the second pillow was the indentation of a head. One of us lifted something from it, and leaning forward, that faint and invisible dust dry and acrid in the nostrils, we saw a long strand of iron-gray hair.

Questions for Discussion

1. Discuss the ways in which Faulkner uses Miss Emily's house as an appropriate setting and as a metaphor for both her and the themes established by the narrative.
2. What are the different uses of the themes of "love," "honor," and "respectability" in the story?
3. Why does Faulkner use this particular narrator? What do you know about him? Can you list his "values," and if so, are they shared by the town? Is this narrator reliable? Does the fact he is male matter?
4. Many critics have read Miss Emily as a symbol of the post-Civil-War South. Discuss the advantages and disadvantages of adopting this stance.
5. What does the character Emily stand for, an insane spinster, a devoted lover or symbol of the past?

About the Author

William Faulkner (1897—1962), is one of the greatest writers America has ever produced, and has become the most frequently and intensely interpreted writers of modern American literature.

Faulkner was born in New Albany, Mississippi and raised in nearby Oxford, and lived there almost all his life. As a poor student, Faulkner left school in his teens and had no further formal education beyond a year as a special student at the University of Mississippi.

However, the man himself never stood taller than five feet, six inches tall, but in the realm of American literature, Faulkner is a giant. More than simply a renowned Mississippi writer, the Nobel Prize-winning novelist and short story writer is acclaimed throughout the world as one of the twentieth century's greatest writers, one who transformed his "postage stamp" of native soil into an apocryphal setting in which he explored, articulated, and challenged "the old verities and truths of the heart." During what is generally considered his period of greatest artistic achievement, from *The Sound and the Fury* in 1929 to *Go Down, Moses* in 1942, Faulkner accomplished in a little over a decade more artistically than most writers accomplish over a lifetime of writing. It is one of the more remarkable feats of American literature, how a young man who never graduated from high school, never received a college degree, living in a small town in the poorest state in the nation, all the while balancing a growing family of dependents and impending financial ruin, could during the Great Depression write a series of novels all set in the same small Southern county —novels that include *As I Lay Dying*, *Light in August*, and above all, *Absalom, Absalom*! —that would one day be recognized as among the greatest novels ever written by an American.

A Rose for Emily is considered by many readers as one of horror. Miss Emily Grierson, a queer old lady in a southern town, is the main character. The story is told in a retroverted order so that suspensions keep up the reader's interest till the end.

Essay

Sinners in the Hands of an Angry God

Jonathan Edwards

—Their foot shall slide in due time

Deut. 32:35

In this verse is threatened the vengeance of God on the wicked unbelieving Israelites, who were God's visible people, and who lived under the means of grace; but who, notwithstanding all God's wonderful works towards them, remained (as ver. 28.) void of counsel, having no understanding in them. Under all the cultivations of heaven, they brought forth bitter and poisonous fruit; as in the two verses next preceding the text. The expression I have chosen for my text, Their foot shall slide in due time, seems to imply the following doings, relating to the punishment and destruction to which these wicked Israelites were exposed.

1. That they were always exposed to destruction; as one that stands or walks in slippery places is always exposed to fall. This is implied in the manner of their destruction coming upon them, being represented by their foot sliding. The same is expressed, Psalm 73:18. "Surely thou didst set them in slippery places; thou castedst them down into destruction."

2. It implies, that they were always exposed to sudden unexpected destruction. As he that walks in slippery places is every moment liable to fall, he cannot foresee one moment whether he shall stand or fall the next; and when he does fall, he falls at once without warning: Which is also expressed in Psalm 73:18, 19. "Surely thou didst set them in slippery places; thou castedst them down into destruction: How are they brought into desolation as in a moment!"

3. Another thing implied is, that they are liable to fall of themselves, without being thrown down by the hand of another; as he that stands or walks on slippery ground needs nothing but his own weight to throw him down.

4. That the reason why they are not fallen already, and do not fall now, is only that God's appointed time is not come. For it is said, that when that due time, or appointed time comes, their foot shall slide. Then they shall be left to fall, as they are inclined by their own weight. God will not hold them up in these slippery places any longer, but will let them go; and then at that very instant,

they shall fall into destruction; as he that stands on such slippery declining ground, on the edge of a pit, he cannot stand alone, when he is let go he immediately falls and is lost.

The observation from the words that I would now insist upon is this. "There is nothing that keeps wicked men at any one moment out of hell, but the mere pleasure of God." By the mere pleasure of God, I mean his sovereign pleasure, his arbitrary will, restrained by no obligation, hindered by no manner of difficulty, any more than if nothing else but God's mere will had in the least degree, or in any respect whatsoever, any hand in the preservation of wicked men one moment. The truth of this observation may appear by the following considerations.

1. There is no want of power in God to cast wicked men into hell at any moment. Men's hands cannot be strong when God rises up. The strongest have no power to resist him, nor can any deliver out of his hands.—He is not only able to cast wicked men into hell, but he can most easily do it. Sometimes an earthly prince meets with a great deal of difficulty to subdue a rebel, who has found means to fortify himself, and has made himself strong by the numbers of his followers. But it is not so with God. There is no fortress that is any defense from the power of God. Though hand join in hand, and vast multitudes of God's enemies combine and associate themselves, they are easily broken in pieces. They are as great heaps of light chaff before the whirlwind; or large quantities of dry stubble before devouring flames. We find it easy to tread on and crush a worm that we see crawling on the earth; so it is easy for us to cut or singe a slender thread that any thing hangs by: thus easy is it for God, when he pleases, to cast his enemies down to hell. What are we, that we should think to stand before him, at whose rebuke the earth trembles, and before whom the rocks are thrown down?

2. They deserve to be cast into hell; so that divine justice never stands in the way, it makes no objection against God's using his power at any moment to destroy them. Yea, on the contrary, justice calls aloud for an infinite punishment of their sins. Divine justice says of the tree that brings forth such grapes of Sodom, "Cut it down, why cumbereth it the ground?" Luke xiii. 7. The sword of divine justice is every moment brandished over their heads, and it is nothing but the hand of arbitrary mercy, and God's mere will, that holds it back.

3. They are already under a sentence of condemnation to hell. They do not only justly deserve to be cast down thither, but the sentence of the law of God, that eternal and immutable rule of righteousness that God has fixed between him

and mankind, is gone out against them, and stands against them; so that they are bound over already to hell. John iii. 18. "He that believeth not is condemned already." So that every unconverted man properly belongs to hell; that is his place; from thence he is, John viii. 23. "Ye are from beneath." And thither he is bound; it is the place that justice, and God's word, and the sentence of his unchangeable law assign to him.

4. They are now the objects of that very same anger and wrath of God, that is expressed in the torments of hell. And the reason why they do not go down to hell at each moment, is not because God, in whose power they are, is not then very angry with them; as he is with many miserable creatures now tormented in hell, who there feel and bear the fierceness of his wrath. Yea, God is a great deal more angry with great numbers that are now on earth: yea, doubtless, with many that are now in this congregation, who it may be are at ease, than he is with many of those who are now in the flames of hell. So that it is not because God is unmindful of their wickedness, and does not resent it, that he does not let loose his hand and cut them off. God is not altogether such an one as themselves, though they may imagine him to be so. The wrath of God burns against them, their damnation does not slumber; the pit is prepared, the fire is made ready, the furnace is now hot, ready to receive them; the flames do now rage and glow. The glittering sword is whet, and held over them, and the pit hath opened its mouth under them.

5. The devil stands ready to fall upon them, and seize them as his own, at what moment God shall permit him. They belong to him; he has their souls in his possession, and under his dominion. The scripture represents them as his goods, Luke 11:12. The devils watch them; they are ever by them at their right hand; they stand waiting for them, like greedy hungry lions that see their prey, and expect to have it, but are for the present kept back. If God should withdraw his hand, by which they are restrained, they would in one moment fly upon their poor souls. The old serpent is gaping for them; hell opens its mouth wide to receive them; and if God should permit it, they would be hastily swallowed up and lost.

6. There are in the souls of wicked men those hellish principles reigning, that would presently kindle and flame out into hell fire, if it were not for God's restraints. There is laid in the very nature of carnal men, a foundation for the torments of hell. There are those corrupt principles, in reigning power in them, and in full possession of them, that are seeds of hell fire. These principles are

active and powerful, exceeding violent in their nature, and if it were not for the restraining hand of God upon them, they would soon break out, they would flame out after the same manner as the same corruptions, the same enmity does in the hearts of damned souls, and would beget the same torments as they do in them. The souls of the wicked are in scripture compared to the troubled sea, Isa. 57:20. For the present, God restrains their wickedness by his mighty power, as he does the raging waves of the troubled sea, saying, "Hitherto shalt thou come, but no further;" but if God should withdraw that restraining power, it would soon carry all before it. Sin is the ruin and misery of the soul; it is destructive in its nature; and if God should leave it without restraint, there would need nothing else to make the soul perfectly miserable. The corruption of the heart of man is immoderate and boundless in its fury; and while wicked men live here, it is like fire pent up by God's restraints, whereas if it were let loose, it would set on fire the course of nature; and as the heart is now a sink of sin, so if sin was not restrained, it would immediately turn the soul into a fiery oven, or a furnace of fire and brimstone.

7. It is no security to wicked men for one moment, that there are no visible means of death at hand. It is no security to a natural man, that he is now in health, and that he does not see which way he should now immediately go out of the world by any accident, and that there is no visible danger in any respect in his circumstances. The manifold and continual experience of the world in all ages, shows this is no evidence, that a man is not on the very brink of eternity, and that the next step will not be into another world. The unseen, unthought-of ways and means of persons going suddenly out of the world are innumerable and inconceivable. Unconverted men walk over the pit of hell on a rotten covering, and there are innumerable places in this covering so weak that they will not bear their weight, and these places are not seen. The arrows of death fly unseen at noon-day; the sharpest sight cannot discern them. God has so many different unsearchable ways of taking wicked men out of the world and sending them to hell, that there is nothing to make it appear, that God had need to be at the expense of a miracle, or go out of the ordinary course of his providence, to destroy any wicked man, at any moment. All the means that there are of sinners going out of the world, are so in God's hands, and so universally and absolutely subject to his power and determination, that it does not depend at all the less on the mere will of God, whether sinners shall at any moment go to hell, than if

means were never made use of, or at all concerned in the case.

8. Natural men's prudence and care to preserve their own lives, or the care of others to preserve them, do not secure them a moment. To this, divine providence and universal experience do also bear testimony. There is this clear evidence that men's own wisdom is no security to them from death; that if it were otherwise we should see some difference between the wise and politic men of the world, and others, with regard to their liableness to early and unexpected death: but how is it in fact? Eccles. ii. 16. "How dieth the wise man? even as the fool."

9. All wicked men's pains and contrivance which they use to escape hell, while they continue to reject Christ, and so remain wicked men, do not secure them from hell one moment. Almost every natural man that hears of hell, flatters himself that he shall escape it; he depends upon himself for his own security; he flatters himself in what he has done, in what he is now doing, or what he intends to do. Every one lays out matters in his own mind how he shall avoid damnation, and flatters himself that he contrives well for himself, and that his schemes will not fail. They hear indeed that there are but few saved, and that the greater part of men that have died heretofore are gone to hell; but each one imagines that he lays out matters better for his own escape than others have done. He does not intend to come to that place of torment; he says within himself, that he intends to take effectual care, and to order matters so for himself as not to fail.

But the foolish children of men miserably delude themselves in their own schemes, and in confidence in their own strength and wisdom; they trust to nothing but a shadow. The greater part of those who heretofore have lived under the same means of grace, and are now dead, are undoubtedly gone to hell; and it was not because they were not as wise as those who are now alive: it was not because they did not lay out matters as well for themselves to secure their own escape. If we could speak with them, and inquire of them, one by one, whether they expected, when alive, and when they used to hear about hell ever to be the subjects of that misery: we doubtless, should hear one and another reply, "No, I never intended to come here: I had laid out matters otherwise in my mind; I thought I should contrive well for myself—I thought my scheme good. I intended to take effectual care; but it came upon me unexpected; I did not look for it at that time, and in that manner; it came as a thief—Death outwitted me: God's wrath was too quick for me. Oh, my cursed foolishness! I was flattering myself, and pleasing myself with vain dreams of what I would do hereafter; and when I was saying, Peace and safety, then suddenly destruction came upon me."

10. God has laid himself under no obligation, by any promise to keep any natural man out of hell one moment. God certainly has made no promises either of eternal life, or of any deliverance or preservation from eternal death, but what are contained in the covenant of grace, the promises that are given in Christ, in whom all the promises are yea and amen. But surely they have no interest in the promises of the covenant of grace who are not the children of the covenant, who do not believe in any of the promises, and have no interest in the Mediator of the covenant.

So that, whatever some have imagined and pretended about promises made to natural men's earnest seeking and knocking, it is plain and manifest, that whatever pains a natural man takes in religion, whatever prayers he makes, till he believes in Christ, God is under no manner of obligation to keep him a moment from eternal destruction.

So that, thus it is that natural men are held in the hand of God, over the pit of hell; they have deserved the fiery pit, and are already sentenced to it; and God is dreadfully provoked, his anger is as great towards them as to those that are actually suffering the executions of the fierceness of his wrath in hell, and they have done nothing in the least to appease or abate that anger, neither is God in the least bound by any promise to hold them up one moment; the devil is waiting for them, hell is gaping for them, the flames gather and flash about them, and would fain lay hold on them, and swallow them up; the fire pent up in their own hearts is struggling to break out: and they have no interest in any Mediator, there are no means within reach that can be any security to them. In short, they have no refuge, nothing to take hold of, all that preserves them every moment is the mere arbitrary will, and uncovenanted, unobliged forbearance of an incensed God.

. . .

Questions for Discussion

1. This is a sermon preached very long time ago. Please find people's attitude towards religion at that time. To what kind of audience is Edwards addressing?
2. How does Edwards try to persuade people to believe in God again?

About the Author

    Jonathan Edwards (1703—1758), born in E. Windsor, Conn., the fifth of

11 children in a strict Puritan home, entered Yale College at 13. In 1727 he was named a pastor at his grandfather's church in Northampton, Mass. His sermons on "Justification by Faith Alone" gave rise to a revival in the Connecticut River Valley in 1734, and in the 1740s he was also influential in the Great Awakening. In 1750 he was dismissed from the Northampton church over a disagreement on who was eligible to take communion, and he became pastor in Stockbridge in 1751. He died of smallpox shortly after accepting the presidency of the College of New Jersey (now Princeton University). A staunch Calvinist, he emphasized original sin, predestination, and the need for conversion. His most famous sermon, *Sinners in the Hands of an Angry God*, vividly evokes the fate of unrepentant sinners in hell.

Nature (excerpt)

Ralph Waldo Emerson

Introduction

Our age is retrospective. It builds the sepulchers of the fathers. It writes biographies, histories, and criticism. The foregoing generations beheld God and nature face to face; we, through their eyes. Why should not we also enjoy an original relation to the universe? Why should not we have a poetry and philosophy of insight and not of tradition, and a religion by revelation to us, and not the history of theirs? Embosomed for a season in nature, whose floods of life stream around and through us, and invite us by the powers they supply, to action proportioned to nature, why should we grope among the dry bones of the past[1], or put the living generation into masquerade out of its faded wardrobe? The sun shines today also. There is more wool and flax in the fields. There are new lands, new men, new thoughts. Let us demand our own works and laws and worship.

Undoubtedly we have no questions to ask which are unanswerable. We must trust the perfection of the creation so far, as to believe that whatever curiosity the order of things has awakened in our minds, the order of things can satisfy. Every man's condition is a solution in hieroglyphic to those inquiries he would put. He acts it as life, before he apprehends it as truth. In like manner, nature is already, in its forms and tendencies, describing its own design. Let us interrogate the great apparition that shines so peacefully around us. Let us inquire, to what end is nature?

All science has one aim, namely, to find a theory of nature. We have theories of races and of functions, but scarcely yet a remote approach to an idea of creation. We are now so far from the road to truth, that religious teachers dispute and hate each other, and speculative men are esteemed unsound and frivolous. But to a sound judgment, the most abstract truth is the most practical. Whenever a true theory appears, it will be its own evidence. Its test

---

[1] An echo of Ezekiel 37. 1—14, especially 37. 4, where God tells Ezekiel to "Prophesy upon these bones, and say unto them, O ye dry bones, hear the word of the lord". Although Emerson had left the ministry, he was still writing as a prophet.

is, that it will explain all phenomena. Now many are thought not only unexplained but inexplicable; as language, sleep, madness, dreams, beasts, sex.

Philosophically considered, the universe is composed of Nature and the Soul. Strictly speaking, therefore, all that is separate from us, all which Philosophy distinguishes as the NOT ME①, that is, both nature and art, all other men and my own body, must be ranked under this name, NATURE. In enumerating the values of nature and casting up their sum, I shall use the word in both senses;—in its common and in its philosophical import. In inquiries so general as our present one, the inaccuracy is not material; no confusion of thought will occur. Nature, in the common sense, refers to essences unchanged by man; space, the air, the river, the leaf. Art is applied to the mixture of his will with the same things, as in a house, a canal, a statue, a picture. But his operations taken together are so insignificant, a little chipping, baking, patching, and washing, that in an impression so grand as that of the world on the human mind, they do not vary the result.

Chapter I
NATURE

To go into solitude, a man needs to retire as much from his chamber as from society. I am not solitary whilst I read and write, though nobody is with me. But if a man would be alone, let him look at the stars. The rays that come from those heavenly worlds, will separate between him and what he touches. One might think the atmosphere was made transparent with this design, to give man, in the heavenly bodies, the perpetual presence of the sublime. Seen in the streets of cities, how great they are! If the stars should appear one night in a thousand years, how would men believe and adore; and preserve for many generations the remembrance of the city of God which had been shown! But every night come out these envoys of beauty, and light the universe with their admonishing smile.

The stars awaken a certain reverence, because though always present, they are inaccessible; but all natural objects make a kindred impression, when the

---

① Emerson takes the term from Thomas Carlyle's *Sartor Resartus* (1833—1834), where it appears as a translation of the recent German philosophical term for everything but the self. Kant first brought forward "something outside me" in his *Critique of Pure Reason*; later Fichte used "non-Ego" to refer to objective things.

mind is open to their influence. Nature never wears a mean appearance. Neither does the wisest man extort her secret, and lose his curiosity by finding out all her perfection. Nature never became a toy to a wise spirit. The flowers, the animals, the mountains, reflected the wisdom of his best hour, as much as they had delighted the simplicity of his childhood.

When we speak of nature in this manner, we have a distinct but most poetical sense in the mind. We mean the integrity of impression made by manifold natural objects. It is this which distinguishes the stick of timber of the wood-cutter, from the tree of the poet. The charming landscape which I saw this morning, is indubitably made up of some twenty or thirty farms. Miller owns this field, Locke that, and Manning the woodland beyond. But none of them owns the landscape. There is a property in the horizon which no man has but he whose eye can integrate all the parts, that is, the poet. This is the best part of these men's farms, yet to this their warranty-deeds give no title.

To speak truly, few adult persons can see nature. Most persons do not see the sun. At least they have a very superficial seeing. The sun illuminates only the eye of the man, but shines into the eye and the heart of the child. The lover of nature is he whose inward and outward senses are still truly adjusted to each other; who has retained the spirit of infancy even into the era of manhood①. His intercourse with heaven and earth, becomes part of his daily food. In the presence of nature, a wild delight runs through the man, in spite of real sorrows. Nature says, —he is my creature, and maugre② all his impertinent griefs, he shall be glad with me. Not the sun or the summer alone, but every hour and season yields its tribute of delight; for every hour and change corresponds to and authorizes a different state of the mind, from breathless noon to grimmest midnight. Nature is a setting that fits equally well a comic or a mourning piece. In good health, the air is a cordial of incredible virtue. Crossing a bare common, in snow puddles, at twilight, under a clouded sky, without having in my thoughts any occurrence of special good fortune, I have enjoyed a perfect exhilaration. Almost I fear to think how glad I am. In the woods too, a man casts off his years, as the snake his slough, and at what period soever of

---

① An echo of Samuel Taylor Coleridge's *Biographia Literaia*, Chapter 4, in which Coleridge defines the character and privilege of genius as the ability to carry the feelings of childhood into the powers of manhood.

② In spite of.

life, is always a child. In the woods, is perpetual youth. Within these plantations of God, a decorum and sanctity reign, a perennial festival is dressed, and the guest sees not how he should tire of them in a thousand years. In the woods, we return to reason and faith. There I feel that nothing can befall me in life, no disgrace, no calamity (leaving me my eyes), which nature cannot repair. Standing on the bare ground, —my head bathed by the blithe air, and uplifted into infinite space, —all mean egotism vanishes. I become a transparent eye-ball①; I am nothing; I see all; the currents of the Universal Being circulate through me; I am part or particle of God. The name of the nearest friend sounds then foreign and accidental: to be brothers, to be acquaintances, —master or servant, is then a trifle and a disturbance. I am the lover of uncontained and immortal beauty. In the wilderness, I find something more dear and connate② than in streets or villages. In the tranquil landscape, and especially in the distant line of the horizon, man beholds somewhat as beautiful as his own nature.

The greatest delight which the fields and woods minister, is the suggestion of an occult relation between man and the vegetable. I am not alone and unacknowledged. They nod to me, and I to them. The waving of the boughs in the storm, is new to me and old. It takes me by surprise, and yet is not unknown. Its effect is like that of a higher thought or a better emotion coming over me, when I deemed I was thinking justly or doing right.

Yet it is certain that the power to produce this delight, does not reside in nature, but in man, or in a harmony of both. It is necessary to use these pleasures with great temperance. For, nature is not always tricked in holiday attire, but the same scene which yesterday breathed perfume and glittered as for the frolic of the nymphs, is overspread with melancholy today. Nature always wears the colors of the spirit. To a man laboring under calamity, the heat of his own fire hath sadness in it. Then, there is a kind of contempt of the landscape felt by him who has just lost by death a dear friend. The sky is less grand as it shuts down over less worth in the population.

---

① The most famous phrase in the essay, endlessly ridiculed and explicated. As Sealts says in *The Composition of Nature*, Emerson is not "merely repeating what he had already said about the implications of the preceding sentence on the bare common." When the speaker leaves the village for the woods, "the level of discourse is significantly shifted along with the setting, and the ensuing episode takes place on what Emerson would later call another 'platform' of experience."

② Related.

Part Two American Literature

Questions for Discussion

1. How does the author think about the past?
2. What is the author's definition of nature? How do you think about the definition?
3. How does the author define poet?
4. "Standing on the bare ground,—my head bathed by the blithe air, and uplifted into infinite space, —all mean egotism vanishes. I become a transparent eye-ball; I am nothing; I see all; the currents of the Universal Being circulate through me; I am part or particle of God." What is your understanding of it?
5. What ideas does the author express here?

About the Author

   Ralph Waldo Emerson (1803—1882) is an American lecturer, poet, philosopher, essayist, and the leading exponent of New England Transcendentalism.

   Emerson was born in Boston, Massachusetts. He graduated from Harvard University at the age of 18, and later entered and graduated from the Harvard Divinity School. In 1829 Emerson married Ellen Louisa Tucker, who died in 1831 from consumption. Emerson became sole pastor at the Second Unitarian Church of Boston in 1830. Three years later he had a crisis of faith, and resigned from his post. In 1835 Emerson married Lydia Jackson and lived with her at the east end of the village of Concord, where he settled into his life of conversations, reading and writing, and lecturing, which furnished a comfortable income.

   His major works include: *Nature* (1849), *Essays* (1841), *Essays: Second Series* (1844), *Representative Men* (1850), and *The Conduct of Life* (1860). As an essayist Emerson was a master of style. He encouraged American scholars to break free of European influences and create a new American culture.

   Nature, a collection of essays was Emerson's first book, which appeared when he was 33. It consists of 8 chapters entitled respectively Nature, Commodity, Beauty, Language, Discipline, Idealism, Spirit, and Prospects. In it Emerson emphasized individualism and rejected traditional authority. He also believed that people should try to live a simple life in harmony with nature and with others.

Walden

Henry David Thoreau

Chapter II: Where I Lived, and What I Lived For

At a certain season of our life we are accustomed to consider every spot as the possible site of a house. I have thus surveyed the country on every side within a dozen miles of where I live. In imagination I have bought all the farms in succession, for all were to be bought, and I knew their price. I walked over each farmer's premises, tasted his wild apples, discoursed on husbandry with him, took his farm at his price, at any price, mortgaging it to him in my mind; even put a higher price on it —took everything but a deed of it—took his word for his deed, for I dearly love to talk—cultivated it, and him too to some extent, I trust, and withdrew when I had enjoyed it long enough, leaving him to carry it on. This experience entitled me to be regarded as a sort of real-estate broker by my friends. Wherever I sat, there I might live, and the landscape radiated from me accordingly. What is a house but a sedes, a seat? —Better if a country seat. I discovered many a site for a house not likely to be soon improved, which some might have thought too far from the village, but to my eyes the village was too far from it. Well, there I might live, I said; and there I did live, for an hour, a summer and a winter life; saw how I could let the years run off, buffet the winter through, and see the spring come in. The future inhabitants of this region, wherever they may place their houses, may be sure that they have been anticipated. An afternoon sufficed to lay out the land into orchard, wood-lot, and pasture, and to decide what fine oaks or pines should be left to stand before the door, and whence each blasted tree could be seen to the best advantage; and then I let it lie, fallow, perchance, for a man is rich in proportion to the number of things which he can afford to let alone.

My imagination carried me so far that I even had the refusal of several farms—the refusal was all I wanted—but I never got my fingers burned by actual possession. The nearest that I came to actual possession was when I bought the Hollowell place, and had begun to sort my seeds, and collected materials with which to make a wheelbarrow to carry it on or off with; but before the owner gave me a deed of it, his wife—every man has such a wife—changed her mind and wished to keep it, and he offered me ten dollars to release him. Now, to speak the truth, I had but ten cents in the world, and it surpassed my arithmetic to tell, if I was that man who had ten cents, or who had a farm, or ten dollars, or all together. However, I let him keep the ten dollars and the farm too, for I had carried it far enough; or rather, to be generous, I sold him the farm for just what I gave for it, and, as he was not a rich man, made him a present of ten dollars, and still had my ten cents, and seeds, and materials for a wheelbarrow left. I found thus that I had been a rich man without any damage to my poverty. But I retained the landscape, and I have since annually carried off what it yielded without a wheelbarrow. With respect to landscapes,

"I am monarch of all I survey,

My right there is none to dispute."

I have frequently seen a poet withdraw, having enjoyed the most valuable part of a farm, while the crusty farmer supposed that he had got a few wild apples only. Why, the owner does not know it for many years when a poet has put his farm in rhyme, the most admirable kind of invisible fence, has fairly impounded it, milked it, skimmed it, and got all the cream, and left the farmer only the skimmed milk.

The real attractions of the Hollowell farm, to me, were: its complete retirement, being, about two miles from the village, half a mile from the nearest neighbor, and separated from the highway by a broad field; its bounding on the river, which the owner said protected it by its fogs from frosts in the spring, though that was nothing to me; the gray color and ruinous state of the house and barn, and the dilapidated fences, which put such an interval between me and the last occupant; the hollow and lichen-covered apple trees, nawed by rabbits, showing what kind of neighbors I should have; but above all, the recollection I had of it from my earliest voyages up the river, when the house was concealed behind a dense grove of red maples, through which I heard the house-dog bark. I was in haste to buy it, before the proprietor finished getting out some rocks, cutting down the hollow apple trees, and grubbing up some young birches which had sprung up in the pasture, or, in short, had made any more of his improvements. To enjoy these advantages I was ready to carry it on; like Atlas, to take the world on my shoulders—I never heard what compensation he received for that—and do all those things which had no other motive or excuse but that I might pay for it and be unmolested in my possession of it; for I knew all the while that it would yield the most abundant crop of the kind I wanted, if I could only afford to let it alone. But it turned out as I have said.

All that I could say, then, with respect to farming on a large scale—I have always cultivated a garden—was, that I had had my seeds ready. Many think that seeds improve with age. I have no doubt that time discriminates between the good and the bad; and when at last I shall plant, I shall be less likely to be disappointed. But I would say to my fellows, once for all, as long as possible live free and uncommitted. It makes but little difference whether you are committed to a farm or the county jail.

Old Cato, whose "De Re Rustica" is my "Cultivator," says—and the only translation I have seen makes sheer nonsense of the passage—"When you think of getting a farm turn it thus in your mind, not to buy greedily; nor spare your pains to look at it, and do not think it enough to go round it once. The oftener you go there the more it will please you, if it is good." I think I shall not buy greedily, but go round and round it as long as I live, and be buried in it first, that it may please me the more at last.

The present was my next experiment of this kind, which I purpose to describe more at length, for convenience putting the experience of two years into one. As I have said, I do not propose to write an ode to dejection, but to brag as lustily as chanticleer in the morning, standing on his roost, if only to wake my neighbors up.

When first I took up my abode in the woods, that is, began to spend my nights as well as days there, which, by accident, was on Independence Day, or the Fourth of July, 1845, my house was not finished for winter, but was merely a defence against the rain, without plastering or chimney, the walls being of rough, weather-stained boards, with wide chinks, which made it cool at night. The upright white hewn studs and freshly planed door and window casings gave it a clean and airy look, especially in the morning, when its timbers were saturated with dew, so that I fancied that by noon some sweet gum would exude from them. To my imagination it retained throughout the day more or less of this auroral character, reminding me of a certain house on a mountain which I had visited a year before. This was an airy and unplastered cabin, fit to entertain a travelling god, and where a goddess might trail her garments. The winds which passed over my dwelling were such as sweep over the ridges of mountains, bearing the broken strains, or celestial parts only, of terrestrial music. The morning wind forever blows, the poem of creation is uninterrupted; but few are the ears that hear it. Olympus is but the outside of the earth everywhere.

  The only house I had been the owner of before, if I except a boat, was a tent, which I used occasionally when making excursions in the summer, and this is still rolled up in my garret; but the boat, after passing from hand to hand, has gone down the stream of time. With this more substantial shelter about me, I had made some progress toward settling in the world. This frame, so slightly clad, was a sort of crystallization around me, and reacted on the builder. It was suggestive somewhat as a picture in outlines. I did not need to go outdoors to take the air, for the atmosphere within had lost none of its freshness. It was not so much within doors as behind a door where I sat, even in the rainiest weather. The Harivansa says, "An abode without birds is like a meat without seasoning." Such was not my abode, for I found myself suddenly neighbor to the birds; not by having imprisoned one, but having caged myself near them. I was not only nearer to some of those which commonly frequent the garden and the orchard, but to those smaller and more thrilling songsters of the forest which never, or rarely, serenade a villager—the wood thrush, the veery, the scarlet tanager, the field sparrow, the whip-poor-will, and many others.

  I was seated by the shore of a small pond, about a mile and a half south of the village of Concord and somewhat higher than it, in the midst of an extensive wood between that town and Lincoln, and about two miles south of that our only field known to fame, Concord Battle Ground; but I was so low in the woods that the opposite shore, half a mile off, like the rest, covered with wood, was my most distant horizon. For the first week, whenever I looked out on the pond it impressed me like a tarn high up on the side of a mountain, its bottom far above the surface of other lakes, and, as the sun arose, I saw it throwing off its nightly clothing of mist, and here and there, by degrees, its soft ripples or its smooth reflecting surface was revealed, while the mists, like ghosts, were stealthily withdrawing in every direction into the woods, as at the breaking up of some nocturnal conventicle. The very dew seemed to hang upon the trees later into the day than usual, as on the sides of mountains.

  This small lake was of most value as a neighbor in the intervals of a gentle rain-storm in August, when, both air and water being perfectly still, but the sky overcast, mid-afternoon had all the serenity of evening, and the wood thrush sang around, and was heard from shore to shore. A lake like this is never smoother than at such a time; and the clear portion of the air above it being, shallow and darkened by clouds, the water, full of light and reflections, becomes a lower heaven itself so much the more important. From a hill-top near by, where the wood had been recently cut off, there was a pleasing vista southward across the pond, through a wide indentation in the hills which form the shore there, where their opposite sides sloping toward each other suggested a stream flowing out in that direction through a wooded valley, but stream there was none. That way I looked between and over the near green hills to some distant and higher ones in the horizon, tinged with blue. Indeed, by standing on tiptoe I could catch a glimpse of some of the peaks of the still bluer and more distant mountain ranges in the northwest, those true-blue coins from heaven's own mint, and also of some portion of the village. But in other directions, even from this point, I could not see over or beyond the woods which surrounded me. It is well to have some water in your neighborhood, to give buoyancy to and float the earth. One value even of the smallest well is, that when you look into it you see that earth is not continent but insular. This is as important as that it keeps butter cool. When I looked across the pond from this peak toward the Sudbury meadows, which in time of flood I distinguished elevated perhaps by a mirage in their seething valley, like a coin in a basin, all the earth beyond the pond appeared like a thin crust insulated and floated even by this small sheet of interverting water, and I was reminded that this on which I dwelt was but dry land.

Though the view from my door was still more contracted, I did not feel crowded or confined in the least. There was pasture enough for my imagination. The low shrub oak plateau to which the opposite shore arose stretched away toward the prairies of the West and the steppes of Tartary, affording ample room for all the roving families of men. "There are none happy in the world but beings who enjoy freely a vast horizon"—said Damodara, when his herds required new and larger pastures.

Both place and time were changed, and I dwelt nearer to those parts of the universe and to those eras in history which had most attracted me. Where I lived was as far off as many a region viewed nightly by astronomers. We are wont to imagine rare and delectable places in some remote and more celestial corner of the system, behind the constellation of Cassiopeia's Chair, far from noise and disturbance. I discovered that my house actually had its site in such a withdrawn, but forever new and unprofaned, part of the universe. If it were worth the while to settle in those parts near to the Pleiades or the Hyades, to Aldebaran or Altair, then I was really there, or at an equal remoteness from the life which I had left behind, dwindled and twinkling with as fine a ray to my nearest neighbor, and to be seen only in moonless nights by him. Such was that part of creation where I had squatted,—

"There was a shepherd that did live,

And held his thoughts as high

As were the mounts whereon his flocks

Did hourly feed him by."

What should we think of the shepherd's life if his flocks always wandered to higher pastures than his thoughts?

Every morning was a cheerful invitation to make my life of equal simplicity, and I may say innocence, with Nature herself. I have been as sincere a worshipper of Aurora as the Greeks. I got up early and bathed in the pond; that was a religious exercise, and one of the best things which I did. They say that characters were engraven on the bathing tub of King Tching-thang to this effect: "Renew thyself completely each day; do it again, and again, and forever again." I can understand that. Morning brings back the heroic ages. I was as much affected by the faint hum of a mosquito making its invisible and unimaginable tour through my apartment at earliest dawn, when I was sitting with door and windows open, as I could be by any trumpet that ever sang of fame. It was Homer's requiem; itself an Iliad and Odyssey in the air, singing its own wrath and wanderings. There was something cosmical about it; a standing advertisement, till forbidden, of the everlasting vigor and fertility of the world. The morning, which is the most memorable season of the day, is the awakening hour. Then there is least somnolence in us; and for an hour, at least, some part of us awakes which slumbers all the rest of the day and night. Little is to be expected of that day, if it can be called a day, to which we are not awakened by our Genius, but by the mechanical nudgings of some servitor, are not awakened by our own newly acquired force and aspirations from within, accompanied by the undulations of celestial music, instead of factory bells, and a fragrance filling the air—to a higher life than we fell asleep from; and thus the darkness bear its fruit, and prove itself to be good, no less than the light. That man who does not believe that each day contains an earlier, more sacred, and auroral hour than he has yet profaned, has despaired of life, and is pursuing a descending and darkening way. After a partial cessation of his sensuous life, the soul of man, or its organs rather, are reinvigorated each day, and his Genius tries again what noble life it can make. All memorable events, I should say, transpire in morning time and in a morning atmosphere. The Vedas say, "All intelligences awake with the morning." Poetry and art, and the fairest and most memorable of the actions of men, date from such an hour. All poets and heroes, like Memnon, are the children of Aurora, and emit their music at sunrise. To him whose elastic and vigorous thought keeps pace with the sun, the day is a perpetual morning. It matters not what the clocks say or the attitudes and labors of men. Morning is when I am awake and there is a dawn in me. Moral reform is the effort to throw off sleep. Why is it that men give so poor an account of their day if they have not been slumbering? They are not such poor calculators. If they had not been overcome with drowsiness, they would have performed something. The millions are awake enough for physical labor; but only one in a million is awake enough for effective intellectual exertion, only one in a hundred millions to a poetic or divine life. To be awake is to be alive. I have never yet met a man who was quite awake. How could I have looked him in the face?

We must learn to reawaken and keep ourselves awake, not by mechanical aids, but by an infinite expectation of the dawn, which does not forsake us in our soundest sleep. I know of no more encouraging fact than the unquestionable ability of man to elevate his life by a conscious endeavor. It is something to be able to paint a particular picture, or to carve a statue, and so to make a few objects beautiful; but it is far more glorious to carve and paint the very atmosphere and medium through which we look, which morally we can do. To affect the quality of the day, that is the highest of arts. Every man is tasked to make his life, even in its details, worthy of the contemplation of his most elevated and critical hour. If we refused, or rather used up, such paltry information as we get, the oracles would distinctly inform us how this might be done.

I went to the woods because I wished to live deliberately, to front only the essential facts of life, and see if I could not learn what it had to teach, and not, when I came to die, discover that I had not lived. I did not wish to live what was not life, living is so dear; nor did I wish to practise resignation, unless it was quite necessary. I wanted to live deep and suck out all the marrow of life, to live so sturdily and Spartan-like as to put to rout all that was not life, to cut a broad swath and shave close, to drive life into a corner, and reduce it to its lowest terms, and, if it proved to be mean, why then to get the whole and genuine meanness of it, and publish its meanness to the world; or if it were sublime, to know it by experience, and be able to give a true account of it in my next excursion. For most men, it appears to me, are in a strange uncertainty about it, whether it is of the devil or of God, and have somewhat hastily concluded that it is the chief end of man here to "glorify God and enjoy him forever."

Still we live meanly, like ants; though the fable tells us that we were long ago changed into men; like pygmies we fight with cranes; it is error upon error, and clout upon clout, and our best virtue has for its occasion a superfluous and evitable wretchedness. Our life is frittered away by detail. An honest man has hardly need to count more than his ten fingers, or in extreme cases he may add his ten toes, and lump the rest. Simplicity, simplicity, simplicity! I say, let your affairs be as two or three, and not a hundred or a thousand; instead of a million count half a dozen, and keep your accounts on your thumb-nail. In the midst of this chopping sea of civilized life, such are the clouds and storms and quicksands and thousand-and-one items to be allowed for, that a man has to live, if he would not founder and go to the bottom and not make his port at all, by dead reckoning, and he must be a great calculator indeed who succeeds. Simplify, simplify. Instead of three meals a day, if it be necessary eat but one; instead of a hundred dishes, five; and reduce other things in proportion. Our life is like a German Confederacy, made up of petty states, with its boundary forever fluctuating, so that even a German cannot tell you how it is bounded at any moment. The nation itself, with all its so-called internal improvements, which, by the way are all external and superficial, is just such an unwieldy and overgrown establishment, cluttered with furniture and tripped up by its own traps, ruined by luxury and heedless expense, by want of calculation and a worthy aim, as the million households in the land; and the only cure for it, as for them, is in a rigid economy, a stern and more than Spartan simplicity of life and elevation of purpose. It lives too fast. Men think that it is essential that the Nation have commerce, and export ice, and talk through a telegraph, and ride thirty miles an hour, without a doubt, whether they do or not; but whether we should live like baboons or like men, is a little uncertain. If we do not get out sleepers, and forge rails, and devote days and nights to the work, but go to tinkering upon our lives to improve them, who will build railroads? And if railroads are not built, how shall we get to heaven in season? But if we stay at home and mind our business, who will want railroads? We do not ride on the railroad; it rides upon us. Did you ever think what those sleepers are that underlie the railroad? Each one is a man, an Irishman, or a Yankee man. The rails are laid on them, and they are covered with sand, and the cars run smoothly over them. They are sound sleepers, I assure you. And every few years a new lot is laid down and run over; so that, if some have the pleasure of riding on a rail, others have the misfortune to be ridden upon. And when they run over a man that is walking in his sleep, a supernumerary sleeper in the wrong position, and wake him up, they suddenly stop the cars, and make a hue and cry about it, as if this were an exception. I am glad to know that it takes a gang of men for every five miles to keep the sleepers down and level in their beds as it is, for this is a sign that they may sometime get up again.

Why should we live with such hurry and waste of life? We are determined to be starved before we are hungry. Men say that a stitch in time saves nine, and so they take a thousand stitches today to save nine tomorrow. As for work, we haven't any of any consequence. We have the Saint Vitus' dance, and cannot possibly keep our heads still. If I should only give a few pulls at the parish bell-rope, as for a fire, that is, without setting the bell, there is hardly a man on his farm in the outskirts of Concord, notwithstanding that press of engagements which was his excuse so many times this morning, nor a boy, nor a woman, I might almost say, but would forsake all and follow that sound, not mainly to save property from the flames, but, if we will confess the truth, much more to see it burn, since burn it must, and we, be it known, did not set it on fire—or to see it put out, and have a hand in it, if that is done as handsomely; yes, even if it were the parish church itself. Hardly a man takes a half-hour's nap after dinner, but when he wakes he holds up his head and asks, "What's the news?" as if the rest of mankind had stood his sentinels. Some give directions to be waked every half-hour, doubtless for no other purpose; and then, to pay for it, they tell what they have dreamed. After a night's sleep the news is as indispensable as the breakfast. "Pray tell me anything new that has happened to a man anywhere on this globe"—and he reads it over his coffee and rolls, that a man has had his eyes gouged out this morning on the Wachito River; never dreaming the while that he lives in the dark unfathomed mammoth cave of this world, and has but the rudiment of an eye himself.

...

Questions for Discussion

1. What kind of book is *Walden*?
2. Why Thoreau decided to live in the woods instead of in the city?

About the Author

Henry David Thoreau (1817—1862), U. S. thinker, essayist, and naturalist. Born in Concord, Mass., Thoreau graduated from Harvard University and taught school for several years before deciding to become a poet of nature. Back in Concord, he came under the influence of R. W. Emerson and began to publish pieces in the Transcendentalist magazine *The Dial*. In the years 1845—1847, to demonstrate how satisfying a simple life could be, he lived in a hut beside Concord's Walden Pond; essays recording his daily life were assembled for his masterwork, *Walden* (1854). His *A Week on the Concord and Merrimack Rivers* (1849) was the only other book he published in his lifetime. He reflected on a night he spent in jail protesting the Mexican-American. War in the essay *Civil Disobedience* (1849), which would later influence such figures as M. Gandhi and M. L. King. In later years his interest in Transcendentalism waned and he became a dedicated abolitionist. His many nature writings and records of his wanderings in Canada, Maine, and Cape Cod display the mind of a keen naturalist. After his death his collected writings were published in 20 volumes, and further writings have continued to appear in print.

Once More to the Lake

E. B. White

One summer, along about 1904, my father rented a camp on a lake in Maine① and took us all there for the month of August. We all got ringworm② from some kittens and had to rub Pond's Extract on our arms and legs night and morning, and my father rolled over in a canoe with all his clothes on; but outside of that the vacation was a success and from then on none of us ever thought there was any place in the world like that lake in Maine. We returned summer after summer—always on August 1st for one month. I have since become a salt-water man, but sometimes in summer there are days when the restlessness of the tides and the fearful cold of the sea water and the incessant wind which blows across the afternoon and into the evening make me wish for the placidity of a lake in the woods. A few weeks ago this feeling got so strong I bought myself a couple of bass hooks and a spinner and returned to the lake where we used to go, for a week's fishing and to revisit old haunts.

I took along my son, who had never had any fresh water up his nose and who had seen lily pads only from train windows. On the journey over to the lake I began to wonder what it would be like. I wondered how time would have marred this unique, this holy spot—the coves and streams, the hills that the sun set behind, the camps and the paths behind the camps. I was sure that the tarred road would have found it out and I wondered in what other ways it would be desolated. It is strange how much you can remember about places like that once you allow your mind to return into the grooves that lead back. You remember one thing, and that suddenly reminds you of another thing. I guess I remembered clearest of all the early mornings, when the lake was cool and motionless, remembered how the bedroom smelled of the lumber it was made of and of the wet woods whose scent entered through the screen. The partitions in the camp were thin and did not extend clear to the top of the rooms, and as I was always

---

① A state of the northeast United States. It was admitted as the 23rd state in 1820. Augusta is the capital and Portland the largest city. It has a population of 1,233,223.

② A kind of contagious skin diseases caused by several related fungi, characterized by ring-shaped, scaly, itching patches on the skin. [医]金钱癣,轮癣

the first up I would dress softly so as not to wake the others, and sneak out into the sweet outdoors and start out in the canoe, keeping close along the shore in the long shadows of the pines. I remembered being very careful never to rub my paddle against the gunwale for fear of disturbing the stillness of the cathedral.

The lake had never been what you would call a wild lake. There were cottages sprinkled around the shores, and it was in farming country although the shores of the lake were quite heavily wooded. Some of the cottages were owned by nearby farmers, and you would live at the shore and eat your meals at the farmhouse. That's what our family did. But although it wasn't wild, it was a fairly large and undisturbed lake and there were places in it which, to a child at least, seemed infinitely remote and primeval.

I was right about the tar: it led to within half a mile of the shore. But when I got back there, with my boy, and we settled into a camp near a farmhouse and into the kind of summertime I had known, I could tell that it was going to be pretty much the same as it had been before—I knew it, lying in bed the first morning, smelling the bedroom, and hearing the boy sneak quietly out and go off along the shore in a boat. I began to sustain the illusion that he was I, and therefore, by simple transposition, that I was my father. This sensation persisted, kept cropping up all the time we were there. It was not an entirely new feeling, but in this setting it grew much stronger. I seemed to be living a dual existence. I would be in the middle of some simple act, I would be picking up a bait box or laying down a table fork, or I would be saying something, and suddenly it would be not I but my father who was saying the words or making the gesture. It gave me a creepy sensation.

We went fishing the first morning. I felt the same damp moss covering the worms in the bait can, and saw the dragonfly alight on the tip of my rod as it hovered a few inches from the surface of the water. It was the arrival of this fly that convinced me beyond any doubt that everything was as it always had been, that the years were a mirage and that there had been no years. The small waves were the same, chucking the rowboat under the chin as we fished at anchor, and the boat was the same boat, the same color green and the ribs broken in the same places, and under the floor-boards the same fresh-water leavings and debris—the dead helgramite, the wisps of moss, the rusty discarded fishhook, the dried blood from yesterday's catch. We stared silently at the tips of our rods, at the dragonflies that came and went. I lowered the tip of mine into the water, tentatively, pensively dislodging the fly, which darted two feet away, poised, darted two feet back, and came to rest again a little farther up the rod. There had been no years between the ducking of this dragonfly and the other one—the one that was part of memory. I looked at the boy, who was silently watching his fly, and it was my hands that held his rod, my eyes watching. I felt dizzy and didn't know which rod I was at the end of.

We caught two bass, hauling them in briskly as though they were mackerel, pulling them over the side of the boat in a businesslike manner without any landing net, and stunning them with a blow on the back of the head. When we got back for a swim before lunch, the lake was exactly where we had left it, the same number of inches from the dock, and there was only the merest suggestion of a breeze. This seemed an utterly enchanted sea, this lake you could leave to its own devices for a few hours and come back to, and find that it had not stirred, this constant and trustworthy body of water. In the shallows, the dark, water-soaked sticks and twigs, smooth and old, were undulating in clusters on the bottom against the clean ribbed sand, and the track of the mussel was plain. A school of minnows swam by, each minnow with its small individual shadow, doubling the attendance, so clear and sharp in the sunlight. Some of the other campers were in swimming, along the shore, one of them with a cake of soap, and the water felt thin and clear and insubstantial. Over the years there had been this person with the cake of soap, this cultist, and here he was. There had been no years.

Up to the farmhouse to dinner through the teeming, dusty field, the road under our sneakers was only a two-track road. The middle track was missing, the one with the marks of the hooves and the splotches of dried, flaky manure. There had always been three tracks to choose from in choosing which track to walk in; now the choice was narrowed down to two. For a moment I missed terribly the middle alternative. But the way led past the tennis court, and something about the way it lay there in the sun reassured me; the tape had loosened along the backline, the alleys were green with plantains and other weeds, and the net (installed in June and removed in September) sagged in the dry noon, and the whole place steamed with midday heat and hunger and emptiness. There was a choice of pie for dessert, and one was blueberry and one was apple, and the waitresses were the same country girls, there having been no passage of time, only the illusion of it as in a dropped curtain—the waitresses were still fifteen; their hair had been washed, that was the only difference—they had been to the movies and seen the pretty girls with the clean hair.

Summertime, oh, summertime, pattern of life indelible, the fadeproof lake, the woods unshatterable, the pasture with the sweetfern and the juniper forever and ever, summer without end; this was the background, and the life along the shore was the design, the cottages with their innocent and tranquil design, their tiny docks with the flagpole and the American flag floating against the white clouds in the blue sky, the little paths over the roots of the trees leading from camp to camp and the paths leading back to the outhouses and the can of lime for sprinkling, and at the souvenir counters at the store the miniature birchbark canoes and the postcards that showed things looking a little better than they looked. This was the American family at play, escaping the city heat, wondering whether the newcomers in the camp at the head of the cove were "common" or "nice," wondering whether it was true that the people who drove up for Sunday dinner at the farmhouse were turned away because there wasn't enough chicken.

It seemed to me, as I kept remembering all this, that those times and those summers had been infinitely precious and worth saving. There had been jollity and peace and goodness. The arriving (at the beginning of August) had been so big a business in itself, at the railway station the farm wagon drawn up, the first smell of the pine-laden air, the first glimpse of the smiling farmer, and the great importance of the trunks and your father's enormous authority in such matters, and the feel of the wagon under you for the long ten-mile haul, and at the top of the last long hill catching the first view of the lake after eleven months of not seeing this cherished body of water. The shouts and cries of the other campers when they saw you, and the trunks to be unpacked, to give up their rich burden. (Arriving was less exciting nowadays, when you sneaked up in your car and parked it under a tree near the camp and took out the bags and in five minutes it was all over, no fuss, no loud wonderful fuss about trunks.)

Peace and goodness and jollity. The only thing that was wrong now, really, was the sound of the place, an unfamiliar nervous sound of the outboard motors. This was the note that jarred, the one thing that would sometimes break the illusion and set the years moving. In those other summertimes, all motors were inboard; and when they were at a little distance, the noise they made was a sedative, an ingredient of summer sleep. They were one-cylinder and two-cylinder engines, and some were make-and-break and some were jump-spark, but they all made a sleepy sound across the lake. The one-lungers throbbed and fluttered, and the twin-cylinder ones purred and purred, and that was a quiet sound, too. But now the campers all had outboards. In the daytime, in the hot mornings, these motors made a petulant, irritable sound; at night, in the still evening when the afterglow lit the water, they whined about one's ears like mosquitoes. My boy loved our rented outboard, and his great desire was to achieve single-handed mastery over it, and authority, and he soon learned the trick of choking it a little (but not too much), and the adjustment of the needle valve. Watching him I would remember the things you could do with the old one-cylinder engine with the heavy flywheel, how you could have it eating out of your hand if you got really close to it spiritually. Motor boats in those days didn't have clutches, and you would make a landing by shutting off the motor at the proper time and coasting in with a dead rudder. But there was a way of reversing them, if you learned the trick, by cutting the switch and putting it on again exactly on the final dying revolution of the flywheel, so that it would kick back against compression and begin reversing. Approaching a dock in a strong following breeze, it was difficult to slow up sufficiently by the ordinary coasting method, and if a boy felt he had complete mastery over his motor, he was tempted to keep it running beyond its time and then reverse it a few feet from the dock. It took a cool nerve, because if you threw the switch a twentieth of a second too soon you would catch the flywheel when it still had speed enough to go up past center, and the boat would leap ahead, charging bull-fashion at the dock.

We had a good week at the camp. The bass were biting well and the sun shone endlessly, day after day. We would be tired at night and lie down in the accumulated heat of the little bedrooms after the long hot day and the breeze would stir almost imperceptibly outside and the smell of the swamp drift in through the rusty screens. Sleep would come easily and in the morning the red squirrel would be on the roof, tapping out his gay routine. I kept remembering everything, lying in bed in the mornings—the small steamboat that had a long rounded stern like the lip of a Ubangi, and how quietly she ran on the moonlight sails, when the older boys played their mandolins and the girls sang and we ate doughnuts dipped in sugar, and how sweet the music was on the water in the shining night, and what it had felt like to think about girls then. After breakfast we would go up to the store and the things were in the same place—the minnows in a bottle, the plugs and spinners disarranged and pawed over by the youngsters from the boys' camp, the Fig Newtons and the Beeman's gum. Outside, the road was tarred and cars stood in front of the store. Inside, all was just as it had always been, except there was more Coca-Cola and not so much Moxie and root beer and birch beer and sarsaparilla. We would walk out with a bottle of pop apiece and sometimes the pop would backfire up our noses and hurt. We explored the streams, quietly, where the turtles slid off the sunny logs and dug their way into the soft bottom; and we lay on the town wharf and fed worms to the tame bass. Everywhere we went I had trouble making out which was I, the one walking at my side, the one walking in my pants.

One afternoon while we were there at that lake a thunderstorm came up. It was like the revival of an old melodrama that I had seen long ago with childish awe. The second-act climax of the drama of the electrical disturbance over a lake in America had not changed in any important respect. This was the big scene, still the big scene. The whole thing was so familiar, the first feeling of oppression and heat and a general air around camp of not wanting to go very far away. In mid-afternoon (it was all the same) a curious darkening of the sky, and a lull in everything that had made life tick; and then the way the boats suddenly swung the other way at their moorings with the coming of a breeze out of the new quarter, and the premonitory rumble. Then the kettle drum, then the snare, then the bass drum and cymbals, then crackling light against the dark, and the gods grinning and licking their chops in the hills. Afterward the calm, the rain steadily rustling in the calm lake, the return of light and hope and spirits, and the campers running out in joy and relief to go swimming in the rain, their bright cries perpetuating the deathless joke about how they were getting simply drenched, and the children screaming with delight at the new sensation of bathing in the rain, and the joke about getting drenched linking the generations in a strong indestructible chain. And the comedian who waded in carrying an umbrella.

When the others went swimming my son said he was going in, too. He pulled his dripping trunks from the line where they had hung all through the shower and wrung them out. Languidly, and with no thought of going in, I watched him, his hard little body, skinny and bare, saw him wince slightly as he pulled up around his vitals the small, soggy, icy garment. As he buckled the swollen belt suddenly my groin felt the chill of death.

Questions for Discussion

1. In this essay, the author tries to make a comparison between the lake he was revisiting and the lake in his memory. Was the lake the same as it had been many years before? What does the author want to tell by making such a comparison?
2. Did the father and the son have the same enthusiasm about the trip to the lake?
3. In the whole essay more than once the author had an illusion that he was his father and his boy was him. What does this contribute to the subjects of this article?
4. What thought does the author convey in this article?
5. If you value this essay, why do you value it? If you don't, why don't you?

About the Author

Elwyn Brooks White (1899—1985), a leading American essayist and literary stylist of his time, is known for his crisp, graceful, and relaxed style.

White was born in Mount Vernon, New York, as the son of a prosperous piano manufacturer. He graduated from Cornell University, Ithaca, N. Y., in 1921 and was a reporter and freelance writer before joining The *New Yorker* magazine as a writer and contributing editor in 1927. There he met his wife, Katherine Sergeant Angell, the magazine's first fiction editor and for 11 years he wrote for the magazine editorial essays and contributed verse and other pieces. White's favorite subjects were the complexities of modern society, failures of technological progress, the pleasures of urban and rural life, war, and internationalism. He was skeptical about organized religion, and advocated a respect for nature and simple living.

Between writing columns, White also published children's books. His three books for children—*Stuart Little* (1945), *Charlotte's Web* (1952), and *The Trumpet of the Swan* (1970)—are considered classics. In 1959 he revised and published a book by the late William Strunk, Jr., *The Elements of Style*, which became a standard style manual for writing in English. Among White's other works are *Points of My Compass* (1962), *Letters of E. B. White*, edited by D. L. Guth, appeared in 1976, his collected essays in 1977, and *Poems and Sketches of E. B. White* in 1981. He was awarded the gold medal for essays and criticism of the National Institute of Arts and Letters, and a Pulitzer Prize special citation in 1978. He held honorary degrees from seven American colleges and universities, and was a member of the American Academy.

Once More to the Lake is an essay first published in Harper's magazine in 1941. This narrative essay chronicles E. B. White's pilgrimage back to a lakefront resort he visited as a child.

Bibliography

[1] Abrams M H. A Glossary of Literary Terms [M]. Beijing: Foreign Language Teaching and Research Press, 2004.

[2] Abrams M H. The Norton Anthology of English Literature: The Major Authors [M]. 7th ed. New York: W. W. Norton, 2001.

[3] Baym N. The Norton Anthology of American Literature [M]. 6th ed. New York: W. W. Norton, 2003.

[4] Beaty J. The Norton Introduction to Literature [M]. Shorter 8th ed. New York: W. W. Norton, 2002.

[5] Ferguson M, Salter M J, Stallworthy J. The Norton Anthology of Poetry [M]. Shorter 4th ed. New York: W. W. Norton, 1997.

[6] Cassill R V. The Norton Anthology of Short Fiction [M]. Shorter 3rd ed. New York: W. W. Norton, 1986.

[7] Worthen W B. The Harcourt Brace Anthology of Drama [M]. 2nd ed. Fort Worth: Harcourt Brace College Publishers, 1996.

[8] 傅俊. 英国戏剧读本 [M]. 上海：上海外语教育出版社, 2006.

[9] 桂扬清. 英美文学选读 [M]. 北京：中国对外翻译出版公司, 1996.

[10] 胡荫桐. 英国文学教程 [M]. 天津：南开大学出版社, 1994.

[11] 黄源深. 英国散文选读 [M]. 北京：外语教学与研究出版社, 1996.

[12] 秦寿生. 英美文学名篇选读 [M]. 北京：高等教育出版社, 2000.

Recommended Websites

http://www.bartleby.com/230/

http://www.online-literature.com/

http://www.readbookonline.net/

http://www.gutenberg.org/